T0372815

ALGORITHMS

Algorithms: Technology, Culture, Politics develops a relational, situated approach to algorithms. It takes a middle ground between theories that give the algorithm a singular and stable meaning in using it as a central analytic category for the contemporary society and theories that dissolve the term into the details of empirical studies.

The book discusses algorithms in relation to hardware and material conditions, code, data, and subjects such as users and programmers, but also "data doubles." The individual chapters bridge critical discussions on bias, exclusion, or responsibility with the necessary detail on the contemporary state of information technology. The examples include state-of-the-art applications of machine learning, such as self-driving cars, and large language models, such as GPT.

The book will be of interest to everyone engaging critically with algorithms, particularly in the social sciences, media studies, STS, political theory, or philosophy. With its broad scope, it can serve as a high-level introduction that picks up and builds on more than two decades of critical research on algorithms.

Tobias Matzner is a professor of Digital Cultures and Digital Humanities at Paderborn University, Germany. His research focuses on the intersections of technology, culture, and politics, with a particular focus on algorithms and machine learning.

ALGORITHMS

Technology, Culture, Politics

Tobias Matzner

Routledge
Taylor & Francis Group

LONDON AND NEW YORK

First published 2024
by Routledge
4 Park Square, Milton Park, Abingdon, Oxon OX14 4RN

and by Routledge
605 Third Avenue, New York, NY 10158

Routledge is an imprint of the Taylor & Francis Group, an informa business

© 2024 Tobias Matzner

British Library Cataloguing-in-Publication Data
A catalogue record for this book is available from the British Library

Library of Congress Cataloguing-in-Publication Data
Names: Matzner, Tobias, author.
Title: Algorithms : technology, culture, politics / Tobias Matzner.
Description: Milton Park, Abingdon, Oxon ; New York, NY : Routledge, 2024. I
Includes bibliographical references and index.
Identifiers: LCCN 2023018363 (print) I LCCN 2023018364 (ebook) I
ISBN 9781032290614 (hardback) I
ISBN 9781032290591 (paperback) I ISBN 9781003299851 (ebook)
Subjects: LCSH: Algorithms.
Classification: LCC QA76 .M3573 2024 (print) I LCC QA76 (ebook) I
DDC 518/.1—dc23/eng/20230725
LC record available at https://lccn.loc.gov/2023018363
LC ebook record available at https://lccn.loc.gov/2023018364

ISBN: 978-1-032-29061-4 (hbk)
ISBN: 978-1-032-29059-1 (pbk)
ISBN: 978-1-003-29985-1 (ebk)

DOI: 10.4324/9781003299851

Typeset in Sabon
by MPS Limited, Dehradun

Für Leander

CONTENTS

ACKNOWLEDGMENTS

The first roots of this book go back to when I was working at the International Centre for Ethics in the Sciences and Humanities in Tübingen. I want to thank Regina Ammicht Quinn for providing an environment in which such ideas could grow.

The trajectory that led from these thoughts to writing this book, and that brought me via New York to Paderborn, would not have been possible without the support of Rahel Jaeggi and Alice Crary.

I had the fortune and pleasure to write this book while working with my incredible team at Paderborn University: Birte de Gruisbourne, Christian Schulz, and Sonja Dolinsek. Thank you so much for sharing so many thoughts, discussions, and draft readings that allowed the ideas here presented to form.

Thanks to everyone at the department of Media Studies in Paderborn for making it such a great place to work in.

I want to thank Amira Möding for keeping the exchange going on everything algorithmic and beyond.

The many people I could speak with at my university, conferences, workshops, on social media, and in restaurants are far too numerous to list, yet this book would not be possible without them.

I am indebted to Emily Briggs and Lakshita Joshi at Routledge for their commitment and support in turning all these thoughts into a book.

Special thanks to the developers of Zotero and the community at Leo.org – two groups of people that enabled essential algorithmic constituents for writing this book.

The gratitude that my partner Judith deserves has yet to find a form of expression apt for academic publications.

PART I

1

TOWARD A RELATIONAL THEORY OF ALGORITHMS

Algorithms are not neutral! Algorithms are not just a tool that can equally be used for good and bad things! How often one needs to repeat these sentences is one of the more frustrating (and sometimes still astonishing) aspects of working on a political or social perspective on algorithms. They are almost a platitude among researchers on the matter. Yet, the mindset that these sentences confront still structures other fields of research, public discussions, productions of technology, hopes for the future, and more.

This book considers that "algorithms are not neutral!" not as its result but as its starting point. Decades of research have not only firmly established algorithms as cultural, social, and political. They have also opened up many questions. How should "not neutral" be understood? How can political concepts such as discrimination, exclusion, or responsibility best be linked to the technical details of algorithms? How exactly do social and cultural biases and norms find their way into algorithms? How can we make sense of the interplay of the manifold factors that have been shown to influence algorithms: training data, programmers' biases, material resources, coding conventions, the distribution of labor, and much more? How to do justice to the many individual perspectives on algorithms?

Such questions are discussed in this book using algorithms as an analytical perspective that brings out how the technical or material and the political or cultural are related. It also discusses the possibilities and limits of such a perspective because, despite the prominence of the term "algorithm," its use for critical analysis is by no means a matter of course.

In fact, the field of research on algorithms can be described as exhibiting a tension between abstraction and dissolution (Matzner 2022). The first pole of this tension consists of works that use the term algorithm as the central

DOI: 10.4324/9781003299851-2

term for analyses on a rather abstract level. In an oft-cited remark, Scott Lash wrote that a "society of ubiquitous media means a society in which power is increasingly in the algorithm." Yet, for him, that means dealing with a new form of algorithmic rules that are "far different from the sorts of rules that human scientists have dealt with over the decades" (Lash 2007, 70–71). On an even bigger scale, Totaro and Ninno attempt an update of Ernst Cassierer in showing that "the hegemony of algorithmic logic" is the form in which "function has come to dominate the culture of the modern world" (2014, 4). Arguing for an opposing view but with equally abstract and broad historical scope, accelerationist thinkers consider algorithms as a distinctive new mode of reasoning (Parisi 2019) or, in its (somehow) historical-materialist extension, as a new hope for revolution (Srnicek and Williams 2015).

In more concrete, detailed, and often socially or politically accented studies, an abstract use of algorithms often denotes the essential quality that distinguishes the use of algorithms. For example, the notion of algorithmic governmentality (Rouvroy 2013) is theoretically opposed to other, non-algorithmic forms of governmentality. Similarly, Striphas diagnoses the emergence of an algorithmic culture (Striphas 2015). There are a lot more examples, many of which will re-appear in this book: algorithmic identity (Cheney-Lippold 2011), trading (MacKenzie 2018), journalism (Kotenidis and Veglis 2021), accountability (Diakopoulos 2015), and much more. My use of the term abstraction has much more in common with this latter group of texts than with the first one.

However, critics engage particularly with the idea of an essential quality of – or deriving from – algorithms. Already in 2015, Ziewitz complained about an "algorithmic drama" in current research that "introduces algorithms as powerful and consequential actors in a wide variety of domains" (Ziewitz 2016). As a too good to be true example for this drama, while I am writing this introduction, the media are full of stories about an algorithm called GPT-3 that has been given the appearance of exactly such an actor in its more well-known form as the chatbot ChatGPT. The question: "will this actor replace us/me?" overshadows much more pressing ones about the functionalities, data, assumptions, practices, rhetoric, biases, safeguards, and much more that make up this algorithm. In this sense, Nick Seaver cautions: "if the idealized algorithm is supposed to be generic, stable, and rigid, the actual algorithmic system is particular, unstable, and malleable." In consequence, he urges to "contribute some much-needed empiricism and particularism to critical discourses on algorithms" (Seaver 2018). Similarly, Paul Dourish argues against the danger of "taking an essentializing view of algorithms." Rather, he describes his research perspective: "with respect to ethnographic responsibility, I note that 'algorithm' is a term of art within a particular professional culture" (Dourish 2016, 2). As such, he delineates algorithms from "things they are often confused with, but properly distinct from" (Seaver 2017, 3). Dourish lists these "others" of algorithms as "automation," "code," "architecture," and "materialization." He thus wants to put algorithms in their appropriate theoretical place among and in relation to many other, equally important concepts. He explicitly claims that this is "not to dissolve the algorithm in a sea of relations, but rather to understand how algorithm [...] comes to play the particular role that it does" (Dourish 2016, 2). For others, however, understanding the role of the algorithm entails its dissolution. For example, Seaver writes "[P]ress on any algorithmic decision and you will find many human ones [...]. There is no such thing as an algorithmic decision; there are only ways of seeing decisions as algorithmic" (Seaver 2018). Luke Munn adds many more factors that need to be considered regarding algorithms today, such as their distributed nature, the change from programming to software engineering, or their complex materiality (Munn 2018, chap. 0). All of these factors will also be central in this book, as discussed in Chapters 4 and 5. Munn's analysis oscillates between placing algorithms within a complex "ecology" (Munn 2018, 22) and dissolving algorithms entirely by reducing them to a product of other things: "intersections where software and hardware, labor, and nature come together to produce key algorithmic operations" (Munn 2018).

In sum, such works dissolve the position of algorithms as a central analytical category, either by placing them as one among many relevant elements or by dissolving the algorithm itself into one or many constituents, such as human decisions, software, hardware, labor, nature, etc. Algorithms remain only as the object or occasion of analysis.

Munn also brings up the problem of scale. As just described, he thinks that it is necessary to "break [the algorithmic] ecology down into components and unravel its technical underpinnings" (Munn 2018, 23). However, the focus can also become too small, were

> the researcher, like the computer scientist, zooms in on a particular technical procedure—facial recognition, for example. This hyperfocus allows for the fine-tuning of a specific routine, typically foregrounding issues of efficiency and accuracy. But this blinkered approach also works to frame the algorithmic as abstracted and apolitical, divorced from the messy realities of gender and culture, class and capital. The result is all too clean—a technical but apolitical detail.
>
> (Munn 2018, 24)

Munn's worry is very close to the reason why I want to present a perspective that takes a middle ground between the poles of abstraction and dissolution. However, he frames the problem slightly differently, as a matter of the right degree of dissolution, as it were. His middle ground is achieved using Levi Bryant's concept of the machine (heavily inspired by Deleuze and Guattari). A "machine" in this sense is a general ontological concept that can be applied to anything, living and non-living, and is defined by its operation "joined to other machines, a process that Bryant calls structural coupling" (Munn 2018, 24). Focusing on such coupled machines provides Munn with "sub-selections of the material totality which feel strategic and significant." Thus, he stays within the general tendency of dissolution, yet with an attention to retaining a meaningful focus within the complex systems it yields. The connection to "the messy realities of gender and culture, class, and capital" is achieved through the flat ontology that informs Bryant's theory: "machinic framing is 'flattening,' allowing the technical to productively intersect with those elements deemed social, political, or cultural" (Munn 2018, 25).

In Chapter 3, I argue in great detail that such an ontologization of the political counteracts the very motives that animate it. Rather, I propose a politicization of ontology. I show that this makes a certain level of abstraction necessary, but a situated abstraction, not an essentializing one. My approach thus aims at a middle ground between abstraction and dissolution. It shares the skepticism toward too abstract and essentializing notions of algorithms that leads to an emphasis on particular and empirical detail. At the same time, a certain level of abstraction is necessary for first getting a meaningful scope for some sustained or long-term phenomena and second to connect the detailed and particular to the social, cultural, economic, and political issues that also concern Munn. As already mentioned, this notion of abstraction is more related to the second group of works that I have introduced above when discussing the pole of abstraction.

I will show that algorithms can be understood as a research perspective that provides a link between the abstract and the concrete. Algorithms thus are considered relational. They are abstractions that need to be complemented by different particular and concrete things. While all of these matter, they cannot be analyzed at the same time. Different relations thus give insight into different forms of situatedness. I give a theoretically grounded argument for this claim in Chapter 3, but I want to use the remainder of this chapter to provide an intuition for this view that will be amended with a short historical argument in Chapter 2.

*

In the last decade, many important books, articles, and op-eds have focused on algorithms as social, ethical, and political issues. They have done pioneering work in analyzing bias and discrimination brought about by contemporary applications of machine learning and AI, including by now canonical cases like ProPublica's investigation into racial bias in recidivism prediction (Angwin and Larson 2016). This case is noteworthy not only for its bias, but for what it attempts to do. When I speak publicly about algorithmic discrimination and mention this case, often the audience is taken aback by the very idea of an algorithmic recidivism prediction. There are two interrelated sets of issues here: first that algorithms perform the task in a biased fashion; second that (assumed) algorithmic capabilities bring about changes in society, which in this case make something like automatic recidivism prediction seem a good idea to begin with. There are more striking examples: there have been papers claiming to guess homosexuality or criminality from face photographs (Wang and Kosinski 2018; Wu and Zhang 2016). Such uncanny reincarnations of physiognomy have been quickly debunked (Bowyer et al. 2020; Hirschman 2017). Yet, they show that the social relevance of algorithms is not just based on what they do in the narrow sense of their application but also on what they do to society in a wider sense: which practices and worldviews they challenge or contradict and which ones they sustain, legitimize, or enable in the first place. Titles like "Automating Inequality" (Eubanks 2017), "Race after Technology" (Benjamin 2019), "Algorithms of Oppression" (Noble 2018), "Weapons of Math Destruction" (O'Neil 2017), "Cloud Ethics" (Amoore 2020), or "The Black Box Society" (Pasquale 2015) have collected and detailed the many forms in which algorithms are entangled with racism, sexism, social discrimination, exploitation, and other forms of asymmetrical power relations. All of them show the close entanglements of the two aspects I mentioned: algorithms often produce outcomes that are discriminatory or unjust, but they also support, enable, suggest, or legitimize existing and new forms of domination and inequality. To understand this impact, a wide perspective is necessary. Such algorithmic practices are often not as novel or "disruptive" as their advocates claim; there are complex historical continuities and global conditions at play. Thus, the aforementioned books are not just about technology but as much or even more about society, politics, and economics, about racism, sexism, and class (or succeeding structures of economic discrimination). They are historical, going back at least to the founding moments of the US (where most of these texts in the English-speaking world come from) or to colonialism. They are books about pre-digital systems of recording information about people, sorting and administrating them. They are books about struggles between corporate, state, and citizen power.

The use of the term "algorithms" in such social and critical texts derives from a common sense idea of algorithms as it is often used in computer science, where algorithms are a particular form of abstraction, i.e. the abstract formulation of the general approach to a problem. E.g. the "Bubble Sort" algorithm is based on the idea that numbers in a list can be sorted by comparing each number to its successor and exchanging the two if the succeeding number is smaller than its predecessor. After a few runs through the list, there will be no more exchanges necessary, and the list is sorted. This verbal description of the algorithm could be formalized, and usually in computer science such formalisms come with additional demands, such as unambivalent meaning or using only a defined set of elementary operations to describe the algorithm, in this case, e.g. comparing and exchanging. Yet, the oft-evoked analogy that cooking recipes are also algorithms, which are usually formulated less precisely ("add salt to taste"), illustrates that often the central idea behind the concept "algorithm" is to express a general approach to a problem or task that abstracts from all the details of a particular execution. In consequence, the abstraction can be put into a more rigid formalism based on a formal model of computing – Turing machines as discussed in Chapter 2 being one of them. Yet, this would still be a formalism that abstracts. Using the example of Bubble Sort, it would abstract from the concrete realization of the list, the representation of the numbers, the processing of the exchange, etc. Adding these details, the algorithm could be written down in a particular programming language, yet it would still abstract from, e.g. the concrete processes in memory chips or the machine language that the CPU needs to run the program. So already here, we see different forms (not levels!)[1] of abstraction with different complements.

Following this intuition, it makes sense to say that Google's search algorithm is based on the idea that many incoming links as well as the ranking of the sites that contain the link are influential for the placement in the results list. This is not precise enough for a mathematical formulation, so here we deviate from one influential form of using the term in computer science. Yet it still follows the same intuition to express a general principle.

It is this general approach and outcome that often matters for the social, political, and ethical analyses. For example, Virginia Eubanks illustrates in many detailed studies how algorithms continue logics and processes that have made "welfare" a technology of exclusion of the poor (Eubanks 2017). Yet, she does not discuss code or hardware very much. She is concerned with links between institutional or bureaucratic and algorithmic processes that are very hard to delineate when one just looks at individual lines of code or bits on a disk, for example.

This is not just due to complexity. Most of the mentioned authors analyze algorithms by observing their use – in ethnographic studies with those who apply them, by speaking to those affected, and by analyzing the data they produce. An abstracted grasp of what goes on is achieved, that is, an algorithm is described, not based on a pre-existing approach but based on the performativity of its application. This moves the term algorithm another step away from the common sense meaning in computer science – from a specification toward a dynamic concept embedded in practice. Here is an illustration using the recipe analogy: when I just had moved out of home, I used

1 This is discussed in detail in Chapter 4.

to call my mother – a renowned cook – asking for recipes of dishes I tried to reproduce in my own kitchen. She would usually answer by asking for some time to cook the dish again, taking notes of the steps performed and quantities used while doing so, for she had so habitualized the process that she could not just tell me. Thus, we deal with a much more performative idea of the algorithm: not the idea that drives an execution but what emerges during the execution. This is different from so-called "black box studies" that conceive of such observations of the execution as a more or less precise approximation of the "true" algorithm hidden in the black box of the machine. In the performative view, which I begin to develop here, the execution is part of the algorithm, not just an approximate representation of it.

Still, I think algorithm is a good term for this level of analysis, a certain abstracted grasp of "what goes on." For example, at one point in her book, Virginia Eubanks describes her observations in an Office of Children, Youth and Families in Pittsburgh where an algorithmic risk assessment tool for children is used. She voices her surprise that the case of an endangered young child gets a much lower risk score by the algorithm than the case of a teenager that both she and the childcare worker she accompanies judge as less severe. Eubanks finds out that the algorithm overrates prior contact with public services (Eubanks 2017, 141). This pertains to the detail of how the algorithm calculates risk scores but is already in a form that allows it to connect to social terms. In order to do so, she need not talk about or even know the concrete coding instructions or operations in chips and on disks – although the reason for the overrating *might* be located in such particularities. Yet, even if it were, the abstract formulation "the algorithm overrates prior contact with public services" is needed in order to single out the particular coding instructions or operations in chips and on disks that are relevant for bringing about that result. In other words, the level of abstraction on which Eubanks describes the algorithm allows forming a relation between the social issues – risk, exposure, contact with public services – and the concrete specifics that might cause a wrong estimation of these issues – formulae, datasets, coding instructions, etc.

In consequence, although abstraction is necessary to connect to social, historical, ethical, and political perspectives, this is just one end of what should be understood as a relation: algorithms as a relation that always ties the abstract to the concrete. I will call these concrete elements the *complements* of the algorithm: hardware, networks, program code, but also programmers, users, and subjects that are captured in data. I call them complement, because they do not determine or constitute the algorithm, but rather algorithm and their complements co-constitute each other. In this sense, algorithms are treated as *complementary abstractions*.

I will quickly walk through a few exemplary arguments for this relational view that are discussed in the book.

The sentence that started this section: "algorithms are not neutral!" is often continued: "... because they are made by humans" (Noble 2018, 2), or as I quoted Seaver above, every algorithmic decision can be reduced to a human decision. Such a statement implicitly reduces algorithms to channels or carriers of human politics, presumptions, and prejudice. First of all, though, they are not neutral carriers; they shift, warp, increase, and decrease the impact of these human "inputs." Second, a lot hinges on the meaning of the word "making" in "made by humans." Most authors who voice such claims, including those cited above, do not claim that all algorithms are intentionally laden with politics. In contrast, one of the problems voiced is that implicit or unreflected bias and structural inequalities find their way into the algorithm. This can happen via training data (O'Neil 2017) but also things like the demographic composition of programming teams have been found to impact the results of algorithms (Campolo et al. 2017).

Regarding training data, I will discuss in Chapter 6 that data are not just a given input, the features of which are consequentially reflected by algorithmic models – including biases. Such views are suggested by ways of talking about data in metaphors of natural resources just waiting to be excavated and continue a long line of thought considering data a just given – as the etymology of the word says – and not made (Rosenberg 2013). Yet, specific algorithms need specialized forms of data and digital platforms put a lot of effort into making people produce such data (Mühlhoff 2020). So while data are socially and politically biased, they do not simply imprint this bias onto the algorithm. How and to what extent this happens always depends on how the data are biased toward a particular algorithm. Furthermore, in many instances, the algorithm itself, not just its data-based outputs, needs to be considered as an extension of biased practices. An example would be the way in which predictive policing continues the injustices of existing forms of policing (Benjamin 2019; Browne 2015). In this sense, data and the algorithm constitute each other.

The view that other socio-cultural factors such as the programmers' demography reflect in the algorithm is discussed in Chapter 5. Many problems can be indeed attributed to a lack of thought or critical reflection of programmers. However, if the circumstances of programming are said to reflect in the algorithms, this implies a dualism of a human world with power, politics, etc., and technology as its product, carrier, channel, or representation. The problems of this implication go beyond just acknowledging that algorithms are at best distorted or warped channels of the prejudices of their makers. Many of the conditions of programming are themselves dependent on algorithms in the sense that, for example, paths of dependencies exist, where already existing technologies form and constringe the possibilities of programmers (Rieder 2020, 133). Furthermore, as I discuss in Chapter 7, the cultural and social practices said to reflect in the algorithm are increasingly structured by the algorithms themselves. For example, we currently witness algorithmic versions of fame (based on followers and social media feeds) or suspicion (based on hidden data collection, databases of security agencies, and automated vetting) (Matzner 2016). Here algorithms enable new forms of verdicts or judgments about humans – which come with their very own forms of discrimination or injustice. Thus, they are hard to track, because they are different from human verdicts (Mann and Matzner 2019). In sum, the important studies on how algorithms are made and by whom need to be united with those that study what using algorithms does to societies and the subjects living in them. Both are related via the technical particularities of algorithms – leading again to a co-constitutive view.

In Chapter 5, I discuss the common claim in political discussions of algorithms that access to source code is the key factor for political or ethical scrutiny. In consequence, its inaccessibility is problematized, often by evoking the metaphor of a black box (Kitchin 2017; Pasquale 2015). This black box can mean different things. Sometimes it is used to refer to those having access to the source code but prohibiting access to keep their trade secrets – or even to keep their criminal activities – hidden (Pasquale 2015). In other uses, the black box refers to the problem of deriving the concrete, formalized steps of a program by just using it – sometimes this is referred to as a black box study (Kitchin 2017). In the context of machine learning, even programmers themselves cannot foresee and explain the "behavior" of their software – which has led to the field of explainable AI (Rohlfing et al. 2020).

All of these evocations of black boxes have their reason. To varying degrees, however, they follow a determinist idea of executing code as a chain of purely technical translations (Galloway 2006b): source code into machine code into steps executed by a processor (Berry 2011). Technical here also implies that, at least theoretically, all of these translations can be reversed, that is with enough knowledge and resources, the algorithm could be read by following the steps a computer does. Computer scientists and hackers call this aptly "reverse engineering." In consequence, relating the social and political issues with source code would suffice; a separate inquiry to the related complements would be a matter of just following determinate paths.

Wendy Chun has engaged with this view (Chun 2008). She shows that each of the steps of translation cannot be reduced to each other as the view of them as a technical relation claims. In contrast, each of these steps is not a translation but a creation. For example, the simple command to add two values in program code becomes an entire – machine specific – sub-program in machine code (Chun 2008, 306). The electronic states "representing" these values, in turn, need to be stabilized with all kinds of technical finesse that turn jumpy and continuous electric voltages into (halfway) discrete values. Based on these examples, Chun argues that "source code thus only becomes source after the fact"(Chun 2008, 307). Pertaining to detailed studies on programming, such as Rieder's (2020), this can easily be extended to algorithms. Thus, code is constituted after the fact by the algorithm that is running as much as that algorithm is an execution of code.

Of course, such a critique of code as a central or even essential element must not lead to the inverted view. With the universalist presumptions of cybernetics and grandiose misreading of Turing's notion of a universally programmable computer (including mistaking computing machinery as essentially materialized versions of a said computer), in particular, feedback logics and hardware have been frequent candidates of such essentialisms.[2] They are also implicated in theories that use ideology as a means to theorize interfaces, software, or algorithms (Galloway 2006b; 2012). Quite generally, this inverts the start and end of the chain of translations from code to chips, where one element determines the rest, but similar arguments apply. For example, today the hardware often is in the notorious "cloud." As I discuss in Chapter 4, this entails that often the hardware that runs a program is dynamically allocated only at the moment of execution. The same search on a search engine that is executed in a data center in the US, when repeated a second later, could be executed in a data center in India. Thus, not only does code become code "after the fact," as Chun writes, the same holds also for computers, networks, storage, etc. The algorithm only becomes the algorithm when executed on hardware, yet the hardware at the same time becomes the hardware during execution.

Most algorithms today are interactive in the sense that they depend on users' inputs. Many textbooks still describe algorithms as receiving input at the beginning, doing some processing, and giving output at the end. Yet, this is an image that dates back to the days of big expensive computers when running a program meant to hand in a neatly organized stack of punched cards containing input and program, which was run somewhere by experts, and receiving the results hours or days later on another punched card or printout. Today using a computer means constantly typing, clicking, pinching, and talking. It means that central parameters of the algorithms are no longer defined by programmers but derived from user inputs or capturing usage data, e.g. rankings of search results or entries in feeds. In consequence, algorithms are not merely executed but they have users, which I discuss in Chapter 7. These users with their inputs influence what algorithms do. Strategies such as search engine optimization show that clever users can even entice algorithms to work on their behalf by feeding them particular forms of

---

2 Just showing why this is a simplified view, however, does not grasp the problem entirely, because here technological determinism also serves to produce its advocate and author of the texts in a heroic fashion as one of the few persons that can stand the humiliation of humanism this view entails. The problem is, in fighting them, one automatically becomes a hero fighting the hero. Thus, I will restrict the engagement with this heroism to a couple of footnotes but develop a politically rather than heroic posthumanist theory in Chapter 3.

input. While search engine optimization is mostly a professional activity in PR and advertising, quotidian users also have an imaginary of the algorithms they use that structure their practices, e.g. when using social networking sites (Bucher 2017; Schulz 2022). Pentenrieder (2020) has shown that food delivery riders deliberately adjust their routes and cycling speed to trick the dispatching algorithm into providing them with more profitable orders. Importantly, these user imaginaries of the algorithm usually do not conform to the logic implemented in the program. Yet, this does not mean that they are "wrong." This would only make sense if indeed the implemented algorithm was the only decisive element. Yet as these examples show, both the users' actions – driven by their imaginary – and the programmed logic together produce the algorithm that effectively is executed.

This relation between algorithms and users may be particularly salient in contemporary applications driven by user data. However, it also structures other applications. Already in 2005, Philip Brey discusses the question "What kind of tool is a computer" (Brey 2005, 383). He distinguishes the perspective of the programmers from the perspective of the users. For the first, computers are "physical symbol systems" (Brey 2005, 393) citing Newell and Simon (1976)). For the latter, a computer might be a convenient information processor but also a music player or a game and much more. Thus, to understand what a computer does, neither perspective can be reduced to the other. Programmers need to deal with data strings, (sub)programs, and procedures while the computer would not do for the users that which they use for if they had to deal with these too, instead of "clicking, 'dragging,' and scrolling" (Brey 2005, 395) or enjoying music rather than decoding mp3 files.

However, in Brey's text, these two groups are just assumed as given. I have already discussed that programmers cannot just determine technology by writing code or algorithms. Similarly, many users' practices are deeply shaped by technology. Thus, Lucas Introna proposes a view similar to Brey's but extends it using Barad's (2007) concept of intra-action, where algorithms and their users both are the result of a particular practice. This particular Baradian version of a co-constitutive relation will be discussed in detail in Chapter 3 as a basis for my own view. It already establishes one aspect of the need for a situated practice, which will also be a central topic: a computer *is* neither a machine driven by programmer's code nor a machine that users use. Both amount to a specific "cut" in Barad's terms, a certain distribution of subjects and the objects they act on that derives from a particular practice. Thus, switching from analyzing the relation of users and algorithms to programmers and algorithms or code and algorithms or hardware and algorithms does not yield a better or deeper perspective but a *different* perspective.

This illustrates another important issue in the analysis of algorithms. The different complements of algorithms need not just be summed up to get the full view. Rather, each of the relations to a complement that are discussed in this book allows us to discuss specific things that only can be grasped from this perspective while others need a different perspective. Chapter 3 will argue in detail why the strive of a unifying or essentializing should be avoided – both for epistemological and political reasons.

Before that, in Chapter 2, I will enhance the relational approach that I have begun to describe here with a view toward three genealogical roots of algorithms in their contemporary form: the works of mathematicians such as Gödel, Turing, and Church struggling with the foundations of computability, cybernetics, and automated data processing via tabulation machines. Chapters 4–7 then discuss different co-constitutive relations of algorithms and their complements: algorithms and matter, algorithms and code, algorithms and data, algorithms and subjects; and algorithms and humans. These chapters are written in a rather self-contained fashion, so that they do not presuppose the other ones in part II – even if there are many links and overlaps to other chapters. Only Chapter 7 on subjects probably should be read after Chapters 5 on code and 6 on data.

2

ALGORITHMS AS RELATIONAL FROM THE BEGINNING

Three historical sketches

Often, the history of algorithms begins with the etymological roots of the term "algorithm" in the name of the Persian mathematician محمد بن موسى الخوارزمى (Muḥammad ibn Mūsā al-Khwārizmī) where "al-Khwārizmī" used to be latinized as "Algorithmi." This scholar wrote several influential books on mathematics, including one whose title led to the world of algebra: الكتاب المختصر في حساب الجبر والمقابلة (al-Kitāb al-mukhtaṣar fī ḥisāb al-jabr wal-muqābala). This translates as "The Compendious Book on Calculation by Completion and Balancing" and one essential operation, al-jabr, completion, led to the name algebra.

With this root, the term algorithm is tied to calculation or computation in a quite general manner and the term indeed often changed its use. In medieval Latin discourse, it was often used to denote the decimal number system, since a second influential text of al-Khwārizmī's was his "Book on Indian computation" that described decimal numbers. The current use of the term is rather recent.

Thus, the modern term "algorithm" cannot be clarified much by its etymology. Rather, it needs to be understood against very specific developments in Western mathematics at the end of the 19th and early 20th centuries when the foundations of mathematics have been debated from a new angle. Two other historic roots of contemporary computing are often discussed: the proliferation of mechanical data processing via punch cards, which also started around the turn of the century, and – a bit more recent – the rise of a presumably new universal science called cybernetics. In the following, I will discuss each of these and use them to further substantialize the

DOI: 10.4324/9781003299851-3

understanding of algorithms that I will develop in this book. Importantly, I do not argue that these historical moments or developments define algorithms. Rather, I want to show that my view is compatible with these histories, although it is clearly motivated by both contemporary developments of technology and much more recent critiques of ontology and epistemology. These historic moments also serve as good illustrations for my approach because many readers that deal with algorithms in one form or the other may already know them.

The foundations of mathematics and the limits of computation

The 19th century had seen impressive progress in mathematics, which in particular brought about a more formally precise description of its most elementary basis. In particular, Georg Cantor had established set theory over a series of papers starting in 1874 (Cantor 1883). It actually dealt with the question of how many real numbers exist. The method and way of thinking he employed, however, led him todevelop a formal way of treating sets and operations on sets like uniting or intersecting them. This theory provoked a bit of a sensation because it included so-called "transfinite" numbers, that is, numbers that are greater than infinite, which was a very counterintuitive notion. Cantor managed to give it a defined meaning. His set theory allowed to derive the important properties of numbers from just a couple of basic axioms about sets. In fact, it allowed to understand numbers as sets. And it also allowed to define numbers greater than infinite. Back in Cantor's days, famous mathematicians found that idea outrageous, in particular the famous Leopold Kronecker. His critique was already a prefiguration of a conflict that would develop a few decades later under the name formalism vs. intuitionism. Where intuitionists held that mathematical objects are essentially matters of thought that can merely be expressed formally, formalists thought that mathematical objects are nothing else than their formal expression. Cantor's definition of numbers through the axioms of set theory was an important step toward this formalist idea.

This is exemplary of the movement of axiomatization that spread in the 19th century in Europe. Frege tried to develop a kind of calculus of sets which was meant to ground arithmetic using only his own and very influential formalism of logic. Russel famously found an error in Frege's formalism but the idea caught on. Russell and Whitehead (1927) went on to write the three-volume monumental "Principia Mathematica" where they invented a complex and lengthy formalism with the same aim: to ground the entirety of mathematics in a small set of formally defined axioms and nothing more than the rules of logic to apply them. There was some debate about whether all the choices the authors made were as self-evident as they claimed. Furthermore, the book was very difficult to understand. Lorain Daston reports that "[i]t became a standing joke that the proofs [...] were so exhaustive and exhausting that it took until page 362 of the first volume to get to the proof of the proposition that '1+1=2,' and then only as a promissory note, 'when arithmetical addition has been defined'"(Daston 2019, 326 citing Whitehead and Russell, 1:362).

Still, with such very formal expressions of the basics of mathematics at hand, an intriguing idea had come up: if mathematical theories can be proven by deriving them from a set of axioms by applying rules of logic step by step and these steps themselves can be formally expressed, could mathematics in its entirety be a purely formal affair? The most famous expression of this idea is known as Hilbert's program. David Hilbert developed it in the 1920s after the first disappointments with attempts of finding a universal basis for the entirety of mathematics. He still hoped that any area of mathematics could be defined by a finite consistent set of axioms. Proving a theory in that field would then mean proceeding from these axioms in a purely formal manner to produce a formula that expresses the theory. This led to a consequential question: when are such proofs possible? This question became known by the German name Hilbert and his co-author Ackermann used for it in their 1928 introduction to logics: "Entscheidungsproblem" or in English "decision problem." In the opening section on the Entscheidungsproblem, Hilbert and Ackermann quite clearly state their formalist hopes:

> Mathematical logic provides more than just a more precise language by a formal expression of modes of deduction. Once a logical formalism is fixed, one can expect *that a systematic, so to speak calculatory, treatment* of the logical formulae is possible [...].
> (Hilbert and Ackermann 1928, 72, my translation and emphasis)

Such a treatment has to answer two questions in particular. The first asks whether a given logical formula can become true at all (if it is "satisfiable"); the second asks whether the formula is true in general (if it is "universally valid"). Both questions relate to each other: if a formula is true in general, its negation cannot be satisfiable, and vice versa. In their description of the Entscheidungsproblem, Hilbert and Ackermann transferred these questions according to their formalist expectations. They said, "the Entscheidungsproblem is solved if one knows *a procedure [Verfahren] that allows to decide in a finite number of steps* if a given logical expression is universally valid or satisfiable" (Hilbert and Ackermann 1928, 73, my translation).

In that form, the traditional question in logic, whether a theorem follows from the axioms, becomes the search for a finite procedure, a procedure that can be executed in a purely formal manner in a finite number of steps. It is this procedure that Hilbert and Ackermann mention quite casually in their definition of the Entscheidungsproblem that is an important root of the contemporary understanding of algorithms.

Hilbert's program did not live long. It was hotly debated already when he formulated it, mainly by the aforementioned school of thought called intuitionism. Mathematical objects are intuitions of minds, they argued, and not just elements of formal systems on paper. The biggest blow to Hilbert's program, however, did not come from such external critiques but from within. In 1931, Kurt Gödel, who began his career as a follower of Hilbert's program, published one of the most consequential papers in mathematics. He showed that any formal system of axioms that is consistent and at least allows the definition of natural numbers can express propositions which are neither provable nor refutable within that system (Gödel 1931). For a system to be consistent just means that the axioms do not allow contradictory statements – and of course that is a presupposition of any sound theory. The second requirement, the ability to express the natural numbers, is of course not very severe given that Hilbert had hoped to formalize mathematics in general which is much more than just basic arithmetic on integers. However, Gödel's result is just a very general result showing that an undecidable proposition can always be constructed. It does not say anything about the propositions that actually can be derived from axioms. Formal axiomatic systems are used for all kinds of subject areas and a lot of important results have been proven using them although they are all incomplete in Gödel's sense. Thus, his results put an end to Hilbert's idea that mathematics can be an *entirely* formal process. This does not mean that formal systems cannot do all kinds of relevant things.

For that reason, the Entscheidungsproblem lived on. In contrast to Gödel, who showed that not *all* expressions can be proven or refuted, the Entscheidungsproblem only asks if there is a procedure to decide if a particular expression can be proven or refuted. Thus, the Entscheidungsproblem limits the scope from all expressions to one. However, it also introduces a new element: the aforementioned procedure that only needs a finite number of steps. This procedure, in turn, gave the question of the Entscheidungsproblem a generality quite similar to the results of Gödel. Hilbert and Ackermann had asked if there was a procedure for *any* single expression to decide its provability. Hilbert and Ackermann themselves provided such a procedure for a very small and constricted part of logics. However, answering if such a procedure exists for any expression would first need an understanding of such procedures in general. In other words, it would need a mathematical formalism that would not only allow to formulate such procedures but to say something about their scope, possibilities, and limits. In other words, Hilbert already had formulated that such procedures should consist only of purely formal steps in a finite number. Yet, what was needed was a formal understanding of these procedures themselves.

Such a formal understanding of decision procedures was found by two mathematicians independently but in close succession: Alonso Church and Alan Turing. In fact, both dealt with a related problem, namely, what a formal understanding of calculation or computation could mean. Yet, once that was solved, it quickly became clear that the formalisms of computation they had found could also serve to decide the Entscheidungsproblem: there is no such procedure for all expressions.

Church found the solution a few years before Turing, yet my explanation here starts with Turing's approach since it has been more influential in the present understanding of algorithms. Turing attempted a formal definition of what it means to compute. He did so by considering what a human computer would do when calculating on paper. He then simplified this process to make it mathematically tractable while maintaining the same functionality. For example, Turing assumed that computing entails reading certain symbols and then writing down a symbol. To make things simpler, he assumed that each symbol would get exactly one square on a piece of paper. He further assumed the paper to be just one strip of paper rather than a normal sheet, so that when scanning symbols, the machine can just move left or right, not up and down. Of course, one can do any computation that is possible on a sheet of paper also on a sufficiently long strip, although that would make the process much more complicated for a human computer – but it is mathematically easier. The fact that Turing admitted an infinitely long tape (as he called the strip of paper) already shows that his interest was in the limits of computability in a mathematical sense (not in a practical sense). He further assumed that a human computer has a "state of mind" and that this state determines the outcome of the calculation. For example, a person adding numbers using pen and paper might remember that the sum of the current column of digits already exceeds ten so that one has to be carried over to the next column. Since such states of mind influence the result, and at the same time computing was meant to be a purely formal affair, Turing assumed that the human computer would write down their state of mind – much like a person doing the addition with pen and paper, marking down a little number to not forget the carryover. Now, Turing argued, we could assume a person who "works in such a desultory manner" that the computer writes down the entire state of mind after each step of the computation in order to be able to resume it later on (Turing 1937, 253). Again, this is not very practicable. Yet, Turing is again interested only in two properties: first, a person working in this manner theoretically could do the same thing as a person just calculating without writing down the state of mind – even if it would be much more complex as a process; second, this guarantees that everything needed for the calculation is written down so that the result of the next step can be expressed as a rule depending only on the symbol that is read from the tape and the state of mind that can also be read from the paper. Thus, the rules can be such a purely formal thing that Hilbert was after. The fact that Turing assumes here that there are only a finite number of clearly discernible mental states again speaks to the fact that his line of thought only tells us something about the possibilities of a formal system and not so much about psychological precision – although his own wording suggests the latter.

Based on this intuition, Turing devised what is known as a Turing "machine," although it was just a mathematical construct. Such a machine is essentially a set of rules that all look the same. They depend on two "inputs": the last symbol that the machine has read from the tape and the current state of the machine, and it produces three "outputs": it moves the machine a definite number of steps to the left or right on the tape, it specifies the symbol to write on the tape, and it specifies the new state of the machine.

After a finite number of steps, the machine halts and then the result can be found in a predefined location on the tape.

Turing showed that using such simple rules, most numbers that we deal with can be computed. This included infinitely long numbers, but only up to a given precision, because a requirement is that the machine only runs a finite number of steps. For example, it is possible to formulate rules so that a machine reads a given number n from the tape and then prints the first n digits of the number π on the tape. This precision n has to be fixed (to limit the number of steps the machine runs) but it can be set arbitrarily high. Although Turing himself does not use the word in his paper, such a list of rules for a Turing machine is one of the most influential ways of formalizing what an "algorithm" is.

Turing used this newfound formalism for computing to achieve a result quite similar to Gödel. He showed that it is possible to define a machine by a finite set of rules, each single of them clear, precise, and purely formal. Yet, we can never know if this machine, once it starts to execute, will ever halt. This knowledge, however, is crucial for Turing machines. They are required to only run a finite number of steps and then the result is computed. Thus, for each algorithm on a Turing machine, it is essential to show that it will halt. In fact, this property (usually called "to terminate" later on) is a central part of any definition of algorithms in the realm of computer science. Why is that so? If it is impossible to determine beforehand that the machine will eventually halt, it leaves its users in a weird situation: the machine runs and runs and the users never know if it will spit out the result in the next minute, or hour, or year – or never. In other words, they never know if they just need some more patience or will never have a result.

In consequence, Turing found a limit to computation quite similar to the limit Gödel found for proofs. Gödel stated that each set of axioms that can express numbers can also express propositions that cannot be proven using these axioms. Similarly, Turing found that the formalism of Turing machines can express machines that it cannot compute (in the sense that we never know if it terminates).

Turing's interest (in this paper) was not to compute specific things, i.e. to build a computer and find algorithms for it. His interest was the possibility of the existence of a clearly stated algorithm that results in a machine of which we never know if it ever will halt. Thus, for him, the algorithm is not important for what it computes – to the contrary its entire sense is to show that it does not compute. Rather, it is important for the *relationship* it establishes between Turing's formalism and mathematical properties: computation and its limits. It is this relational manner, in which Turing also uses another algorithm in the last section of his paper. He shows that the Entscheidungsproblem can be translated into a Turing machine. Although the formalism of Turing machines was devised to compute numbers, Turing used a trick that already Gödel had used and that is a fundament of machinic computation to the very day: he translated the symbols of Hilbert's logical calculus into numbers and thus showed that a Turing machine could be defined that would compute the Entscheidungsproblem – if it did not have the halting problem, too. Thus, by showing that the Entscheidungsproblem can be expressed using a Turing machine and that we will never know if this Turing machine will ever halt, Turing showed that the Entscheidungsproblem has no solution.

Again, the sense of the algorithm that Turing invented to implement Hilbert's calculus was not to compute anything in particular. In fact, it served to show that the very thing it is meant to compute cannot be computed since we cannot know if the machine will ever halt. Again, the sense of this algorithm was to establish a *relationship*; the relationship between two formalisms: Hilbert's functional calculus, which was concerned with logic, and Turing's model of computation. By establishing this relation, Turing could use his insights into computability to answer a question from logic, the Entscheidungsproblem.

Although the notion of the algorithm would live on to denote mere sequences of instructions for Turing machines or similar formal mechanisms, it is this relational sense at the very root of the contemporary notion of the term "algorithm" that I build on in this book.

This view emphasizes that algorithms attain their meaning only in relation to an underlying model of computation. The word algorithm became a precise mathematical concept the moment it started to denote lists of instructions for Turing machines – not just lists of instructions like recipes or similar things that are often used to illustrate what an algorithm is.

At the same time, the properties of these models of computation are understood only by finding certain algorithms. As we just saw, Turing found an algorithm for his machine that implements Hilbert's calculus and thus allows us to say something about the Entscheidungsproblem. He also found an algorithm for a Turing machine of which it is impossible to say if it will ever halt, thus establishing the limits of this model of computation. This is what I call mutual complementarity: the algorithm only makes sense regarding a model of computation, but the model of computation can only be understood via the (possibility of) existence of particular algorithms. For Turing himself, that complement even figures in his use of language. He does not speak of Turing machines that are consequently programmed by a list of rules. Rather, a list of rules, in his words, is a machine.

Of course, Turing did so in order to show the limits of computation in general, not just the limits of Turing machines. However, he was well aware that such a thing could never be proven without a formal notion of computation. What he did show was that his notion of computation is equivalent to Church's notion: "effective calculability." He also gave various explanations for why he thought that what a Turing machine does can be seen as equivalent to what a human being doing computation does. However, this can be nothing more than a convincing story, because human activities and concepts in natural language like "compute" or "calculate" do not admit mathematical proofs. In fact, there are many things of which we would arguably say they are computable, but which are not computable in Turing's sense. For example, the question of whether the face in front of a smartphone is the owner's face today is regularly used to unlock the device. Thus, of course, the computer in the phone can compute the answer to the question: is this face the owner's face? However, the underlying algorithm does not compute in Turing's sense. For him, computation is a matter of determinist execution that arrives at a definite answer. The phone uses a neural network, which solves the question only with a certain probability (it is never 100% sure it's the face) in a high number of cases (it does occasionally fail as all users of such phones know). On the other hand, there are things that clearly are computable in Turing's sense, but not in any practical sense of the term. For example, contemporary encryption mechanisms usually use keys that are a sequence of 2^{2048} zeroes and ones. That is a number with 617 decimal digits – a very large number but clearly a finite number. Since Turing only asks that a machine terminates in a finite number of steps, there is a very simple solution: build a machine that tries each key and it will find the decryption in maximum 2^{2048} steps. This is computable in Turing's sense. However, the security of such an encryption mechanism clearly relies on the fact that such systematic testing is not computable in a sensible time span on any computer that currently exists.

This illustrates a core feature of considering algorithms as relations: algorithms only make sense regarding a specific idea of computation.

Church, in his approach to computation or as he calls it "effective calculability," makes explicit use of the term "algorithm." However, he does not specify algorithms himself. Rather, he proves statements of the form: under this and that condition, an algorithm for the effective calculation for this and that exists. He is not interested in the specific algorithms. For his mathematical task, it is enough to know that it exists. To know that means in other words: under specific conditions, we know the relation of some formula to the model of effective calculability. Thus again, the algorithm here is used in a relational manner.

Punch cards and mechanical data processing

During the times just described, when European and American mathematicians were debating the foundations of mathematics, (electro-)mechanical data processing was already an established technology. Telegraphy had led to a variety of appliances to transform symbols into electricity and back. Jacquard looms, but also mechanical pianos, harmoniums, or barrel organs, used punched cards or punched tape as a data carrier. Usually, Herman Hollerith is credited with bringing this technology to the realm of administrative data processing. His "Electric Tabulating System" was the topic of his doctoral thesis in 1889 and of a patent issued in the same year (Hollerith 2020). He proposed to use punch cards for his own work at the United States Census Bureau to facilitate the compiling of statistics and went on to found the Tabulating Machine Company, the successor of which still exists under the name of IBM. In the beginning, his machines were basically electromagnetic counters, which could be set to a specific entry on the card, i.e. a position of holes, and which would count the occurrence of holes, i.e. entries, at this position and display their number on a dial. Later on, his company added more complex functions such as arithmetic operations on the counts. In particular, machines for sorting the cards were added to the product range. This meant that punch cards were no longer just carriers for the input of certain electro-mechanical processes – now these processes operated on the cards themselves. The input was a batch of cards and the output was a sorting of these into several different batches based on some entries on the cards. This allowed queries akin to the possibilities of modern databases. Such machines, known as unit recording equipment, attained widespread use before the advent of digital computers in businesses, administration, and government.

Punched cards went on to become a common data carrier for programmable computers. Yet Hollerith's machines were not programmable in this sense. They were efficient machines that were built to a set of limited functions: sort cards by specific entry, count occurrences of values, and perform simple arithmetic on values, e.g. add them. Later instances of unit recording equipment usually sported control panels that could be easily rewired to perform different functions. This rewiring can be considered a kind of programming. Yet the term would only attain the meaning it has today in the context of computing once programs were no longer configurations of the machine but loadable data as well.[1]

---

1 This is discussed in detail in Chapter 5.

Still, these hard-wired functions like sorting or counting are of course algorithms, even if they would not necessarily have been called that way. Here algorithms are not broken down into several formal steps but into discrete components of the machine. In a sense, the algorithm is nothing more than these components. They attain their meaning however by the function – or algorithm they provide. This is again a mutually constitutive structure. This case, however, illustrates the need to open up the perspective. Because the relation here is not just the one between a function and the machine. Like the algorithm for Church and Turing established the relation of a formalism to some fundamental mathematical properties, here it establishes a relation between a machine and the need for a function to be performed efficiently. The machine as a material algorithm gives no new understanding of sorting or counting *per se* but enables a much more efficient execution. This efficiency is essential for the algorithm. It does not just sort; humans could do that, but it sorts efficiently. This was the reason for the success of the early data processing machinery, both in celebrated cases like the 1890–1895 US census, which is usually the prominent application mentioned in history books, and in cases many would prefer to be forgotten, like the role of the German subsidiary of IBM, Dehomag, in organizing the holocaust (Aly and Roth 2004). Thus, the algorithm is insufficiently understood as a relation of machinery to sorting or querying. Rather, it is the relation of machinery to sorting and querying in the context of late 19th- and early 20th-century data processes in business, governments, and the military, with aspects such as its growing amounts of data, demands for time efficiency, and the spreading of statistical decision making.

Thus, it would be too easy to say – as is often done – that the formalisms or models of computation in the first case and the machines in the latter just execute the algorithm. In both cases, we deal with a relation of mutual constitution. For example, Hollerith's machines quickly changed what efficiency regarding sorting and querying of data means. From the beginning on, for example, the data sorted with Hollerith's machines were data about persons. Thus, from the very beginning, the rather simple electromechanic switches that would find a hole in the card to make contact or not open up the entire predicament that later on would be the matter of profound studies on the relationship between sorting people and data processing (Bowker and Star 2000; Lyon 2003; Sandvig 2014). Being sortable means to reduce social complexity to a definite value, as definite as hole/no hole; it means to be more efficiently administered by means of state administration and surveillance, etc. This also illustrates that the meaning of computing cannot be just clarified by its theoretical scope and limits that Turing, Church, and others inquired about. Up to this day – all the buzz about AI notwithstanding – two of the most successful applications of computers are the database and the spreadsheet. Here, computations are often nothing more than a couple of sums, averages, etc. They are not used for being able to compute quite complex things; rather, they are used because they allow the fast processing of a lot of data.

With this observation, the relational understanding of algorithms needs to be enhanced. It concerns a relation between something abstract or general and something concrete or particular: in the case of Turing and Church, the relation of the abstract notion of computability to specific formalisms; in the case of Hollerith, the broad social phenomenon of efficiency within the context of administration and accounting with a particular form of machinery.

Cybernetics

Cybernetics is maybe the most-discussed historical root of modern computing. For many analysts, critical as well as euphoric, computing is essentially the ultimate realization of the cybernetic worldview. In light of this almost seamless identification of computing with cybernetics, it is important to note that in the beginning, cybernetics and algorithms, as they emerged from the work of mathematicians like Turing, actually were quite different ways of thought. Algorithms, as they have been understood in computer science until today, are related to formally codified, individual steps of execution with certain mathematical properties – in particular that they terminate. Furthermore, they follow instrumental logic. Algorithms are considered to turn a given input into a defined output. As soon as the first computers were actually built, the mathematical and formal possibilities that concerned Turing and Church thus were filled with concrete engineering: algorithms were meant to do stuff, to solve problems.[2]

The machines that cyberneticians built were meant to solve problems, too. Yet in their view machines could solve problems not because they were programmable with formal, discrete steps. Rather, they could solve problems because the problem and the machine were ontologically of the same order: issues of communicating and controlling information, in particular through feedback loops. What is more, according to cybernetics, processes never terminate; at best they stabilize in particular states. To put it in oversimplified terms: for a Turing machine view, computers are useful because they are special; they are universally programmable, that is, they can run every computable algorithm. The challenge is to find these algorithms. For the cybernetic view, computers are useful because they are not special, because they do what also happens in nerves and cells, in social processes, and in mechanical devices – communication and control of information. (Note that here I am comparing the internal meanings of two common views on computing – not my own.)

---

2 Famously, Turing himself was involved to build a computer to help decrypt German radio messages during the Second World War.

The new "ultra-rapid computing machine"(Wiener 2019, 8) as Norbert Wiener calls it in 1948 was thus just a very convenient way of organizing information transfer. Yet, for cybernetics, it does not matter if that organization is done with formal, individual steps or by other means. In fact, Wiener still unproblematically crosses over what would become a defining opposition later on: analog or digital, continuous or discrete. For his, essentially physical, perspective, the move from one to the other is as easy as turning a sum into an integral. See, for example, his introduction to the chapter on time series from his defining book "Cybernetics":

> There is a large class of phenomena in which what is observed is a numerical quantity, or a sequence of numerical quantities, distributed in time. The temperature as recorded by a continuous recording thermometer, or the closing quotations of a stock in the stock market, taken day by day, or the complete set of meteorological data published from day to day by the Weather Bureau are all time series, continuous or discrete [...].
> (Wiener 2019, 85)

How then did formal computing and algorithms become an essential part of the cybernetic worldview, for some even the most exemplary or clear instance? First, there are personal and biographical similarities. Wiener himself lists a couple of "migrant[s] from the field of mathematical logic to cybernetics" such as John von Neumann, Walter Pitts, Claude Shannon, and himself (Wiener 2019, 23). In fact, in the beginning, these ties were quite visible. For example, McCulloch and Pitts had done some inquiry into neural activity which led them to develop an abstraction of neurons that is the root of today's artificial neural networks. Yet, they tried to prove that these neurons could be described by a formal calculus, quite akin to the formal methods Hilbert and Ackermann had looked for (McCulloch and Pitts 1943). They did not yet realize that the potential of artificial neural networks lies in continuous activation functions and output in terms of value ranges – rather than the "all or none process" that they modeled to make the net compatible with the discrete symbols of logic. Used in this continuous manner, artificial neural networks can approximate functions that are not efficiently computable in Turing's sense. They are, though, still describable in the language of feedback and control that cybernetics would go on to develop, which is one of the reasons it is used much today, where artificial neural networks have become a central technique of computing.

A second relation is that both the mathematical and physical work of people like von Neumann and Wiener were indeed helpful for engineering, e.g. a much better understanding of stabilizers or control units. A lot of cyberneticians also contributed to the success of computing machines during the Second World War. Wiener himself emphasized the importance of his work on controlling anti-aircraft guns for his later thought; some influential cyberneticians such as Vannevar Bush or John von Neumann worked on the Manhattan Project; and quite generally, the military was a prominent driver of the development of early computing, both during the Second World War and the ensuing Cold War. Thus, most historians of cybernetics emphasize the important role of the military (Bowker 1993) if not putting it as the central category (Galison 1994).

In cybernetics, this military setting merged with an already ongoing, larger movement that brought quantitative and scientific rigor to fields that had traditionally been influenced a lot by the humanities, such as psychology or sociology. The second prominent development along this line is of course behaviorism. Only with regard to this self-conception as uniting matters from philosophy, society, and science can the importance of cybernetics conceiving itself as a newly universal science be understood. Importantly, this did not only entail applying scientific methods to new areas, although some of its proponents voiced it that way. In fact, it changed some fundamental premises of what was considered science itself. As Bowker explains, since Boyle, science was built on the idea of bracketing society in the laboratory: "Boyle excluded all traces of social interest from the laboratory and denied that he was talking about anything other than nature." In contrast to these "traditional sciences [that] operated behind the walls of the laboratory, cybernetics was everywhere you went. Where traditional sciences repudiated all possible mention of society, cybernetics proclaimed that it could produce the best possible description thereof" (Bowker 1993, 122). The same goes for humans, animals, and machines. This view allowed the cyberneticians to consider the concrete functioning of their theories and machines not as particular acts of engineering with a limited scope and use (as all machines) or as results pertaining to a specific field of knowledge (as all results from laboratories). Rather, they considered them as evidence or demonstrations that their universal science was true.

This is a very rough account and the intersections of cybernetics and algorithms – both among practitioners and academic analyses – are so manifold that they come up in many places in this book. Here, they are just a short hint at the fact that the oft-assumed proximity or even equation of algorithms with cybernetics is no matter of course. Furthermore, even this very short discussion highlights another important aspect of the relations of algorithms. Here, algorithms and their efficacy are enabled by factors and circumstances which are often not reflected by the programmers or users themselves – such as the particularities of wartime engineering in the US in this case. Quite as the situation and necessities of data processing for governance and businesses influenced – and were influenced by – the sorting and counting algorithms of unit processing equipment, here the influence was the situation in the war or some trends in the scientific community in the first half of the 20th century. As we have seen, the cyberneticians themselves would not consider their algorithms and machines as products of – and thus in constitutive relation to – this particular situation. For them, this was just the occasion for novel insights into what they essentially considered ontological.

This means that a relational account of algorithms also needs to take relations into account that are not reflected by users, programmers, etc. In fact, such observations have led people to see algorithms or software as inherently ideological (see, for example, Galloway (2006b) or Kittler (1992)). Yet, this is not the way I want to go here, because this presumes to find a reality behind the algorithm or software. Rather, neither algorithms nor something behind, below, or above them are the essence of computers and digital technology. As has already been discussed in the last chapter, algorithms are a situated research perspective. They ask for specific relations that connect a wider, abstract perspective with a concrete particular aspect. Asking for algorithms allows us to understand the relation of that aspect – formalism, machinic efficiency, wartime needs or desires – to algorithms. These aspects complete or complement the algorithm in a constitutive manner: as we have seen, Turing or Church conceived of algorithms as formalisms; in a sense, in unit recording equipment, the machine is the algorithm. Yet a pure reduction would not work here. In consequence, we need to understand the algorithms not only by their constitutive elements but also by what they do: show the limits of computing, speed up accounting, etc. Thus, these doings of algorithms also bestow the specific sense on their constitutive elements: Turing's formalism became famous because it could show the limits of computing. Unit recording did not just sort but sort specific things with specific meanings made to be sorted that way. In this sense, we deal with a mutual complement. A complement though that is always situated and directed. In all applications of algorithms, there are issues of formalism (or as I will call it in a later chapter: code), material conditions, data, and subjects that form the chapters of this book. Depending on how we inquire about algorithms, different of these relations come to the fore.

3

THEORIZING COMPLIMENTARY ABSTRACTIONS

From ontological to radical situatedness

The last two chapters have argued for a relational view of algorithms. This will be spelled out in this chapter. In the first chapter, I have already shortly mentioned Lucas Introna's work on algorithms, which is based on Karen Barad's "agential realism." Introna fuses the insight that there are different perspectives on algorithms, such as users and programmers, with algorithms as situating subjects themselves. In consequence, algorithms are not a given object which is then considered from different perspectives that are somehow "external" to algorithms. Both users and programmers are what they are also because of algorithms. Thus, the object of observation (the algorithm) and the observers (users, programmers) co-constitute each other. This also entails that it does not make much sense to rank or judge the different perspectives as more or less ideological, as more or less removed from the essential processes, etc. All of these verdicts would need an algorithm that is independent of the different perspectives so that it can be used as a reference for comparing them.

In contrast, as Introna describes it, an algorithm "is an algorithm because it is enacted as such by a heterogeneous assemblage of actors, imparting to it the very action we assume it to be doing" (Introna 2016, 23). We can think of many different perspectives on such enacting or on elements of it: this line of code compares two variables, the processor executes this instruction, and the administrator uses this algorithm to make a judgment. Any such description, however, would both focus on a particular "element" and halt the dynamics of this praxis. In Introna's Baradian terms, it would "cut" it:

> [A]ny cut of, or in, the temporal flow would not just be constitutive of the answer as to what it "is" that is actually being done (comparing, swapping, sorting, administering, etc.); it would also be constitutive of

DOI: 10.4324/9781003299851-4

what we take the actor to be as such: is the actor the programmer, the code, the administrator, the compiler, the central processing unit, the manager, and so on? The answer is: it depends on how or where we make the cut. This is what Barad [...] calls the "agential cut".

(Introna 2016, 23)

The formulation of "making" the cut in this quote should not be understood as if this was an arbitrary choice. This becomes clear from the general topic of Introna's text, which deals with "governing algorithms." Thus, the actors in this paragraph are not only constituted through the cuts discussed but also otherwise situated, e.g. through governmental power structures. Introna argues that Barad's performative view, if applied to algorithms, is a good starting point for clarifying the relationship between algorithms and governance. This is the case, Introna argues, because governance needs to be understood from a performative perspective as well: "the argument would be that the governance of algorithms, or through algorithms, must itself be understood as practices of governmentality in order to understand the doing of governance" (Introna 2016, 30).

In the next section, I will begin to discuss Barad's theory as a starting point for integrating a view of algorithms with social and political perspectives – while doing justice to the technical detail. However, it needs some amendments. This can be seen in Introna's text, too. The particular form of governing through algorithms that he discusses is plagiarism detection software. He shows that in order to understand its impact, one needs to consider the increasing role of the private sector in education and the commodification of universities (the text is from the 2010s UK). In consequence, actors shift their roles: "the student is now increasingly enacted as a customer, the academic as a service provider, and the academic essay (with its associated credits) is enacted as the site of economic exchange – academic writing for credit, credit for degree, degree for employment, and so forth" (Introna 2016, 33). These shifts entail the need for various forms of governance. Here, the plagiarism detection algorithm comes in as a technology of governing in order to guarantee the "value" of the academic essay in the aforementioned exchange. However, the algorithm does not just execute one element, originality control, of this general shift toward a more economically driven university. It also changes it: Turnitin – the algorithm Introna analyzes – rates the originality of a text by checks against a database. Thus, originality, once a disputed criterion to be judged by human readers, is turned into a task of pattern matching. Here is an example of how – in my words – data complement an algorithm in constituting *the specific way* in which the algorithm does what it does: rate originality.

This still means that Turnitin needs a trained user, because a good academic text is not 100% original; it has quotes, lists of references, etc. Thus, a user needs to check where in the text and to which extent the overlaps are found. This shows that the algorithm is also designed presuming a specific relation between user and algorithm (Introna 2016, 33).

Through both relations, database and algorithm as well as user and algorithm, elements that are external to that relation are changed, so this change needs to be understood against the wider context of commodification and exchange that Introna discusses. In the relation of database and algorithm, this would be originality; in the relation of user and algorithm, something like the sense of academic writing exercises. It may be telling that for discussing these aspects, Introna does not refer directly to Barad's vocabulary that he introduced before, because particularly such relations between something quite specific such as a database and something that can only be understood as part of a larger context that spans much more than the present case, e.g. the commercialization of the university, are very hard to grasp in Barad's framework. Furthermore, as I will show, there are some difficulties to reconcile the political claims in Introna's analysis fully with Barad's theory. Thus, she provides a great starting point for a relational, co-constitutive view but will be amended with thoughts from Foucault, Haraway, and Butler.

Since this relational concept forms the basis for the rest of this book, I will discuss it in great detail to make sure that the quite different aspects that will be discussed later on can be covered using this theoretical perspective.

Barad's intra-active ontology

Barad develops her theory out of Niels Bohr's reflection on quantum mechanics. She gives an original interpretation of his work that she calls "Bohr's philosophy-physics" (Barad 2007, chap. 3) which she then ontologizes into her agential realism.[1]

Bohr is concerned with the problem that on the quantum level, measurements interfere with what is being measured. In particular, this makes some measurements mutually exclusive. Barad describes a thought experiment of measuring the position of an electron (Barad 2007, 110 et seqq.). This could be done using a photon, a light particle, that will bounce off the electron and hit a photographic plate, leaving a mark. For a precise measurement of position, this plate needs to be fixed. If one wanted to measure the impulse of the electron, the photographic plate would need to be movable, and the movement caused by the impact of the electron would need to be recorded. Since something cannot be movable and fixed at the same time, if one of these properties is determinate (say position), the other (momentum) cannot be. The apparatus does not only

---

1 This two-step shift from Bohr to Barad's ontology is not explicit in Barad's texts and has been carefully reconstructed by Thomas Nyckel (2022), whose detailed re-reading has provided important input for my reconstruction of Barad's thought.

enable, but at the same time also precludes determinate, knowable things. For Barad, following Bohr, this is the reason that it does not make sense to say these qualities exist independent of measuring. "[T]he measurement apparatus is the condition of possibility for determinate meaning for the concept in question [e.g. position, momentum] [...]" (Barad 2007, 127).

According to Bohr's theory, such apparatuses themselves (in contrast to the objects "within" the apparatus) are observable without difficulty. In fact, the possibility to communicate and reproduce them is the central condition of objectivity for Bohr (Barad 2007, 143). Barad finds fault with these humanist assumptions in Bohr's thinking, that is, assuming a human subject that can objectively observe and instrumentally deal with the apparatus (Barad 2007, 145). Here Barad takes up suggestions from Foucault and Butler that the subject itself is also constituted by a specific practice. She uses the Foucauldian notion to redescribe apparatuses as part of "discursive practices" that bring about the objects of science as well as the scientist as a subject itself. Thus, she includes the knowing subject in the theory (Barad 2007, 150–152).

This is where Introna picks up Barad's theory. Different apparatuses or different material-discursive practices yield different subjects and objects: not just scientist and measuring device but, for example, also programmer and code or user and movie watching machine. Yet, ontologically, they are all the same; neither is closer to the truth, more essential, etc. However, as I will argue in the following text, Barad's way of theorizing this at the same time makes it lose its political thrust – even if it is inspired by Foucault and Butler.

Barad herself claims to proceed in a more rigorous manner than both Butler and Foucault who are "limited to the domain of human social practices" (Barad 2007, 145). Barad attempts to overcome this "anthropocentrism" by extending the concepts derived from Bohr to a general ontology. In this view, all subject–object distinctions are just particular "cuts" of what she calls "intra-actions." The change from "interaction" to "intra-action" emphasizes that the relation precedes the relata, i.e. the subjects and objects are secondary to the intra-action in which they emerge. Intra-actions are ontological. Barad thus posits that the intra-action that yields an electron and a photon with certain properties and the intra-action that yields a scientist and their instruments all are ontologically the same. In this regard, Barad can be subsumed under those thinkers advocating for a radically symmetric ontology between humans and non-humans.[2]

---

2 For this reason, Barad is also considered one of the prime representatives of "new materialist" feminists, although otherwise, she does not share too much with the Spinozist or vitalist forms of thought prevalent in this discourse. Indeed, a lot of her other concerns, how practices relate to phenomena, how the subject–object split is secondary to a practice, etc., share a lot more with a Post-Heideggerian phenomenology.

Accordingly, Barad also criticizes Foucault and Butler for not paying enough attention to matter. Although she acknowledges a certain importance of materiality in Foucault, when she describes his notion of discursive practices as "local sociohistorical material conditions" (Barad 2007, 147), she keeps emphasizing that this is too limited. Countering this claim, Thomas Lemke has shown that the relevance of the material becomes even more obvious when turning to the notion of *dispositif* in Foucault (Lemke 2021, chap. 4). Barad particularly attacks Butler in claiming that she reduces matter to "the passive product of discursive practices" (Barad 2007, 151). Again, many have criticized this as a misreading of Butler (Ahmed 2008; Lemke 2021, chap. 3). Yet, I do not think that a lacking concern for matter is even an independent claim in Barad. What she is concerned with is that neither Butler nor Foucault discusses matter aside from human practices. Thus, I guess her critique of lacking attention to matter can be subsumed into her critique of anthropocentrism. I will discuss these issues of anthropocentrism in the last section of this chapter. First, with the basics of Barad's view now established, I want to discuss how she integrates wider sociotechnical aspects into her ontology. Coming from feminist science studies, she is very much concerned with issues like gender, race, and other forms of domination.

Politics in Barad's ontology

The question of whether Barad's discussion is adequate to physics, her privileging scientific practices, or her lack of historicizing her perspective has been discussed at length (Pinch 2011; Rouse 2004). Still, Barad's work has inspired a wide range of critical analyses of all kinds of practices, including the one by Introna just mentioned. The critical and political impact of Barad's work thus can be acknowledged as highly productive and inspiring, despite the problems that the aforementioned critics have pointed out. What I will engage with is this critical and political potential – showing that there are some problems in Barad's thought that might run counter to this potential that can be amended with thoughts by Haraway, but also moments in Butler and Foucault that Barad does not consider.

The way in which Barad includes social and political issues in her ontology is well illustrated by her reading of a particular incident in a laboratory. In the early days of quantum physics, in 1922, German scientists Otto Stern and Walter Gerlach conducted an experiment that would lead to the introduction of the concept of "spin" into physical theory (Barad 2007, 166). The experiment included directing a beam of silver atoms onto a plate, where it should leave a visible mark. At first, the physicists were disappointed since the mark did not form. Only when Stern looked closely at the plate, suddenly the mark became visible. They figured that Stern, who smoked cheap cigars containing lots of sulfur, had held the plate close enough to his face that his sulfurous breath reacted with the silver, turning it into a much more visible black sulfide – known from the tarnishes on silverware.

Here Barad points to a fact well known from STS and laboratory studies: a laboratory or the agencies of observation have more constituents than what is commonly considered as such. Barad also emphasizes that the cigar might be incidental to Stern and Gerlach, but its presence is no accident. The fact that Stern smoked cheap cigars is part of his "gendered and classed performance of masculinity" (Barad 2007, 167).

Thus, Barad makes a point that is also important for algorithms. The context of practice matters, not only for conducting measurements but also for programming, for example. Furthermore, this context does not only matter through salient factors but through things that might seem accidental – Stern's social position or the demography of a programming team – but which have important consequences and are not that accidental at all – as discussed in Chapter 5.

Barad emphasizes that she does not want to say that "social factors determine scientific investigations" (Barad 2007, 167). By ontologizing Bohr's philosophy-physics, apparatuses lose their dualist character and become recursive and networked. "Apparatuses are themselves material-discursive phenomena, materializing in intra-action with other material-discursive apparatuses" (Barad 2007, 203). In consequence, she describes gender and class themselves as material-discursive practices, thus as dynamic and ongoing, not just a one-way influence. In Barad's words, this would be an example of what it means that apparatuses intra-act: "material practices that contributed to the production of gendered individuals also contributed to the materialization of this particular scientific result" (Barad 2007, 167).

Here is another advantage that Barad's perspective holds for the analysis of algorithms – or technology in general: it allows describing co-constitutive relations. This might not be very salient in the present example because the impact of the experiment on male cigar smoking probably is negligible. However, in algorithms, a social factor that structures a program, for example, a hiring algorithm that disadvantages non-male candidates, can clearly have an effect on the practices that produce gender if widely enough applied. Since in Barad, both practices or apparatuses intra-act, in this case, material practices that contributed to the production of gendered individuals and an algorithm, both co-constitute each other.

However, there is also a difficulty emerging here. Gender and class can matter only because of a specific object: the cigar. It is a surprising addition to the experimental setup but it is clear addition that leaves a mark, a visible mark instead of an invisible mark. Thus, without thematizing this, Barad's notion of intra-action relies very much on a kind of indexicality. To be sure, she reworks the simple idea of one primary object producing a secondary mark, as classic examples of indexicality, e.g. a paw leaving a mark in soil, are often described. Yet, Barad's intra-active take remains a version of indexicality in the sense that the production of material marks is key, which she takes from Bohr's concept of objectivity, "permanent marks ... left on bodies which define the experimental conditions" (Barad 2007, 119). She continues to use this indexical language also in other examples, such as her text on fetal ultrasonography which I will discuss as follows. Here she talks about "marks on a computer screen" (Barad 2007, 202).

However, the practices that produce gender and class that Barad wants to include in her theory are hard to grasp using such a view. Both Butler and Foucault show that the significance of practices – even very material practices such as torture and incarceration (Foucault 1977) or surgery (Butler 1993) – derives from repeated, sustained acts entangled with power. In Butler's work, this appears as "iteration" or "citation" (Butler 1993); in Foucault, particularly through the need for long-term genealogical perspectives to understand practices. This does not mean that these acts are just a consequence of power in the form of norms, discourse, or dispositifs. In a sense, norms, discourses, or dispositifs are nothing else than their enactment. Thus, one could say they intra-act and this is the reason why Barad thinks she can integrate discursive practices in her ontology. Yet, the important point is that norms, discourses, or dispositifs are nothing else than their *sustained, repeated, or iterated* enactment.

In Wittgenstein's writing, there is a beautiful image that serves as an illustration of this issue. He evokes the relation between a river and the riverbed. One could say that of course the riverbed guides the river. However, in another sense, the riverbed just exists by the water flowing, engraving its own bed. Yet, once the riverbed is there, of course, it would not make much sense to say that the riverbed is just the result of the flow of water. At least the water currently flowing is very much the result of the shape of the riverbed. In Wittgenstein's words: "I distinguish between the movement of the waters on the river-bed and the shift of the bed itself; though there is not a sharp division of the one from the other" (Wittgenstein 1969, §97). That way, a more abstract and long-term phenomenon and current phenomena can be understood to co-constitute each other.

Butler writes, "There is no 'one' who takes on a gender norm. On the contrary, this citation of the gender norm is necessary in order to qualify as a 'one,' to become viable as a 'one'" (Butler 1993, 232). This sounds similar to Barad's moving the subject from a presupposed actor to the product of intra-action. However, in this case, the norms can only be understood as the result of a distributed iteration of the norm. Being a subject is nothing else than being subjected to these norms, but only on a much more abstract and bigger scale are the norms nothing else than the result of (many!) subjects acting this way. They produce a form of meaning that can only be understood as part of something larger, which figures in Foucault's writing as discourse or dispositif and in Butler's as the norm or "heteronormative matrix." In contrast, Barad seems to maintain a form of flat ontology where all relevant elements are present in an intra-action, and thus gender and class need something like a cigar to contribute to a mark on a screen.

This allows us to begin to understand the challenge better that was formulated in the introduction: to describe a co-constitutive relation between the concrete, like an academic essay originality score, and the abstract and contextual, such as the neoliberal university.

Barad herself deals with such issues as well. In fact, there is a second, gradual shift in her work. The first is quite explicit, from Bohr's philosophy-physics to her own ontology. The second is never thematized by Barad herself.[3] Yet, she gradually moves away from a concern for apparatuses, enacting cuts between subjects and objects, phenomena leaving (indexical) marks, and a view on the recursive and networked intra-action of these apparatuses. Instead, describes a specific materialization as brought about by many entangled practices. For example, she has a list of the many intra-actions of the piezoelectric transducers used in ultrasound imaging.

> They "materialize (and are iteratively rematerialized) in intra-action with a multitude of practices, including those that involve medical needs; design constraints (including legal, economic biomedical, physics and engineering ones); market factors; political issues; other R&D projects using similar materials; the educational background of the engineers and scientists designing the crystals and the workplace environment of the engineering firm or lab; particular hospital or clinic environments where the technology is used; receptivity of the medical community and the patient community to the technology; legal, economic, cultural, religious political, and spatial constraints on its uses; positioning of patients during the examination; and the nature of the training of technicians and physicians who use the technology".
>
> (Barad 2007, 204)

Barad's texts are full of such open-ended lists. Her book even features a visualization of these "entangled genealogies," featuring among other things the World Trade Organization, homophobia, aliens, and Einstein's formula "$E = mc^2$" in one complex topology of relations.

Thus, Barad addresses iteration (at the beginning of the quote above), genealogies, and factors that exist on much longer timescales, geographic

---

3 Again, I rely on the careful reconstruction of Barad's thought in Nyckel (2022) in particular pp. 120 et seqq.

extensions, and different levels of abstraction. Yet, there are two issues with the way Barad includes them in her theory. One is ontological-epistemological, one ethical-political, and of course, both are related.

The ontological-epistemological issue essentially deals with the question of how Barad understands the situatedness of practices and knowledge. We already see that with this shift toward many, multiple, and potentially infinite entanglements, we begin to lose the orienting force of a situated perspective that I consider one of the strengths of Barad's thought: one perspective enables one to observe certain things while precluding others. To deal with these in turn, we need yet another perspective that yet again precludes others. With this shift, however, Barad moves more toward a perspective where intra-actions are endlessly concatenated and networked. The question is no longer the interdependence of observing one thing and excluding the other. Rather, the concern becomes whether we see enough – or all – of these connections, and indeed Barad frames responsibility that way (Barad 2007, 391). Barad herself claims to reconcile her care for exclusion with the potentially infinitely entangled relation. Tracing how she does this brings us closer to the way she includes the political into her ontology.

The politics of Barad's ontology

Barad discusses a text on fetal sonography and other fetal treatments by Monica Casper (1994) who criticizes the attribution of agency to fetuses. She argues that acknowledging non-human agency is not simply an ontological extension of agency from the (wrong) restriction of agency to humans. It impacts those who already have agency, which she considers a political more than an ontological issue. In particular, she criticizes that the attribution of agency to the fetus "reduces [women] to technomaterial environments for fetal patients" (Barad (2007, 215) citing Casper (1994, 844)). Thus, Casper is not against non-human agency per se, for example, she demands it for certain animals. Yet, she demands them for political reasons and not as a general ontological extension.

I do not want to discuss Casper's particular claim but the way Barad criticizes it. This case is illustrative because Barad agrees with the problem of the reduction of women (Barad 2007, 217), yet she argues that Casper is referring to the wrong reasons. Barad mentions two problems. The first is not really an issue, though, because Barad wonders if it might not be strategically necessary in some cases to invoke fetal agency (Barad 2007, 216). I guess Casper would agree because she explicitly states that her reasons for precluding fetal agency are a "politics"; they are about "taking sides" (Barad (2007, 215) citing Casper (1994, 853)). The second critique is more profound and more interesting. Barad claims that Casper would (implicitly) draw a *universal* boundary between "who and what gets to be an agent"

(Barad 2007, 216). Instead, Barad argues that the boundary that is drawn between mother and fetus is indeed political – but not as a matter of attributing agency but subjectivity (Barad 2007, 217). How is it possible that Barad reads Casper's boundary as universal, even if Casper explicitly states that it was political? The answer is that Casper chose the wrong attribute: agency. Barad wants to agree with Casper's politics, but for that reason, it needs to be an attribution of subjectivity. Because subjects, as I have already explained, are enacted in phenomena or intra-actions. Agency, though, is not. Here is Barad's definition: "agency cannot be designated as an attribute of subjects or objects, which are themselves constituted through specific practices" (Barad 2007, 218). Instead "[a]gency is a matter of intra-acting; it is an enactment, not something that someone or something has. Agency is a matter of making iterative changes to particular practices through the dynamics of intra-activity" (Barad 2007, 214).

Thus, for Barad, neither the woman nor the fetus has agency, but agency is distributed over the intra-action that produces both. Barad expresses it as "there are fetal enactments" (Barad 2007, 218). Because of this ontological status of agency, Barad cannot but read a preclusion of agency as a universal claim.

Here we begin to see that Barad is very much concerned with politics, including boundaries and exclusions. Yet, all of these political differences or differentiations and boundaries are ontologically the same. All of them are produced by intra-actions in entangled material-discursive practices or apparatuses, and this outlook motivates her political perspective. In contrast, Casper is concerned with the possibilities of agency in a very particular practice, not on the ontological level. Similarly, I have quoted Barad at length with her list of entanglements that intra-act to materialize piezoelectric transducers. These different elements from "the position of patients" to "political issues" can be seen as entangled because they are ontologically the same. Politics, for Barad, is situated within the ontology. In contrast, for Casper, ontology (or at least a part of it, i.e. the distribution of agency) itself is political.

Washick and Wingrove come to a similar conclusion in their discussion of another section where Barad agrees a lot with the politics of a text but considers it too limited. In this case, she discusses Leelas Fernandes' *Producing Workers* – an analysis of the socio-technical subjectifications of workers on a shop floor. Barad follows Fernandes' analysis, particularly her attention to how the machines and the configuration of the shop floor contribute to "producing workers" (Barad 2007, 242). Still, Washick and Wingrove summarize their analysis:

> The multiple possibilities for re-materialized identities and relations that Barad canvasses here elaborate her affirming conclusion that "even when apparatuses are primarily reinforcing [of the status quo], agency is not foreclosed"; indeed "[a]gency never ends; it can never 'run out'" […]. The

distance between this vision of a plentiful futurity and Fernandes' persistent attention to how different workers are differentially constrained is profound: where the latter sees horizons of possibility delimited not deterministically and for all time but rather systematically, the former sees the never exhausted, because never delimitable in advance, scope of intra-acting agencies.

(Washick and Wingrove (2015, 69) citing Barad (2007, 235))

Washick and Wingrove diagnose a difference in situatedness. Fernandes' main concern is how the particular configuration of the shop floor, gendered practices, economic demands, and more "produce" workers as severely constrained subjects. Barad acknowledges this, yet her emphasis is on the general, ontological possibility of change. It is important to note that Fernandes does not doubt this; the limits she sees are "not deterministically and for all time," as Washick and Wingrove write. Yet, they are so systematic that this theoretical possibility does not help much. For Barad, however, the important factor is that change is ontologically *guaranteed* – regardless of how constraining the current apparatuses are. Again, for Barad, the matter is the ontological character of politics, while Fernandes – as Casper in the last example – is concerned with the current political possibilities.

This difference is not just a matter of emphasis – general ontological possibilities vs. current configurations among these possibilities. Rather, Barad's view has a depoliticizing character – in the very attempt to politicize ontology.

This begins to appear in a last example I want to use from Barad's book where she moves political thought to the ontological level. In this case, she engages with a quote from Judith Butler: "It must be possible to concede and affirm an array of 'materialities' that pertain to the body, that which is signified by the domains of biology, anatomy, physiology, hormonal and chemical composition, illness, age, weight, metabolism, life and death" (Barad (2007, 211) citing Butler (1993, 66)). Barad criticizes that "Butler assigns different kinds of materialities to different discursive practices." She counters that "there is an important reason to suspect that these different discursive practices are not separate at all but entangled in specific ways" (Barad 2007, 211). Yet, this is the very matter that Butler is concerned with. Most probably, they are related. Yet, how exactly they are related needs to be shown, which is a matter of critical practice – and Butler would be the least to oppose such disclosure of relatedness. She herself does so when, for example, she discusses how Aristotelian, Foucauldian, and Marxist treatments of matter are related (Butler 1993, 31 et seqq.). Importantly, though, it needs to be shown and it does not suffice to acknowledge that they all are ontologically entangled.

This political work of establishing connections between different practices and contexts is central to the analysis of algorithms. Benjamin (2019),

Eubanks (2017), Noble (2018), and others have emphasized the need to understand algorithms in the current social and historical situation. This entails the ways in which racism, the postcolonial condition, sexism, and other forms of domination continue in algorithmic practices and materialities and how these sustain, change, and shift these power relations. Yet, that is analytical work to be done – as exemplified by these studies – that cannot be relegated to ontology.

All of these texts, quite similar to the ones by Judith Butler or Leelas Fernandes discussed above, are concerned with concrete others, who suffer injustice, violence, and discrimination. To be sure, part of such critical work is to counter narratives of algorithmic objectivity, clarity, or other forms of "closure," as Amoore calls them (2020, 162). It is important to emphasize the possibilities of difference within algorithmic practices and beyond. Yet, this difference is not just a generic ontological possibility for change; it is, in this context, a difference that enables a different – and better – life for specific others in their specific situations.

When paying closer attention to the way the situation of such others needs to be understood, it becomes clearer that this does not just concern a different emphasis on concrete situations rather than general ontology. Rather, it poses some problems to Barad's ontological framework. In other words, ontology cannot solve the political problems for us. In contrast, it may even cause some more. In particular, the situation of such others is certainly relational and part of certain practices, as Barad emphasizes. Yet, these relations are asymmetric and constitutively excluding. These features often figure in the literature as "othering" (Spivak 1985) or "unmarked identities" (Alcoff 2006). There are huge debates on these issues which I summarize here quite abstractly in order to highlight the difference to Barad.

For example, racism brings the difference between whites and non-whites into existence. In this sense, this difference is an intra-action, as Barad would most probably agree. There are no whites and non-whites prior to racist practices. Yet, this relation is different from the cut between an observer and the observed. The latter is – in one important aspect – a symmetric relation. Observer and observed depend on the constitutive practice in the same manner. However, positions such as white, male, and able-bodied work differently. They are constitutively asymmetric: for example, being white *is* not being non-white.

A second and related issue is that the subject positions at the more powerful end of these asymmetric relations also are constituted by repressing or ignoring the dependence on others. This is what is called an unmarked identity. For example, being white permits to ignore the own social situatedness; being white just becomes being (Alcoff 2006). In particular, the presumed autonomy of liberal subjects has been shown to depend on other subjects, while at the same time, this dependence is disavowed (Mills 2011;

Pateman 1988; Rössler 2021). Again, this is not just accidental or an oversight but constitutive of the forms of subjectivity in question.

Both issues are central to understanding the position of those who are concerned by the outcomes of algorithmic processes. They are also necessary for analyzing the operation of algorithmic operations themselves. Many machine-learning technologies work by assuming or defining normalcy and rely on their power to detect or classify conformity or deviance from that norm – thus applying an equally asymmetric relation (Matzner 2018). The need for all kinds of dissimulated or ignored labor and contributions in order to produce the felt increase of autonomy or instrumental value for the users of digital technology has recently been at the center of critical attention (Atanasoski and Vora 2019; Casilli 2017; Gillespie 2018; Mühlhoff 2020).

In her earlier work, Barad derives her treatment of exclusion from the mutual exclusion[4] of measurements. Like the observation of position precludes the observation of momentum, any intra-action that leads to an observation precludes others. In consequence, exclusion in Barad is an ontological relation of two forms of intra-action that each does not constitutively depend on the other. The exclusion just comes from the fact that a thing that needs to be fixed for measuring position needs to be moveable for measuring momentum. Yet, one does not depend on not being the other constitutively, such as being white depends on not being non-white or being male depends on not being non-male. Here, again, Barad maybe underestimates how much the indexical forms of meaning-making she deals with contribute to her thought. A mark is there or not. A form of meaning that constitutively involves an othering exclusion cannot be sufficiently understood from this perspective.

As I have shown, in her later work, Barad's attention shifts away from the boundary-making and exclusions of apparatuses to many entangled practices. Accordingly, she now demands "an accounting of the constitutive practices in the fullness of their materialities, *including the enactments of boundaries and exclusions*, the production of phenomena in their sedimented historiality, and the ongoing reconfiguring of the space of possibilities for future enactments" (Barad 2007, 391, emphasis mine). This requirement, which correspondsto Barad's notion of objectivity, is also the base for her ethics of responsibility. The possibility to include exclusions in this list seems to be a matter of course for Barad. Like in the example of Butler, Barad does not consider the critical and political work that is necessary to make exclusions visible because, for her, they are already ontologically part of the situation, in the same way that the different practices of

---

4 In the language of physics, the right term here would be complementarity. Yet I use that term differently and thus resort to a scientifically speaking imprecise wording.

mattering that Butler describes are already related for her. In other words, exclusion for Barad is within ontology. However, in the case of asymmetric exclusionary relations, ontology *itself* is exclusionary. In consequence, ethics and politics do not derive from ontology but pertain to the ontology itself.

For Barad, the issue is one of a switch of perspectives: that which apparently is given, really is the product of a dynamic, relational ontology. This may have a lot of appeal, because it provides a kind of ontological guarantee for politics and for the possibility to change. At the same time, however, it comes with its own exclusions and forms of power.[5]

Kathryn Yusoff addresses the same problem as the "desire for ontodeliverance" (Yusoff 2018, 82). She discusses debates on the Anthropocene, another area where a political reconfiguration of ontology takes place. Based on the recognition of the scope of human influence on the earth, the demand for a more symmetric relation between the human and the non-human arises. However, as Yusoff remarks, this demand for acknowledging materiality only turns the "God's eye-view" into a "lithic eye" view (Yusoff 2018, 10). It stays within the scope of a general ontological reconfiguration of boundaries, thus ignoring the particular differences embedded in the concrete history of the situation we have come to understand as the Anthropocene. Here, on a global scale and with wide historical scope, Yusoff fervently marks the same type of problem that also led Barad to ignore the particular politics of a fetus with agency or of workers constrained by their machines in the cases discussed above. Yusoff turns to diasporic writers such as Sylvia Wynters or Aimé Césaire for a different perspective. This brings up a final important problem of Barad's ontology: the possibility of contesting voices. If politics is about a reconfiguration of intra-actions *within* ontology, the possibility of someone appearing who sees things *essentially* differently is precluded. For example, someone who does not even agree with the way their own exclusion is understood.

Here, seemingly paradoxically, the ontological guarantee of politics that Barad relies on precludes the need to actually pursue it by those concerned or in the name of or in solidarity with them. Because if change is essentially possible, the need – and obstacles – to concretely pursue it can become invisible. This is not a real paradox, though, if one considers the insight already voiced by Hannah Arendt that any guarantee of politics is actually its end (Arendt 1998, 244).

---

5 Andrea Seier writes not of a guarantee of politics, but that what used to be "strategic interventions" are turned into "scientific truth claims" (Seier 2018, 174). This strange trust in science within a work deeply inspired by science studies is also one of the central elements of Lemke's critique. However, Barad and maybe even more so many of her readers see her observation as inspiring political work. Thus, I want to particularly engage with the question of what a Baradian politics could mean and which political problem it poses.

Radical situatedness

I will now turn to Haraway's notion of situatedness, which – although regarded by many as a predecessor of Barad's work – is more radical in its treatment of situatedness and circumvents this problem of an ontological guarantee of politics.

There are obvious similarities. In *Situated Knowledges*, Haraway like Barad is concerned with a situated form of objectivity. She also emphasizes the productive, emancipatory potential rather than just the disclosure of the apparently given as made. This includes tying meaning and embodiment together: "We need the power of modern critical theories of how meanings and bodies get made, not in order to deny meanings and bodies, but in order to build meanings and bodies that have a chance for life" (Haraway 1988, 580). Some phrases of the text in fact could be from Barad's book, too: "Feminist objectivity is about limited location and situated knowledge, not about transcendence and splitting of subject and object. It allows us to become answerable for what we learn how to see" (Haraway 1988, 583). It also centers on an engagement with the practices, materialities, and technologies that enable our knowledge and acting. Yet, working in critical negotiation with Marxist and feminist standpoint theories, Haraway arrives at a more radical situatedness.

She rigorously defuses hopes for a completely different, emancipatory standpoint. There is the "serious danger of romanticizing and/or appropriating the vision of the less powerful while claiming to see from their positions. To see from below is neither easily learned nor unproblematic." This holds even if one belongs to the "less powerful," such as Haraway's reluctant association with the scare-quoted "we" in her text: "even if 'we' 'naturally' inhabit the great underground terrain of subjugated knowledges" (Haraway 1988, 584). There is also the danger of resorting to an ever-critical position of unmasking doctrine and ideology while remaining unproductive out of fear of spoiling the purity of the own position. "We unmasked the doctrines of objectivity because they threatened our budding sense of collective historical subjectivity and agency and our 'embodied' accounts of the truth, and we ended up with one more excuse for not learning any post-Newtonian physics and one more reason to drop the old feminist self-help practices of repairing our own cars. They're just texts anyway, so let the boys have them back" (Haraway 1988, 578). Accordingly, Harraway urges to stay with the political rather than ontologizing it: "subjugation is not grounds for an ontology; it might be a visual clue" (Haraway 1988, 586).

At the same time, the insight into the becoming of what apparently are given objects and subjects gives even more fuel to the dreams of "high-tech military fields" (Haraway 1988, 577), or, one could add, liberal hopes for increased autonomy through technology (Matzner 2019b). In her *Cyborg*

Manifesto, she puts it quite directly: If we are cyborgs, we are not just the product of a contingent entanglement of discourse and technology, we are not just the result of the general breakdown of the boundary between nature and culture but we are "are the illegitimate offspring of militarism and patriarchal capitalism"(Haraway 1991, 151) in their present form.

Trying to avoid complicity in these developments (as far as this is possible), Haraway's notion of situatedness is about insights that she herself describes as "partial," "modest," "adequate," and "limited." For Haraway, responsibility and objectivity entail admitting partiality and difference (Haraway 1988, 583). Situated knowledge is about the insight that we cannot completely disentangle ourselves from the particular, historic situation we are in, even in the most emancipatory projects. Furthermore, we cannot even fully account for that situation, nor for the way it is made. Barad claims to be able to do the latter because she has an ontology that does the first.

In consequence, the outcome of situatedness for Haraway is not a new ontology but a new politics. "All these pictures of the world should not be allegories of infinite mobility and interchangeability but of elaborate specificity and difference and the loving care people might take to learn how to see faithfully from another's point of view, even when the other is our own machine" (Haraway 1988, 583). Here, she moves directly from "specificity and difference" to learning "to see faithfully from another's point of view" – remembering that this is not "easily learned," let alone guaranteed by ontology. Haraway even mentions this shift from situatedness to politics explicitly: the sense of "partial, locatable, critical knowledges [is] sustaining the possibility of webs of connections called solidarity in politics and shared conversations in epistemology" (Haraway 1988, 584). She emphasizes that such politics and shared conversations are not easy. We cannot just be in touch with any position. Politics involves struggles against the domination inherent to unmarked positions, while resisting the temptation "to lust for and even scramble into that subject position and then disappear from view" (Haraway 1988, 587). It involves repositionings that include violence and resources that are dependent on exploitation or on being the "illegitimate offspring of militarism and patriarchal capitalism." It involves acting on partial grounds, because this is the only way of an interaction that at least allows the hope for evading domination. "The knowing self is partial in all its guises […], always constructed and stitched together imperfectly, and therefore able to join with another, to see together without claiming to be another" (Haraway 1988, 586).

To summarize, for Barad, situatedness means being situated in a relational ontology. For Haraway, the only thing in which knowledge is situated is the insight into its own limits. This includes the own ontology. Yet, it also includes the insight that the own perspective is still connected to others, maybe even those whom one tries to evade or fight – such as Haraway's mentioning of militarism and patriarchal capitalism. Situatedness is not relativism. Relativism is still a "God trick"(Haraway 1988, 586) demanding vision from everywhere – albeit one that has understood that this demand cannot be fulfilled but still maintains it as an excuse to refrain from the impurity of politics. The issue is "not relativism but location" (Haraway 1988, 588). In this location, we still encounter others and what follows from situatedness for these encounters is the need for a different politics.

Thus, while for Barad, ontology guarantees politics, for Haraway, situatedness entails the need for politics. Politics is understood as the encounter of selves that are "partial in all their guises," "always constructed and stitched together imperfectly." Politics is based on the insight that it can never fully comprehend its own conditions of existence, which, for example, comes with the insight that exclusions might be invisible because of a failure to make an encounter with those excluded happen. Haraway's answer to exclusions is not ontology, which runs the risk of just making them more invisible in hopes of "ontodeliverance," but a politics of solidarity. This may be unsatisfying. Acts of solidarity, a different politics might just never happen. Yet, the important takeaway is that any attempt of giving a more satisfying answer by providing a guarantee for politics will produce problems similar to the ones it is trying to solve.

A quite similar insight derives from Foucault's work, as Frieder Vogelmann has convincingly argued. It is this aspect of Foucault's thought that Barad undermines in her way of extending discursive practices to matter.

Foucault is interested in how knowledge comes into existence, how power operates, and how subjectivation takes place (Vogelmann 2017, 202). This performative view is what makes him interesting to Barad. Similar to her work, it allows suspending of commonly presupposed ideas and concepts. For example, Foucault shows "that the questions whether this self is a 'true self,' an authentic or autonomous self, are so pressing to us only because they belong to *our* self-practices" (Vogelmann 2017, 202, emphasis in the original). Yet, the emphasis on our practices already shows that Foucault takes a different turn here than Barad. Like Haraway, his emphasis is on a certain form of limit that is not ontological but situated: "Foucault's critique aims at a diagnosis of the present that does not simply represent to us what is, but renders visible how 'what is' limits us in our thoughts, in our actions, and in our being" (Vogelmann 2017, 203). Vogelmann further describes this diagnosis as a threefold practice, using Foucault's own (a bit particular) use of the concepts of nihilism, nominalism, and historicism (Foucault 2011, 5). Nihilism means to "systematically suspend the core normative distinctions governing our analyses of knowledge, power, and relation to self." This suspension, however, does not directly lead to a different or even better analysis. It first of all opens up the view toward the conditions of existence of these practices. This particularly includes their genealogy. Foucault points "us to the history explaining why we become used to them (historicism)" (Vogelmann

2017, 201). This also opens up the view toward difference, but only to particular, situated alternatives. Foucault's critiques "direct us to the plurality
covered over by these distinctions (nominalism)" (Vogelmann 2017, 207).

In consequence, contrary to Barad's worries, Foucault does not reduce
everything to human practices. He reduces everything to specific practices, at
a specific time, with specific forms of knowledges – and specific forms of
subjectification. These practices, to a varying extent, are structured by
drawing a boundary between the human and the non-human. Yet, these
issues are pressing not because they are a feature of practices in general but
of *our* practices. Thus, there is no reduction to or ontologization of the
human in Foucault because there is no ontologization at all.

"Knowledge and power are only an analytical grid" Vogelmann emphasizes using Foucault's own words: they "are not 'entities, powers (puis-
sances), or something like transcendentals'"(Vogelmann 2017, 202). Neither
are they, one could add, an ontology.

Rather, if the situation matters, we must acknowledge that in most situations, humans matter. Particularly for the situated analytical work that studies
relations that make up a specific context, I have shown that a too principled
symmetrical view can dissimulate the concrete circumstances of particular
others.[6]

This entails that the critical practice itself remains situated. Even if it aims
to critically engage with a particular situation, that situation is not easily
discernible.[7]

> [I]t can do so only by presenting statements to us which are still
> comprehensible to us as subjects of the current truth regime but which
> also transgress the conditions of existence that delimit what can and
> cannot be statements with truth values. Hence Foucault's critique cannot
> award its theoretical concepts an epistemological status that would shield
> them from its own nihilism, nominalism and historicism.
>
> (Vogelmann 2017, 207)

---

6 Even Rosi Braidotti, theorist of the posthuman, makes a similar argument:

> I agree with the distinction Katherine Hayles makes between anthropocentrism and
> anthropomorphism. You can be a posthumanist and post-anthropocentric thinker. In fact,
> in advanced capitalism, in which the human species is but one of the marketable species,
> we are all already post-anthropocentric. But I don't think we can leap out of our
> anthropomorphism by will. We can't. We always imagine from our own bodies – and why
> should we, considering that we still live on a planet populated by humanoids who think of
> themselves as humans, in different ways, with different points of reference?
>
> (Braidotti and Vermeulen 2014)

7 This is also the reason why an empirical praxeology is not an option. See Seier (2018).

Thus, Foucault advances a form of situatedness that gets stuck in the very situation it tries to analyze, while at the same time it knows that it depends in many ways on something beyond that situation.

Generalizing from this analysis, we can discern a radical situatedness based on Haraway and Foucault, in contrast to Barad's ontological situatedness. In radical situatedness, the partiality and limits of the situation are not dependent on ontological analysis. Rather, they are the result of critical practices that make it possible to encounter the constitution of a situation *within the situation* – and as such, they are always also encounters of partiality, of situatedness itself. Such critical practices can be the operations of nihilism, nominalism, and historicism that Vogelmann describes following Foucault. Such practices can be the reflection on technologies that enable our practices and knowledge that Haraway emphasizes in *Situated Knowledges* when she ends with the question of "apparatuses of bodily production" (Haraway 1988). They can also be encounters "with our own machines," as she writes (Haraway 1988, 583). In a similar gesture, media theory and philosophy of technology have particularly emphasized the potential of failure, breakdowns, or similar occurrences as enabling a shifted insight into the technomaterial conditions of our practices, without transcending them. Wittgenstein's aphoristic later work (Wittgenstein 1969; 2009) or Butler's subversive practices are attempts of making us encounter the constitution of meaning while even the meaning of the words they use to do so is not "our own," as Butler puts it (Butler 2005, 35).

This understanding of radical situatedness provides a more systematic reason why I have described algorithms as a co-constitutive relation of something concrete and an abstraction. When we critically engage with a concrete practice, we can use critical practices such as the ones just mentioned that allow us to encounter the conditions and limits of this practice within the present situation. We thus understand how the practice itself is constituted. Yet, this is always only a partial, situated account. In consequence, we have to resort to abstractions to describe the situatedness, like Haraway does when she mentions militarism and patriarchal capitalism, or like Foucault does when he names different forms of governmentality, for example. In his work, discourse and dispositifs are the names of such abstractions. They are particular forms of abstractions, for they are understood as "analytical grids" that are themselves still part of situatedness. These abstractions are, one could say, the way the greater context "looks" from within the situation. The relation is co-constitutive, because, as has already become apparent in many examples in the introduction, the many practices, technologies, material conditions, etc., that can only be grasped as an abstraction are again partially constituted by the concrete situated practice that is currently analyzed.

In sum, whatever is analyzed in the situated partial view is constitutively related to a bigger context that itself can only ever be grasped partially and thus needs to be abstracted. Thus, the concrete and the abstract complement each other. They form a *co-constitutive relation* between the abstract and the concrete. This means that the abstract is not simply removed or distanced from the concrete but is co-constitutively complemented by it: is a *complementary abstraction*. These two terms, co-constitutive relation and complementary abstraction, are my re-description of what Barad calls intra-action, embedded into the notion of radical situatedness here developed.

For the analysis of algorithms, this entails that there is no single definition of algorithms in this book. Rather, algorithms are one form of complementary abstraction that can be used to analyze what is sometimes called information and communication technologies. As I have begun to show in the last chapter, algorithms abstract from their material conditions, the data that are used to "train" them, the concrete code in which they are implemented, and the subjects whose data they process and who use them – while at the same time being complemented by them. With the theoretical perspective developed in this chapter, we can see that when the analysis focuses on one of these elements – particular material conditions such as energy or CPUs, datasets, programming languages, subject positions, etc. – the situatedness and accordingly the abstraction of the algorithm changes. Thus, in each of the complementary relations that are analyzed in the following chapters, algorithms are something different. This corresponds to the early Barad's idea of different "cuts" yielding different phenomena. Introna's analysis that started this chapter shows how useful this perspective is for analyzing algorithms and I maintain this analytical use but from the perspective of radical situatedness.

Each of the different complementary relations that are analyzed in the following chapters also corresponds to different forms of situatedness. The particular relation that is analyzed is part of what constitutes this situation but, of course, there are many more on quite different timespans and extensions.

The politics of radical situatedness

In this regard, it is important to remember that situatedness is no epistemic prison; it is not an argument for relativism. It is possible to move among situations. Haraway just cautions us that gaining another point of view is a political act and "not easily learned."

I have already re-described Barad's notion of different cuts as different co-constitutive relations. Haraway's emphasis on the politics of moving from one form of situatedness to another is her form of dealing with the problem of exclusion. Yet, this is not a consequence of ontological exclusion, as Barad would have it when she describes how every intra-action precludes others. Rather, it is a consequence of the analytical work that is necessary to make sense of a situation. As Vogelmann argues, this entails suspending some distinctions, working toward their history, and considering alternatives covered over by the prevailing practices or technologies. All of this introduces new conditions, is co-constituted by new elements, and thus never escapes what Vogelmann calls nihilism, nominalism, and historicism in Foucault's terms.

My calling these questions which form of situatedness can be analyzed and how "easily learned" this is "politics" refers to Haraway's use of the term and other political concepts such as solidarity. Yet, my use of "politics" is also inspired by Hannah Arendt's thoughts. Her use of the term does not have much to do with what is commonly called politics. Rather, politics is her name for all action that starts from an encounter with someone or something that means a difference to the own situation, while at the same time having to make sense of that encounter from the own situation (Arendt 1998). Such encounters might confirm the own view, express solidarity with it, but also confront it. One central political consequence of Foucault and Haraway, but also many other particularly feminist and postcolonial epistemologies, has been to show the relevance of such encounters. Politics marks acts of (re-)situating based on such encounters that happen on partial grounds, as Haraway calls it.

In relation to the analysis of algorithms, this entails that what can only be understood as an abstraction is the lived reality for others, whom one cannot just simply assume to understand or integrate. In other words, situatedness never stops. In the context of algorithms, particularly in computer science, there are many attempts at fixing political problems, e.g. biased datasets, etc. Yet, while every attempt of integrating another's point of view is worth all the effort, it should not lead to the assumption of having solved the problem once and for all.

While Haraway emphasizes the force and limits situatedness entails, situations, understood as radical situatedness, are still dynamic. Here Barad's view remains pertinent. As I have argued above, in contrast to Barad, however, the different timespans are important. Abstraction also means to consider that even if a practice and its context need to be understood as co-constitutive, this relation probably cannot be understood from one intra-action alone.

Here is another reason why an analysis of algorithms as complementary relations is inherently political. The many acts, repetitions, iterations, and citations – even if considered abstractly – are acts by many different subjects. As Foucault argues, every core distinction that defines a situation covers a plurality of others. Haraway, whose text constantly but reluctantly talks about a "we," is concerned with a different makeup of this group, one that cannot escape power and violence but at least attempts to reduce it.

In consequence, one is never situated alone. Every critical engagement with the situation also questions the makeup of this group or community of actors that constitute the situation. As Butler and Foucault emphasize, those sharing the practice are often enforced by power to do so. Yet, as Linda Zerilli remarks, quite often it can be those sharing a practice that just seems ordinary, normal, or usual without feeling any power or coercion that poses the strongest opposition to critical practice (Zerilli 1998). As I discuss in Chapters 5 and 7, such claims to community are also at work in seemingly technical or economic acts such as distributing labor in a software project.

This detailed discussion of relationality as radical situatedness yields the approach to algorithms that I will use in this book. Algorithms are a perspective; one could say, using the Foucauldian words cited earlier, they are an analytical grid. In my case, they are a research perspective. More precisely, algorithms are a situated perspective. They bring certain things into view, while others get out of view. From a radically situated perspective, algorithms are thus always dependent on the situation that is analyzed. As there are many different forms of governance or power in Foucault, which are precisely not just configurations of a general ontology of governance or power, there are many forms of algorithms in this book. Algorithms are one particular form in which the wider context of the situation can be encountered in the situation, because algorithms in one way or another relate to this context. This can be quite explicit, for example, when algorithms are driven by the imperatives of efficiency in liberal economics; it can be hard to detect, for example, when algorithms covertly continue a history of racist surveillance. Since algorithms remain a radically situated perspective, this context, however, can only be understood in the particular form of abstraction that I have discussed above: a partial, limited encounter of the context from within.

At the same time, algorithms relate to particular, concrete elements that constitute them. They need hardware and energy to be implemented, and to run, they need programmers, users, data, etc. All of these necessary complements, however, are not external to algorithms; they are also changed by algorithms in a co-constitutive relation. One could say that an algorithm describes the intra-action of a particular element and a more abstract context. This particular form of intra-action, though, needs to be understood in the radically situated manner that I have developed here, that is as complementary abstraction.

PART II

4
ALGORITHMS AND MATERIAL CONDITIONS

Screen and hardware essentialism

Material conditions – usually using the more narrow term "hardware" – have often been declared as the essence of computing. Regardless of which programming language is used, which data is employed, and which ideas the programmers had, in the end, it matters what happens in the logic gates of the hardware. Particularly in critical literature and texts from the humanities and social sciences, this reductionism to physical processes, currents flowing, transistors or tubes "switching," etc., is voiced against a contrary movement: ignoring, forgetting, disavowing matter, which exists in several variants. Within socio-cultural studies of digital technologies, there was a wave of texts in the 1980s and particularly the 1990s that emphasized the immaterial aspects of digital media and communication: infinite copies without loss, unrestricted and traceless manipulation, near real-time transfer around the globe on the new (for the general public) internet, etc. (Bolter 2001; Negroponte 1995; Poster 1990). Critics termed such views "screen essentialism" (Kirschenbaum 2008, 27), arguing that they reduce digital media to the features and possibilities that users experienced on their screens. Everything that goes on "behind" the interface is ignored.

Yet, screen essentialism is not the only form of ignoring hardware. Among its critics were writers such as Lev Manovic, who emphasized the importance to distinguish the "computer layer" from the "cultural layer" of digital media (Manovich 2001, 63). Still, the importance of the computer layer for him entailed the study of software, source code, and data structures much more than hardware. One of the bluntest expressions of the anti-materialist Platonism that informed discourses in the 1990s is from the infamous "Declaration of

DOI: 10.4324/9781003299851-6

Independence of Cyberspace," starting with the line, "Governments of the Industrial World, you weary giants of flesh and steel, I come from Cyberspace, the new home of *Mind*" (Barlow 2016 emphasis mine). Later in the text, he adds: "there is no matter here" and "[o]ur identities have no bodies." After its publication in 1996, the text was widely endorsed by both programmers working in Silicon Valley and diverse hacker communities. Both are certainly not screen essentialists in the sense that they get distracted by shiny user interfaces. But they considered computers as controlled by programming languages, much more than as something material.

Thus, ignoring matter is not just an issue with overly idealist cultural theory from the end of the last century. It also structures many prevailing practices in programming and computer science. One of their most influential precursors, cybernetics, was built on the very idea that information could be analyzed and controlled regardless of its "carrier" (Hayles 1999). Already in one of its early influential texts, Rosenblueth, Wiener, and Bigelow define "teleological behavior" as behavior directed by feedback. Thus, all that matters in analyzing behavior is how it reacts to "signals from the goal" (Rosenblueth, Wiener, and Bigelow 1943, 19). How this reaction is realized internally can be quite different and the authors acknowledge these differences. Yet they conclude that "the broad classes of behavior are the same in machines and in living organisms" (Rosenblueth, Wiener, and Bigelow 1943, 22). In consequence, for building machines with a "purpose," all the material differences are not important as long as appropriate forms of feedback can be realized.

A few years later, when the first computers were in operation, the peculiar role of matter can also be observed on the practical level of everyday work. Wendy Chun reports the gendered division of work at the time. There were mathematicians defining the design of the computers and also their applications. Electrical engineers came up with circuitry, new uses of tubes, innovative data carriers, and more. Both were established and recognized fields for predominantly male scientists. Yet, the practice where mathematics met engineering, where algorithms needed to be transformed into matter, was a job for the "ENIAC girls [...] hired as subprofessionals"(Chun 2004, 32). As discussed in Chapter 5, p. 80, at that time, programming meant reconfiguring the hardware using wires and switches. The genealogy of software and programming that is discussed in that chapter also hinges on a division of labor: certainly, no serious computer scientists would deny the importance of hardware when prompted, yet for most, it is someone else's business.

In his "Material History of Bits," Blanchette (2011) details the so-called "stacks" that inform the relation of hardware and software in contemporary computer science. These stacks consist of several layers, where each layer is considered an "abstraction" of the layers below. In contrast to my use of the term, these are precisely not complementary abstractions. Rather, each layer is designed in a way that knowledge of the other layers is not necessary and can be blackboxed. For example, the OSI model of networking (ISO 2000) that was developed to coordinate networking standards starts with a first layer called the "physical layer." It defines the medium, e.g. a certain form of wire, and how the transfer of bits is organized on that medium, e.g. by defining specific voltage levels that are interpreted as "0" and "1," respectively. The next layer, the so-called "data link layer," deals with protocols that organize single bits into meaningful sequences (so-called frames) that introduce error correction, etc. Engineers working on level 2 can already presuppose that they deal with a channel that can transfer bits, not voltages, flashes of light, etc. Thus, whatever happens in the first layer can be ignored and – at least ideally – the physical medium could be changed without any changes necessary on the second and higher layers. There are seven layers in total that deal with routing, specific applications such as WWW, e-mail, and more. The material aspects are in a sense only the stratum on which that stack is built, which clearly focuses on programming network protocols, not the electrical engineering of building networks that is conveniently stowed away in the first layer. The competing and arguably more successful internet protocol suite only works with four layers and does not even include a physical layer but simply presupposes a working physical network (Braden 1989).

In sum, ignorance of material factors is not just a feature of idealist or utopian writers, but a central factor in the division of labor in today's IT landscape. Some of the stacks that Blanchette talks about are official standards such as the ones discussed above. Others structure common practices of organizing software development or of creating programming languages. For example, the functions of a CPU are provided by complex circuitry involving millions of electronic components. Yet, for programmers, they are conveniently represented as a set of a few dozen machine instructions. However, most programmers usually do not directly operate with this machine code but with so-called "higher" programming languages that offer all kinds of functions which need hundreds or thousands of individual machine commands to be executed.[1]

Critics have emphasized the importance of material factors because the ideal separation in these stacks or the more general distinction of software and hardware fails in various regards. Blanchette mentions "efficiency tradeoffs" (Blanchette 2011, 1054) that come with the additional mediation between the layers of a stack. This is a view also common in programming where code that needs to be very efficient is written in machine code rather than a "higher" programming language. Yet, even that is no longer necessarily true because this presupposes a programmer that knows the machine

---

1 See Chapter 5 for a more detailed discussion.

code very well. In the meantime, many compilers that translate code from a higher to a lower level of the stack are better at optimizing than many programmers are.

This relates to a much stronger form of criticism that is voiced by Wendy Chun. She argues that software is a "functional analog to ideology" (Chun 2004, 43) that hides the machine and all the processes that are necessary to make the software work. The aim of that ideology is to "produce" users and programmers as the ones who are in control of their computers. Like in the Althusserian concept of ideology, this is "an imaginary relationship to our hardware" (Chun 2004, 43). In reality, both users and programmers are much less in control and much more dependent, particularly on hardware. In her later text "Code as fetish," Chun no longer uses the notion of ideology, but the related Marxian notion of "fetishization" (Chun 2008). Yet again, she uses hardware, and particularly the necessity to run software on hardware, that is, working hardware, as a lever against the platonic idea that software commands computers. She argues that software is only software "after the fact," which she explains in large parts as after it is executed on hardware – although explicitly speaking against a too reductionist idea of hardware (Chun 2008).

Nevertheless, in both forms, the argument tends to reverse the problem by introducing a kind of hardware essentialism. The notion of ideology clearly presupposes a real to go with the imaginary, even if ideology is considered in an Althusserian sense as inescapable (Althusser 1977) and thus destined to "persist" (Chun 2004). Chun even prints a circuit diagram in both texts that shows logic gates implementing a simple function. Partly, I think this has to be seen as a performative gesture of printing engineering materials in a journal for cultural or critical theory, reminiscent of the provocations of early media theory.[2] Chun also contends that the diagram itself is an idealization because it does not show the careful timing necessary for making gates actually do their work. Yet, this would only mean an even more detailed view of the hardware. Only at the end of the text does Chun gesture toward a broader notion of execution or performance that presupposes an entire structure that "is as institutional and political as it is machinic" (Chun 2008, 322), to which I will return in Chapter 5. Still, the function of Chun's circuit diagram is to illustrate her argument that a computer without software is possible – an algorithm can directly be wired into hardware – but not a computer without hardware.

---

2 This view unites the hopes of some media theorists that exchanging the methods of academic thought for soldering irons could evade the "postmodern" insight of always being too late to understand their own conditions with a specific branch of hackers who use the access to hardware to intercept or manipulate the orderly "execution" of software – where the latter at least recognize that hardware is not a neatly switching mechanism, but full of distortions, cross-talk, imperfections, and other influences that can work in their favor.

Galloway even follows a stronger hardware essentialism, because he extends this theoretical possibility to all software. He writes, "one should never understand this 'higher' symbolic machine as anything empirically different from the 'lower' symbolic interactions of voltages through logic gates. [...] The relationship between the two is *technical*" (Galloway 2006b, 319 emphasis in original).

Here we encounter a problem that re-appears throughout this book: the attempt of explaining from the origin or from fundamental features rather than with regard to the specifics of contemporary technology. In the beginning, computers were indeed without software. Even today, every CPU has a couple of functions hardwired into it that cannot be completely turned into software. Yet, as I will explain in detail as follows, hardware does not just implement an algorithm, as the stack model would have it. While it is theoretically possible to build any programmable algorithm in hardware, computing would not be what it is today technically, culturally, and politically if the hardware itself was not in many regards constituted by software and algorithms.

This argument is partly reflected in another line of critique that emphasizes the importance of hardware. Matthew Kirschenbaum writes mainly against the "screen essentialists," but he also argues that those who give primacy to hardware (in his example Friedrich Kittler) often do so regarding hardware as a universal medium of logic ones and zeros rather than the matter of actual physical processes (Kirschenbaum 2008, 6). He opposes the "formal materiality" of bits that can be altered, transmitted, and copied without loss to the "forensic materiality," where every bit is unique and leaves traces (Kirschenbaum 2008, 10). In a detailed reconstruction of the workings of a hard drive, Kirschenbaum shows that even if a file is erased on the user interface, the operating system just changes an entry in the section of the disk where a kind of table of contents of the disk is stored (on a windows machine). This allows the contents of the file to be overwritten once space is required but until this happens, they remain on the disk. This is an algorithmic process of the operating system that puts the "deletion" of the file into effect without actually changing its contents on the disk. Furthermore, even if these contents are eventually overwritten, this means that a new pattern of differently magnetized areas is created on the disk. Yet, the old pattern and the new one do not fully overlap. A residue of the old pattern still remains that allows forensic experts to reconstruct even the overwritten data (Kirschenbaum 2008, 50–55). This is why there are dedicated programs for securely erasing data that overwrite it many times with specifically created patterns (Kirschenbaum 2008, 44). As this short example shows, Kirschenbaum is no longer concerned with a clear separation of software and hardware. Rather, he distinguishes the way computing appears to users and many programmers as well (if they are not concerned with hardware drivers, file systems, and the like) from the "mechanisms" that, in Kirschenbaum's view, instantiate it in the background. These "mechanisms" comprise software elements like the file system as well as the magnetic pattern on the physical disk. He also shortly talks of error correction, the distribution of the individual bits on the disk, and more functions that are implemented by a dedicated piece of software, so-called "firmware," that is stored on a chip within the drive and not even available to the most machine level programmer. Yet, the fact that most contemporary "hardware" contains a lot of software is not explicitly made mention of.

Still, this emphasis on mechanisms is important for Kirschenbaum because it breaks the way software appears on the formal level. If a file is deleted, it is still there. If a bit is changed, this manipulation does leave a trace. Depending on the concrete circumstances, recovering them might involve different levels of effort. For example, as long as the contents of the file are not overwritten, a simple software tool suffices. To recover the magnetic patterns on the disk, special laboratory equipment is needed. Despite these differences, the traces are there; bits are individual, not interchangeable. For this reason, Kirschenbaum also uses vocabulary that leans toward essentializing these mechanisms or at least he gives them a clear primacy. He, too, talks of "ideology" (Kirschenbaum 2008, 36) and the user's view as "optimized and impoverished, [...] partial and simplistic window onto the diverse electronic records that have accumulated on the surface of the magnetic disk" (Kirschenbaum 2008, 53). (In these sections, the material aspects of the mechanisms are almost always foregrounded compared to the algorithmic ones.)

This primacy of mechanisms should be questioned. It is indeed impressive if a forensic expert can report the contents of an apparently deleted file – maybe even from a destroyed or burnt disk. Yet, what matters is the reconstruction of the text document or sound recording or movie or what else the disk contained, and not just the bit patterns on the disk. In order to do that, it is also necessary to know the algorithms used to create the file, e.g. a video or image compression algorithm, the format in which it was written on the disk (thus a standard that is as bureaucratic as material), and probably also some knowledge about the praxis of the user who created the file.

In consequence, it is certainly "partial" if the material aspects of the file are forgotten. They can have far-reaching socio-political impact such as the availability of forensic evidence in a court or the many traces that data leave when routed through the internet that are collected by secret services (Greenwald 2014). Yet, it would be equally partial to give primacy to the file on the disk, let alone consider it the "real" file compared to the "ideology" of the screen.

Taking the situatedness of the user and most programmers seriously, what a digital file is can only be understood as a co-constitutive process of algorithms and hardware. When a file, say a text file, is opened for use, it is read from the disk. This means that the magnetic patterns on the disk are scanned, coordinated by algorithms in the firmware. The different levels of magnetic resistance that are measured by a sensor in the hard drive are then interpreted as logic bits by another algorithm. Since the material on the disk is not absolutely constant and the sensor inevitably produces noise, not every bit corresponds to the same level of signals from the sensor. As a consequence, algorithms such as "Partial Response/Maximum Likelihood" are used. It estimates if a change in the signal is significant enough with respect to the preceding readings that it should be interpreted as a bit. Thus, the bits are not simply translated piecemeal from a magnetic pattern into a logical pattern but rather dynamically created based on a larger context. This logical sequence is then, in turn, converted into an electric signal to be sent out via the connector of the disk. All of this is additionally protected by algorithms that do error correction, monitor the movement of the disk complemented by another set of sensors, etc. Thus, already before a single bit leaves the disk, a complex interplay of material parts and algorithms takes place. The information from the disk is then mediated by controller chips on the mainboard, the operating system, the application software, again the operating system, and more until it finally appears on yet another piece of hardware: the screen. There it is presented with all the features that make a text file a text file today: searching, cutting, pasting, changing fonts, layouts, etc. This file only exists, one could say, while that entire chain of mediation is in operation from disk to screen that involves many complementary relations of hardware and algorithms. Once the file is saved and the computer shuts down, a bit pattern is stored in a form that allows recreating that chain but that is, in many regards, not the file. Kirschenbaum points in that direction when he writes that "storage [...] is a kind of suspended animation, a coma or walking death" (Kirschenbaum 2008, 97).

However, this is only true for storage on hard drives and similar media. We also talk about "storing" something in the memory of the computer. Yet, if one would apply the same idea of storage to current memory chips, they would not store anything longer than 64 milliseconds. After that interval, the storage is no longer considered reliable because the electronic charge that is used to store information diminishes very quickly. A dedicated software regularly reads the contents of the memory cells and restores the charge – for another 64 milliseconds maximum. In this case, storage is not suspended animation but constant recreation in a dynamic process between material electronic components storing charges and algorithms that control and maintain these charges.

The situated co-constitution of hardware

Analyses like the ones just presented are situated, as explained in Chapter 2. On one level, a historical situatedness structures such analyses itself. In this regard, Kirschenbaum has more in common with Kittler and other hardware essentialists than he would probably like: they all write from a situation in which computers as hardware were actually present on or below desktops and still conceived as a machine that consists of individual parts that occasionally needed to be opened to replace one or the other. The hard drive could be heard rattling under the load of opening a program. The more daring users would etch their own circuit boards and solder their own components on them. This quite accessible form of hardware is a particular episode in the history of computing. Before, computers were removed from users in data centers where batches of punched cards were handed in, or later a connection to a screen and typewriter terminal was established. Today, we are again approximating such a situation where many applications run on a data center accessed by tablets or phones that of course are computers but in a sense really become essentially screens. Thus, a lot of the discussions of "hardware" in relation to software implicitly generalize this timespan of desktop computers.

However, situatedness must also be considered "within" the analysis. For example, for a programmer dealing with the file system, the contents of a file do not matter, but other things such as its size, the frequency it is accessed, etc. A completely different chain of mediation is in place in their practice. Importantly, neither the user nor the programmer is "closer" to the "reality" of the file. Rather, both are differently situated. What is often termed as proximity to some "real" material substrate pertains to the difficulties in relating one form of situatedness to the other.

The possibility of forensic evidence that animates Kirschenbaum's reflections on hard drives has to be considered in this regard. It approximates the complementary relations of matter and algorithms that structure the situation of the user, but for a quite different situation, for example, a court case or a spying operation. To that aim, a completely different set of complementary relations of matter and algorithms is formed, including dedicated laboratory sensors for reading the disk, controlled by appropriate algorithms, and additional forms of storing, transporting, and presenting the results, e.g. in a presentation in court or in a database for the secret service agent. While this second set of relations might approximate the one that structures the situation of the user, it is still completely differently situated. While the user might have created the file as a usual daily task, for the court, the reliability of the reconstruction matters. A user only in rare cases thinks about the reliability of the correspondence between what they see on the screen and what is stored on the disk. A spy, on the other hand, will recontextualize the file in questions of evidence, suspicion, etc. (see Chapter 7, p. 138, on suspicion.)

In consequence, different sets of complementary relations of matter and algorithms will yield different files, even if they involve the very same disk. This, however, does not mean that the process is just a matter of interpretation, a kind of return to an algorithmic idealism. The relation is truly co-constitutive in the sense that the physical pattern on the disk only permits to complement certain algorithms to begin with (those that are equipped to deal with that kind of data) and it also permits certain results. They are no pure algorithmic fabulation.

Kirschenbaum provides an example of such a co-constitution of algorithms by hardware. He reports that the hard disk was a "landmark achievement in computer engineering precisely because it offered a solution for erasable but nonvolatile random access storage" (Kirschenbaum 2008, 70). Before its invention, storage was mainly on magnetic tape that could be read only serially. The introduction of the hard drive thus allowed completely new forms of applications, for example, in accounting, inventory control, shipping, and many other tasks where records have to be processed in a non-linear, often unforeseeable manner. It also permitted new forms of elementary algorithms. For example, most sorting algorithms that are used today (and often provide one of the first examples when introducing "algorithms") presuppose random access to the numbers to be sorted. This is such a common possibility today that it is not even mentioned as a feature that distinguishes sorting algorithms, yet that was not always the case. For example, Hollerith used a sorting algorithm today called "radix sort" that by our standards is very cumbersome, comparing numbers sequentially, digit by digit (Hollerith 2020, 252). Yet, it was an efficient algorithm in times of processing batches of punched cards with electromechanical means.

While such examples of the influence of hardware on the possibilities of algorithms have been studied in media theory and science and technology studies for years, the way in which algorithms increasingly co-constitute hardware is still less salient in debates. For example, contemporary processors are no longer the hardwired algorithms that still haunt media theory. To pick one of many examples, they use a technology called "Out-of-order execution." This means that a processor does not always execute the commands in the way the software they run specifies. The reason is that some commands are faster than others. In particular, the processor itself works much faster than the memory, so commands that read or store data in memory would waste many processor cycles if the processor just waited for the data to be transferred. Instead, a dedicated algorithm in the processor looks for other commands that can be executed in the meantime. Those need be commands that do not depend on the result from commands that should run before them (according to the software) but now will only be executed later. Basically, a special algorithm in the processor reprograms the software at runtime based on the specific features of the concrete hardware that it works with such as access times of memory and hard drives, etc. This algorithm, complemented by the hardware of the entire machine, not just the processor, thus creates the "execution" that is usually attributed to the processor.

This algorithmic reorganizing of commands has consequences for political values like security and privacy. In 2017, two related security vulnerabilities have been disclosed that became known under the names of "Meltdown" (Lipp et al. 2018) and "Spectre" (Kocher et al. 2019). Both have enabled to read data from one program running on a machine by another. For example, a program implemented in a website could access data of totally unrelated banking software if both were running on the same machine at the same time. Usually, both hardware and software mechanisms are in place so that no program can access the data of another. However, with a cleverly designed program, the out-of-order execution can be exploited to make the processor start to fetch data from a forbidden area before the check of access rights is completed and the program is halted for a violation. The processor then discards the pre-fetched data. However, by exploiting another security issue, a so-called side-channel attack, the data can be retrieved (Lipp et al. 2018, 5).

Again, this is a matter of situatedness. Here we deal with a very special attack that is difficult to exploit outside laboratory settings. Thus, for most users, this algorithmic co-constitution of their processor hardware just makes them faster – which is its original motivation. However, for people susceptible to tailored attacks, it can become a concern – like it does for those who work on carrying out or inhibiting such attacks.

Contemporary users of digital media encounter the way in which algorithms increasingly co-constitute hardware once they need replacement parts or repair. Things like refill cartridges for printers have been carrying machine-readable identification numbers for some time. When installed, a special algorithm, usually using some more or less simple form of cryptographic authentication, checks if the part comes from the official manufacturer to discourage or even inhibit no-name alternatives. Even if that alternative used exactly the same materials, it would not function, because "functioning" is no longer only a material and technical but also an economic and legal question enforced by an appropriate algorithm. This technique is carried to its extreme by so-called "part pairing." In this case, the algorithm does not just check if a new part is the right brand. Rather, it accepts only one specific piece. This has, for example, been used in iPhones (Greenlee 2023). It has a display that contains a machine-readable serial number and the phone will only work if the display with the specific number it has been shipped with is attached. Thus, even a repair with an official replacement part is impossible. It can only be done by specially authorized firms for whom Apple reprograms the part pairing algorithm to recognize the new display. Thus, not only no-name parts but also unlicensed or DIY repair with official parts is precluded. The display is not the only part that is paired; the iPhone 12 that was issued in 2022 has 40% of paired parts (Greenlee 2023).

This algorithmic control of hardware is not just a way of making more money for the manufacturer. It also has direct material consequences. For big manufacturers, who attempt to monopolize the repair market with part pairing, many repairs are actually not cost-efficient. There are big differences in loans between the countries where devices are built and their necessary resources extracted, on the one hand, and the countries in which they run their official stores that offer repairs. In consequence, it is often cheaper to just replace the entire device than repair it. The fact that this is so cheap is also enabled by yet another interplay of algorithms and hardware, namely that most devices are networked and attached to some kind of storage on the internet so that no costly transfer of data is necessary if replacing the device. That way, part pairing drives (among other factors, of course) the huge waste of resources that follows from the fact that most electronic devices are discarded instead of repaired once one element is broken.

Furthermore, there are many countries where officially authorized repair is not available. In these countries, part paring algorithms literally turn a broken but repairable piece of hardware into a useless piece of matter. Part pairing can be tricked and circumvented, for example, by removing the chip from the broken part and soldering it on the new one. However, these are very costly operations compared to just installing a replacement part and have varying success rates (Greenlee 2023). In the West, this issue has been politicized with quite some success, so in 2022, the state of New York passed the first law protecting the "right to repair" one's own devices. The European Parliament is planning some initiatives to establish such a right as well (Šajn 2022). Whether these events change the availability of repair also beyond the respective jurisdictions remains to be seen.

Algorithmic-material networks

So far, I have only discussed what most commonly is understood as hardware. However, material conditions for algorithms extend beyond the devices on our desktops or in our hands, in particular to the material infrastructure of networks. High-frequency trading (HFT) impressively illustrate their relevance. Algorithms buy and sell financial products in very short timespans. Profits are made from minute price changes happening in the range of milliseconds – not longer-term market developments. In many cases, algorithms react to events that are known to cause price changes such as certain types of bids and asks being made. Donald MacKenzie (2021) explains the precursors of this kind of trading. For example, at a certain time during the 1990s, two equivalent futures at the Chicago Mercantile Exchange could be traded both in a traditional pit, where human traders gathered to buy and sell and electronically using a special terminal. If the price in one future changed, there was a short timespan until the information spread and the other changed as well. Traders with a quick communication channel between those sitting at the electronic terminals and their colleagues in the pit could profit from the foreseeable price adjustments. While this was still done by human traders, the principle stayed the same once trading was automatized: the observation of one market event is interpreted as a signal for an upcoming price change and orders are made accordingly. In consequence, an advantage in HFT is intrinsically tied to having information before the competitors.

Today, the signals that the algorithms react to are events that appear so quickly that "nanoseconds are important" (MacKenzie 2021, 13). This led to extreme competition in optimizing transmission times. Donald MacKenzie reports the competition of having the fastest connection between the data centers of the exchanges in New York (located in New Jersey) and the Chicago Mercantile Exchange. He cites the physical limit for any signal to travel between these two points, that is, at the speed of light, as 3.94 milliseconds. However, in glass fiber cable, which is the preferred medium for long-distance data cables today, signals are slower. In the shortest theoretically possible cable on the surface of the earth, a signal would need 5.79 milliseconds. Existing cables in the 2000s offered signal travel times of around 8 milliseconds (MacKenzie 2021, 146). In 2010, a new, dedicated cable was laid that was closer to the shortest possible route and reduced travel time to 6.65 milliseconds. This difference of about 1,35 milliseconds was worth an investment of 300–500 million US dollars (the exact numbers are not known) and reportedly paid off. HFT happens so quickly that having an information about an event in a New York exchange 1.35 milliseconds earlier than the competitors means real profit. The cable was not only moved closer to the optimal route, but it also was constructed ignoring best practices such as adding some slack to make the cable less vulnerable or using error correction which permits transmitting more data at the same time (MacKenzie 2021, 141–145). The last aspect is relevant here, because this means that it also omits additional algorithmic mediation at the terminals and the repeaters that connect individual lengths of fiber. In a very real sense, it was attempted to reduce the cable – still a highly complex technical apparatus – to a bare strand of fiber glass.

The next round in this competition was opened when a new connection was created using long sections of wireless transmissions. Since signals are faster in the air than in fiber, by 2016, a link achieved a travel time of only 3.98 milliseconds, only 0.04 milliseconds slower than the physical limit. These signals move in a straight line of sight from sender to receiver, in contrast to the curvature in cable necessary to go around obstacles. It also used analog repeaters that modulate and amplify the physical excitation of the incoming antenna so that a direct physical link is created, even if it changes a few times between microwave signals in air and electric signals in wires. But no digital abstraction and algorithmic processing are involved. However, microwave transmission made the transmission susceptible to other physical influences, e.g. rain, snow, or even a "summer sunrise" shining directly into an antenna (MacKenzie 2021, 154).

All of this sensitivity to location and physical differences in media and all the efforts to reduce algorithmic mediation could be read as an argument that material aspects are more important than algorithms – that all implement more or less the same known and rather simple trading patterns (MacKenzie 2021, chap. 6).

In fact, HFT is a great example of the importance of material aspects, also beyond the narrow conception of hardware: geological location, transmission media, rain, snow, and sunsets. However, there are also algorithmic factors. For example, MacKenzie reports that programmers noted that an algorithm that had placed an order got the information that the order was filled faster than other algorithms, which had to wait until the processing of the order was announced by the software of the exchange. Thus, they started to post "canary orders" at graduated prices that only served to detect the current price level faster than tracking the announcements of the exchange (MacKenzie 2021, 163).

Yet, the most relevant co-constitutive relation of algorithms and matter in HFT takes place on a larger scale. The reasons that few milliseconds could become a decisive factor in the first place are in important aspects algorithmic. Only a fully automated algorithmic trading system can react fast enough that such differences can begin to matter. The relevance of matter was thus preceded and enabled by the development of an algorithmic trading infrastructure that was neither aimed at high frequencies nor at exploiting physical limits. Both were a consequence of a development that started for reasons much more common in the introduction of automation.

Almost ironically, one important reason to introduce electronic trading was to reduce the dependency on location. For example, in both Switzerland and Germany, new futures exchanges were created from the start with electronic trading. This solved the issue of where the benefits of the location of a new exchange should go, a contentious issue, particularly in these federal states (MacKenzie 2021, 57). Similarly, resistance to introducing electronic trading in Chicago was overcome when the London International Financial Futures Exchange became a strong competitor for futures on Asian financial markets. Because of the respective time zones, London opened when the Asian markets were active, and Chicago was closed. "An electronic trading system could counter the threat from London by permitting trading to continue when Chicago's pits were closed" (MacKenzie 2021, 49). Once these electronic exchanges were set up, the signals that were sent to the terminal software in the trading companies could be routed to particular algorithms that automated trading. As explained above, this usually involved using information from one market to trade on another. These self-built automated systems became first a common practice and then a commodity sold to trading companies; that is, dedicated data interfaces for algorithmic trading were officially established. As MacKenzie reports, introducing these was also an issue of various legal and political struggles, apart from the technical ones. Only once algorithmic trading was established in that form did differences in the algorithms themselves decrease to matter, and transmission speed became relevant. Cost efficiency, another common reason for automation, was a decisive factor in this development. HFT margins were so small at the beginning that only newly emerging automated trading firms with little costs could profit from them – in contrast to a traditional bank (MacKenzie 2021, 93). Yet, also this factor is subject to the co-constitutive relation of matter and algorithms. Once HFT had become such a specialized business that it depended on paying for one of the fastest connections, only the biggest companies in the field could afford it (MacKenzie 2021, 145).

In sum, the decisive factor for today's HFT algorithms is the material factor of transmission lines. Yet, the way in which they are decisive and the way in which they can matter in the first place is algorithmically constituted. The influence of matter, however, is not just a question of physics. It is deeply political. The fact that financial markets provide an economic power that permits to pay landowners sums the magnitude of 100,000 US dollars just to lay a cable across their parking lot (MacKenzie 2021, 143) illustrates how socio-economic power is introduced into algorithms via matter as their complement.

The politics of matter: Internet and data centers

The politics of material conditions are more complex and more impactful in the global "undersea network" (Starosielski 2015) that forms an essential part of the internet. Submarine cables connect continents but also run along the shores between major cities that are often located by the sea – for being an important port is one way in which many of today's big cities became big. Nicole Starosielski (2015, chap. 1) traces the history of submarine cables and illustrates in great detail how each political period was imprinted on the cables laid. Colonial powers, particularly Britain, started to connect their colonies with a clear emphasis on the capitals of the "empire." The brake up of colonial empires and the emerging Cold War shifted emphasis on national control over cables but also diversity of routes to ensure the security of the increasingly militarily relevant communication. Slowly, multinational consortia took over with an interest in securing the capacities of their connections over competitors.

All the while, these novel conditions for the network were counteracted by the existing structures. Companies wanted to reuse their facilities. Creating new routes was more expensive, with all the necessary surveying in deep oceans but also securing the landing points which involves permissions to dig from coastal areas, which are often protected areas where construction is restricted, to the next networking hub. Historical monopolists protected their share.

In consequence, today's undersea network is the result of repeated political and economic power struggles from the colonial area to the free market competition of today. Even the oldest of these influences still are present. For example, the United Kingdom, once the center of an empire that operated many telegraph and telephone lines, is still an important hub for traffic in today's internet. This is one of the reasons that Britain's secret service GCHQ could become a major player in the spy operations that have been disclosed in the wake of Edward Snowden's release of secret documents (Greenwald 2014). Furthermore, former colonies often still have much worse connections to the internet that mean much more effort also for individuals to gain access. However, as Lisa Parks reminds, these politics are complex. The idea that connection to the internet is something that everyone would want or at least benefit from is itself a Western perspective that not necessarily coincides with individual attitudes in former colonies (Parks 2015, 132).

While the material network is laden with politics, the algorithms that are used to route traffic through these cables are programmed as if politics did not matter. The design of the internet protocol famously builds on the idea of decentralization. There is no central node and no single algorithm responsible for distributing the traffic. Rather, each node just processes the traffic it receives. For each packet, it checks if it has a connection to the destination; otherwise, it is sent to another server that is part of a route to that destination. The last option is possible, because nodes advertise all the addresses that they can connect to. In a very simplified manner, the process works like this: the internet is made up (as the name says) of many smaller networks. This could be the network of a company, a university, or of a particular provider of internet access. Say node A connects to a network X, and node B connects to another network, Y. A would then advertise that it has a connection to X. B would receive that information and advertise that it has a connection to Y and knows a route to X. A third server, C, receiving the information of B would send all traffic to X and Y to B. If there are several possible routes, it is up to the node to decide how to distribute the traffic; the protocol does not enforce a particular algorithm.[3]

For routing algorithms, all routes are equally trustworthy. There is no standard way (although attempts exist) of checking the reliability of the advertisements. They are just considered true. This means that an attacker can easily derail or "hijack" internet traffic to a particular destination just by advertising a connection to its address – although this happens more often accidentally than maliciously ("BGP Hijacking" 2022). Furthermore,

3 For a more detailed discussion, see Dourish (2015).

routing algorithms cannot determine the quality of the route other than what they can measure at their location (e.g. number of packets coming in and out, signal travel times, etc.). On the level of the standard internet protocol, there is no way to determine which kind of connection the further route entails, through which countries it goes, and whether it involves a satellite or an undersea cable.

The final route that a data packet takes is the consequence of the interplay of many routing algorithms at different nodes of the network and the material connections of these nodes (Sprenger 2015).

Yet, the level of implementing the internet protocol does not suffice to grasp the algorithmic reality of today's internet. Christian Sandvig (2015) retraces the development of the internet from a medium for failsafe point-to-point connections to a medium that is used predominantly for broadcasting content: video platforms, streaming services for audio and video, etc. Technically, though, broadcasting is not a possibility on the internet. Everyone who watches a movie online needs a dedicated connection to the server of the streaming service. This would be impossible for a single server to manage. The same holds for highly used services such as Google, Twitter, Facebook, etc. Thus, when opening one of these sites, although one always uses the same internet address, the connection goes to one among many servers. The internet protocol permits a technology called anycast: many different servers just advise the same address. The contingent logic of internet routing will then direct traffic to any of these servers. For example, streaming providers make sure to have servers close (in terms of network connections) to the large internet service providers for end users. Big companies even move their servers into the data centers of internet providers. Dedicated firms, so-called "content delivery networks" (CDNs), offer the same service for sale. CDNs run many, widely distributed servers that mirror their clients' servers for faster access, stability, and availability.

To add even more complexity, the server that established the connection with the user's machine might delegate the task internally to yet another machine. From the user's perspective, all of this is the same as if connecting to a single machine with its dedicated address. Yet, on the other side of the connection, this multiplication of serves necessitates algorithmic coordination on several levels.

A former site reliability engineer at Twitter describes the internals (as of 2022) at a huge internet service. It runs two pieces of software: one that keeps track of all the servers that are available, and the other one assigns tasks to them, for example, responding to incoming traffic with the right content. If a server fails, the first program will notice and notify the second so that a new server is enlisted. This is usually possible because the entire operation runs on completely redundant hardware, that is, there are twice as many servers as needed for operation under full load. (In this regard, it is important to note that data centers contain so many parts that failure is not an accident but a daily routine.)

All of this happens without human involvement. That way, algorithms constantly reconfigure the network. A server that just answered a user's call on twitter.com might be replaced with a different one on the next visit. Yet, precautions even go further. Since in data centers many servers are stored in racks and an entire rack could fail (they all share the same power connection, for example), the algorithms do not just redistribute the tasks to any server but choose them so that not too many applications are run on the same rack. The software even creates repair tasks for human engineers at the data center. Thus, algorithms do not just constantly reconfigure the physical network by picking servers for requests to run on; they also orchestrate the physical distribution and replacement of these servers if defunct (Tejo 2022). Other big data centers maintain similar processes.

In consequence, what theory neatly separates as networking and hardware stacks intermingles. Routing does no longer just determine the route data takes on the network to a server; it also influences which server eventually processes it. These dynamics of an ad hoc algorithmic configuration of hardware continue within the data centers. Thus, the specific hardware that "executes" software is only determined in the very instance it runs by a complex set of algorithms for load balancing, error detection, etc. In this sense, not only software is only software after the fact (Chun 2008), but also hardware is only hardware after the fact. This holds for all programs that contain elements that are run in data centers, which is the case for most mobile apps. Yet, with the increasing use of software as a service and programming as orchestration, also traditional desktop software moves in that direction.[4]

This complex co-configuration of algorithms and material factors introduces new entanglements with political, economic, and social power. For example, the provider of a web service, the CDN that serves it, and the concrete data center that hosts it can be three different companies in three different jurisdictions. All of them can collect data according to various terms – although the users usually only can "control" the relationship with the provider. In cases of failure, data losses, abuse, etc., responsibility is distributed among these entities. The political details and consequences depend on the respective situation of use and area of application. Generally speaking, the co-constitution of algorithms and material factors speaks to the fact that in a networked world, the question of how hardware influences the software it runs no longer suffices. Rather, algorithms are no longer

---

4 Compare the discussion in Chapter 5, p. 99, on a performative view of software and software as a service.

complemented "just" by a computer sitting somewhere. Rather, they depend on the availability of a service that itself is co-constituted by additional algorithms and material factors. The latter range from CPUs and storage technologies to cables and geography (and natural resources as are discussed as follows).

The politics of matter: Privacy and cloud messaging

To illustrate the intricate politics that this dependence of algorithms on services can introduce, I will use the example of a service that used to be called "Google Cloud Messaging" and is now known as "Firebase." It is a service that Google builds into its Android operating system for smartphones. It is one of many elements that help to solve a particular problem of smartphones as hardware: they are mobile. Of course, that is their main feature. Yet for programmers of networked apps, it poses a problem. Mobile phones, when moving, will use many different physical routes into the net, with changing network addresses. If, for example, a messaging service such as WhatsApp or Signal receives a new message for a client, it needs to know the current address of that client to deliver that message. To that aim, the messaging service would need to track the addresses of all of its clients all the time. Even clients that have been idle for days or weeks would need to be included because one can never know when the next message arrives. The alternative would be that all the clients poll the service regularly to find out if new messages have arrived. This is the way e-mail (often) works. An e-mail client regularly connects to the server and checks for new messages. Yet, this would cause a lot of traffic, and unnecessary traffic, because most of the time the result would be: no new message. On mobile phones, at least in the beginning, data were too expensive for this solution. Furthermore, the polling interval would introduce a delay in the delivery of the message, which is fine for e-mail but not necessarily for the real-time feeling of text messaging. A third option would be to have a constant connection open, which again creates more traffic and also a higher load for the servers because they would have to maintain a connection to every client that is online (not just every client that is sending and receiving messages).

In consequence, the first solution, so-called "push notifications," is predominantly used today. Since the effort of tracking all users is both technically and economically prohibitive for many app developers, Google offers this as a central service called Firebase (a similar service exists on Apple's phones). Instead of the app provider, Google does the tracking. That is, Google's Firebase servers know the current internet address of every phone running Android (in its default configuration and with a working internet connection). An app, say a messaging service, can register with Firebase. If a message arrives for a client, the operator of the messaging service sends a notification to Firebase that a message is pending for that client. Then Firebase in turn sends the information that a message is pending to the client's phone. Finally, the phone connects to the messaging service and retrieves the message. Importantly, the message itself is not delivered via the Firebase service. It just establishes the connection between the phone and an the provider of an app when needed. Firebase is one example of many algorithmic layers that make sure that mobile phones are not just small, lightweight, and portable computers but the globally usable connection to the net that its users are used to. Here an important feature of the hardware that increasingly becomes the main form of using digital computation for many, a mobile phone with a potent internet connection, is enabled by an algorithmic layer. That layer, however, is not just one of the many services that operating systems provide (such as disk access, etc.) but is itself a complex networked service that involves its own data centers, cables, etc.

Theoretically, a mobile phone is a programmable computer on its own,[5] but many of the algorithms one would want to run on a phone depend on such services. This dependence is not only technical but also political. The case of the text messaging app "Signal" is a good example. Signal is renowned for its state-of-the-art encryption of the contents exchanged between its users. Furthermore, it runs servers that do not collect any metadata, thus even if spies gained access to them or there was a legal requirement to share data (which exists in the US where the servers are located), there is nothing to be found. This is the reason that Signal is often recommended as the messaging service with the best privacy protection, while remaining as easily usable as WhatsApp or other similar alternatives.

However, Signal relied almost from the beginning on Google Cloud Messaging and its successor Firebase. These services are only available on phones which run the entire suite of Google services. This means that even with all privacy settings enabled (which is not trivial), the phone will collect data that accrues at Google (Leith 2021), which is also available at least for the "five eyes" secret services. In the default setting, Google will collect huge amounts of data, including the entire contact list, movement, browse and search histories, etc. The contact list is a good example of the ensuing tradeoff because Signal uses the phone number as its identifier. While Signal itself does not store the numbers of its clients (no metadata), they most probably will reside in the contact list and thus also on Google's servers. It is possible to contact someone via Signal without storing the number in the contact list, but that again involves some effort that goes against Signal's idea of making privacy easy to use that led to using the phone number as an identifier in the first place (Marlinspike 2014).

---

5 But see the limits that APIs and App Stores enforce that are discussed in Chapter 5, p. 102.

The details of this configuration are constantly changing with every update and the ramifications of the different elements regarding privacy are debated. Yet, on a general level, Signal's decision to rely on Google Could Messaging/Firebase means that its users gain privacy for messaging but need to have other services present that infringe on their privacy. In sum, the complex requirements to provide an easy and accessible service on mobile and distributed hardware necessitate additional levels of algorithmic mediation. Depending on how these are solved, they have an impact on issues such as privacy. Importantly, there is no easy alternative to Signal's use of Google's services. Setting up an infrastructure that is easy to use, scales well with many users, and maintains the required security and availability is expensive and difficult.

Users who care a lot about privacy often use open-source versions of the Android operating system. Google releases the source of the core functionality of Android, yet without its proprietary services such as Firebase, the app store, or Google Pay. Based on this source code, a variety of alternative Android versions are available, some of them with a particular focus on privacy – which usually entails getting rid of any dependence on Google's services. Since Signal is also open-source software, some programmers developed an alternative Signal client named "LibreSignal" that was intended to run on these "Google free" Androids. Instead of Google Cloud Messaging and later Firebase, it used the third of the alternatives mentioned above: it established a permanent connection with Signal's server. This was possible because Signal offered such connections for users of its desktop client, where a stable internet connection could be presupposed and that ran on desktop operating systems where services like cloud messaging (at that time) were not available. However, the developers and users of LibreSignal were taken aback, if not outright offended, when Moxie Marlinspike, then CEO and main developer of Signal and known as an open-source advocate, demanded that they stop using Signal's servers. "You're free to use our source code for whatever you would like under the terms of the license, but you're not entitled to use our name or the service that we run" ("LibreSignal Issue #37" 2016). When the developers responded that it did not make much sense to open the source code if alternative versions could not connect to Signal, except for building one's own independent messaging service, Marlinspike suggested that this is exactly what they should do: "if you think running servers is difficult and expensive (you're right), ask yourself why you feel entitled for us to run them for your product" ("LibreSignal Issue #37" 2016).

The central idea of free and open-source software is the autonomy to change whatever one dislikes about existing programs to improve them for the own needs. In Chapter 5, p. 94, I discuss the limits of that presumed independence. Here we see another one that emerges in a time of networked technology: the necessity to use a common service. Importantly, the problem is not hardware alone. The developers of LibreSignal even offered to run their own server – if that server would interchange connections with Signal's servers. Yet, even that was denied by Marlinspike ("LibreSignal Issue #37" 2016). He argued that the level of security they needed while maintaining usability was only possible if servers and clients were under their control. The central problem is to algorithmically gather many distributed phones and the provider's servers into one usable network. Signal would rather rely on Google to do this (in important parts) than on the interplay of many pieces of software and many different servers run by different people – even if this comes with the aforementioned privacy issues.

This is not just an issue of more or less privacy. Rather, each solution follows different ideas of privacy. Signal opts for one expertly secured channel that is traded off against a centralized collection of other data at Google. It also follows the more traditional notion of privacy where state surveillance is the main issue and corporate surveillance, such as the one by Google, is considered less problematic (Matzner and Ochs 2019). The LibreSignal developers adhere to a more inclusive idea of privacy where any form of data collection should be minimized and one way to put that into practice is omitting centralized infrastructures. Here the tradeoff is the need to trust many different parties contributing software and a federated server infrastructure that is more susceptible to attacks or accidental leaks of data.

In the meantime, this contentious issue has been defused because Signal now offers an alternative client (probably due to the pressure that had been building in the open-source community). Yet, the direct relation between the co-constitution of algorithms and material infrastructure with issues such as autonomy and privacy that has become apparent in this example remains.

Algorithms for distributed and networked machines: MapReduce

So far, I have discussed the co-constitution of algorithms and material conditions in the example of concrete applications. Two consequential aspects are the increasingly networked and distributed character of "hardware" and the fact that transmission times have become a relevant metric for evaluating algorithms – in addition to the traditional runtime and storage space. These aspects also have consequences on the more abstract level on which algorithms are discussed in computer science and software engineering. Entire new paradigms of how to write algorithms have emerged in reaction. Parallel computing has been around since the 1960s. For quite some time, however, this meant a static computer with many processors and a fixed logic for distributing tasks among them. As has become apparent in the example of Twitter's operation, today's computing is not just parallel but also dynamic and distributed. The computers that do the work are sometimes added to the pool of available machines only at runtime. They might be located at different locations in a data center. As the example of HFT has shown, already this distance is relevant. This is not only true for HFT but also a general result of the disparity between computing power and transmission. If, for example, one computer in a data center has completed a partial result that needs to be sent to another computer through 200 meters of cable, the pure runtime of the signal is roughly 470 nanoseconds. The real delay would be much longer and depend on the networking hardware that connects the two machines. Yet, even if only considering the delay by the pure length of the cable, a typical processor could have computed hundreds of thousands of computing instructions in the time it waits for the signal to arrive.

These very material considerations entail new ways of thinking about algorithms. Processing data fast today means not only devising algorithms that take few processing cycles to compute. These might, in fact, be available in excess. A very central factor is to process data as locally as possible, even for distributed tasks, that is to minimize the need for communication.

One well-known way to do this is the "MapReduce" programming paradigm. Its central idea is to distribute tasks in a way that the individual tasks can be done locally. That is the so-called map phase. Then, only once, are all the intermediary results exchanged and distributed again: the shuffle phase. The re-distributed intermediary results are processed into the final results, again locally. That is the reduce stage. Here is an example that I take from the original publication of MapReduce (Dean and Ghemawat 2004). A common task is to count the occurrence of a word in a large collection of documents. This is, for example, needed for several metrics used in information retrieval but also in the digital humanities to gauge the relevance of that word within the corpus.

To do that counting via MapReduce, for the map phase, each contributing machine is assigned a set of documents. These documents are processed locally by parsing them word for word. For each word, the local process adds "(word,1)" to its storage of intermediate results – nothing more, no counting, no aggregating. Just marking each occurrence of the word, basically saying it has encountered the word one time. In the shuffle phase, all the intermediate results for the same word are distributed to the same machine. For the reduce phase, each of these machines just has to count how many intermediate results, that is, pairs of "(word,1)", it has received. The number of these intermediate results is the number of occurrences of the word in the corpus. The reduce process basically counts all the marks that the map machines have left whenever they encountered a word.

This may sound like a very complicated way of counting words. Yet, in the material context just discussed, it makes sense. First of all, the map phase involves a lot of disk accesses, that is, reading all the files. That is slow (compared to the speed of processing, as has been discussed above) and profits from being done locally. Second, and more importantly, there is only one transmission phase for results. In a more straightforward implementation, there would be a central table of words and counts, and each process, when occurring the word, would increase the count. However, this would mean a costly remote access for every single word that is encountered, because the table would need to be shared by all machines and thus be local only for one. This does not even include the overhead of making sure that no two processes try to access the same value of the table at the same time.

Of course, all of this depends on an efficient organization of both the initial distribution of the data and the shuffle phase. The success of MapReduce is based on the fact that Google released the framework together with a library that did both. The users only had to specify the tasks of the map and reduce stages. Again, the issues that are discussed in Chapter 5 and here begin to intermingle. The efficiency of MapReduce algorithms is complemented both by a particular relation to the material features of hardware (locality) and by code that provides important functions as libraries that I discuss in Chapter 5. Google's initial library was quickly extended into dedicated software packages. The most well-known might be Apache Hadoop, that includes a file system designed particularly for MapReduce. As a so-called "location aware" file system, it keeps track of where each bit of data is stored physically: on which server, in which rack. Hadoop exploits this information by assigning tasks to the machine that already has the data – rather than making the machine that executes the program read the necessary data as it is usually done. This means that only the comparably small code for the map phase has to be transmitted initially, rather than huge amounts of data – adding another step in optimizing locality.

Energy, heat, rare earths, and other resources

As algorithms increasingly are adapted to where the data are, this locality is of course no accident. To begin with, it is determined by where the data center is. This brings the final important material element into the picture: so-called "natural" resources. All of the many things that make up "the internet" or "the cloud" use energy. Estimates vary, yet the global IT industry is usually compared to one of the five largest countries on earth regarding energy use. What is more, most of that energy is wasted and is turned into heat that requires cooling by fans, cooling liquid pumps, and heat exchanges, all of which consume even more energy. Holt and Vonderau (2015, 82) report that up to 90% of the energy that is pulled off the grid can be wasted. Constructing data centers in locations where energy is cheap and some form of cooling is available, e.g. through a cool climate or nearby rivers, can significantly cut costs. It also helps save the planet from the looming climate catastrophe, but so far, I fear that the first reason is more action guiding than the latter. Thus, geographic factors, but also geo-economic ones like the location of power plants or the availability of fast fiber connections influence the material location of data centers. This, in turn, is reflected by many algorithms distributing the load.

Energy is not the only form of resource that is used by the computing industry. The parts that make up the internet, but also all our shiny appliances, need to be built, transported, and some of them maintained. This needs many of the rare elements of the planet, so-called "rare earths." It needs what is known as "conflict resources," that is, minerals that are exploited to finance wars and other conflicts. Yet, also many other resources are extracted in adverse working conditions and with poor payment.

This is a moment where the limits of the situated research perspective I follow become salient. In this chapter, I discuss the co-constitutive relations of algorithms and material factors – not material aspects of computing per se. This would be much too big a topic and many excellent studies have been dedicated to it (Ensmenger 2018; Hazas and Nathan 2019; Parks and Starosielski 2015). At a certain point, the co-constitutive relationship becomes pretty one-way. Certainly, there is a need for rare earths, energy, etc., due to the success of computing that involves all of the relations discussed in this book. Yet, a lot of the specific circumstances in which the mining happens, the energy is created, etc., do not differ too much from other demands of Western industries. It is structured by the same re-appearing patterns of re-emerging colonial structures, global exploitation of cheap labor, waste, and pollution being externalized to the global South, generally externalizing costs by the celebrated industries driving innovation, etc. Ensmenger (2018) draws parallels between the nuclear and the IT industries in this regard. Thus, I will refer the readers to that literature and continue focusing on how resources "look like from the perspective of algorithms" but also how algorithms are co-constituted by resource demands.

Particularly, the externalization of resource usage can be traced to many common elements of algorithmic practices. Often, for example, discussions of hardware would evoke "Moore's Law." This goes back to the electrical engineer Gordon Moore, who in 1965 observed that the complexity of integrated circuits roughly doubled each year (Moore 1965). Depending on what complexity means, this "law" could be interpreted loosely enough that it is said to hold until today. Of course, the rhetoric of turning the development that is the result of huge resource exploitation (among other things) into a kind of natural law is an optimistic and self-congratulatory gesture of engineers. Yet, it also presupposes all the resources needed for that development as a given or even ignores that necessity.

The existence of such a "law" has influences on algorithms. When I was studying computer science in the early 2000s, in a software engineering class, I was taught to weigh the costs of hiring a programmer to optimize an algorithm against the cost of just buying faster hardware that would be available in a foreseeable timespan thanks to Moore's Law. Here the two possibilities of either making the algorithm faster or the machine that runs it were turned into two comparable alternatives as a matter of economic efficiency. The fact that the first would actually save resources – energy by saving computing cycles due to a faster algorithm and many other resources by using existing hardware longer – was not mentioned. And it did not come to my student's mind either, although the climate catastrophe was politically present at the time between the Kyoto Protocol and *An Inconvenient Truth* coming to cinemas. Thus, while algorithm design clearly was influenced by hardware, it was influenced by hardware only in terms of quite specific metrics, usually processing times and storage capabilities. No sustainability, no energy efficiency.

A particularly telling case of this externalization of resource use and pollution is bitcoin. The underlying technology of this "cryptocurrency," the blockchain, solves an interesting algorithmic task. How is it possible to have reliable transactions between two parties that do not trust each other and there is no third party to establish trust either? The solution is the following. Each transaction is recorded in a public ledger. To make sure that no one can manipulate that ledger, all transactions are cryptographically signed. These signatures are designed in a way that they are very hard to compute. Basically, the only way to find them is to try out values. Since there is no central authority that stores the ledger, everyone participating has their own copy. If there are different versions, the majority is considered true. In consequence, an attacker would need to amass more computing power than the honest participants. Otherwise, the correct ledger will always be signed and distributed faster than the false one. Since the task is very difficult, for a large network such as bitcoin, this is deemed unlikely. To keep that procedure safe, a dedicated algorithm adjusts the difficulty of finding the signatures, so that the problem stays difficult with new and more hardware being used.

In this chapter, I have already discussed several algorithms that react to the material conditions of computing: schedulers that recruit new servers to replace failing ones, algorithms that distribute tasks close to the data, etc. Bitcoin reacts to the computing power in its network (by adjusting the difficulty) not for more efficiency, but for security. It is an algorithm that does not get faster with better hardware but adjusts itself to remain difficult. This means that bitcoin hardware will always work at full blast and is thus an incredible waste of energy (Ensmenger 2018). Yet, the paper that proposed the system (Nakamoto 2008) always just speaks of CPU power, as do many discussions of the topic by its users and developers. It is an algorithm that directly operationalizes resource limits, because that is what essentially limits "CPU power," yet without addressing it as such. For those doing the "mining," as the search for signatures in exchange for payment in bitcoins is called, in contrast, much of the aforementioned considerations apply. In particular, they move to countries where energy is very cheap and employ efficient, dedicated hardware.

With the current discussions of climate catastrophe, serious applications begin to address the relationship between algorithms and resources more directly. Particularly in machine learning, the imperative to gather ever more data and the increasing capacities to extract that data (see Chapter 6, p. 122) have led to huge models. They take days to train, even on the hardware that enterprises such as Google or Facebook operate. In the last years, several papers have been published that begin to mention the financial and environmental costs of such models. Bender et al. (2021, 612) add the urge to consider that those benefiting from their use and those suffering the climate impact first most probably live in different parts of the world. In a systematic evaluation of some smaller models, Schwartz et al. (2020) show that in many models, the detection accuracy only increases linearly with an exponential increase of training examples. They also showed that at a certain point in the training process, additional iterations of the training algorithm only led to very small improvements. As a consequence, they call for introducing efficiency metrics in conference publications. Currently, as they show via a review, most publications in machine learning just list the accuracy of the algorithm. Only 10%–20% of the contributions also discuss making the results more efficient (Schwartz et al. 2020, 57).

The authors consider several ways in which the efficiency of an algorithm could be measured. In my words, these correspond to different complementary relations of algorithms and material conditions. First, they propose measuring carbon dioxide emission, which would comprise the relation of the algorithms to the entire infrastructure including energy generation. It could even be made to include the emissions of manufacturing and building, an option that the authors do not discuss. A second option is energy usage, which is still pretty comprehensive but ignores differences in the way that electric energy is created. However, it is much easier to measure using a simple meter on-site than the complex calculation of carbon dioxide emissions, which necessitates information from third parties such as power plants. They also discuss measures such as the number of parameters in a model. This abstracts completely from material factors, although the amount of energy used correlates with that number. However, the authors think this is too imprecise because different algorithms can use these parameters more or less efficiently. Thus, the authors advocate using the number of processor operations[6] as a measure. This is again already quite abstract, because different processors exhibit quite a range of efficiency. Furthermore, all the factors, such as the efficient distribution of tasks in the data center, that have

---

6 To be precise: floating point operations.

been discussed above do not appear in this measure. However, it renders algorithms comparable at the level at which they are discussed in academic research papers. All the authors will implement their algorithms to run the benchmarks that are critical for the success of a paper in machine learning today. Yet, as a research effort, these implementations probably will not be as efficient as they could be. Most importantly, Schwartz et al. observe that "the dramatic increase in computational cost observed over recent years is primarily from modeling and algorithmic choices" (Schwartz et al. 2020, 59). Thus, they look for a measure that attempts to motivate change in these choices even before hardware optimization can come into the picture. To do that, they comply with the culture of benchmarking in machine-learning research discussed in Chapter 6, p. 124. They need a measure that is "comparable between labs" and thus can drive the research competition for more efficient results. Thus, a quite particular view on algorithms – whose genealogy I detail in Chapter 6 – finds its complement in a particular view toward material resource usage: processor cycles. Given such paradigms as MapReduce, that is, algorithms that are optimized for other factors such as locality as well, this might be too idealized a view. On the other hand, given the way research works, it might be a very pragmatic attempt at fostering the development of what the authors of the paper want: green AI.

5
ALGORITHMS AND CODE

Computers are not necessarily programmable in the sense of today's common use of the term. The first computers had a fixed program. Some were built to be easily reconfigurable for different operations through switches or plugboards. Still, each switch and wire had to be set by hand, programs could not simply be loaded and executed. Konrad Zuse's Z3 is usually considered to be the first programmable computer. It was developed starting in 1938 under the administration of the Nazi Ministry of Aviation which funded development through its research branch (Deutsche Versuchsanstalt für Luftfahrt). Fortunately, it did not have any impact on wartime efforts, in contrast to other computers such as the Bombe, Colossus, and ENIAC.

The Z3 used punched celluloid tape to feed the program into the computer. So rather than setting switches or wires by hand, holes in the tape would close contacts that switched the computer to the according state. However, programming in its modern sense hinges on the development of the so-called stored-program computer. These machines can read the program in the same way as input data. This was enabled by still hardwiring some functions, but only very basic operations. These could then be activated by an exchangeable program. This was done using a special type of memory, often called the instruction register. The register is connected to the processor in a way that each different entry in the register activates a different basic function in the processor. Broadly speaking, storing something in memory can be understood as setting a line of switches on and off to signify a series of ones and zeroes. The basic idea is that this row of switches is used as the switches that also configure the processor for a specific operation.

DOI: 10.4324/9781003299851-7

This register is also connected to the main memory where the data and the program resides. Contents from memory can be read into the register, thus determining which instruction is to be executed.

With that setup, programming was possible as the specification of a sequence of basic operations. However, programs had to be written for the specific processor and the operations it provided, including the specific binary sequence (the "setting of switches") that would select these operations on each processor. This is known as machine code and is usually denoted by short abbreviations for each operation instead of the binary number; e.g. "ADD" instead of 00000010.

In a sense, these abbreviations could already be seen as a programming language, because they are geared toward better human understanding – thus they add something that programming in the sense of giving instructions to computers does not need.

Yet, they still required to spell out every step of every operation anew when programming. Grace Hopper described that this was the reason why programming "degenerates into the dull labor of writing and checking programs. This duty now looms as an imposition on the human brain" (Hopper 1952, 243). In fact, this "dull labor" was often designated to women, while men could remain with the more creative work of coming up with programs (Chun 2008).

Hopper is generally credited with the creation of the first compiler. Basically, she created a collection of oft-used routines, each assigned a number. Programming then could be done by stating these numbers. A second, dedicated program, the compiler, would then create the final program by replacing the numbers with the respective routines. In a succeeding version, the numbers for the subroutines were replaced with mathematical terms and English words. A new language for calling the elementary operations that the collection of routines could provide was created – a programming language.

Already at this early stage in the development of programming, several elements of the co-constitutive relation between algorithms and code are discernible. In Hopper's system, two elements begin to emerge, which are often not clearly distinguished when talking about a programming language: one is a language for specifying execution and calling functions, and another is a set of basic functions already provided to programmers, today often called a standard library.

Hopper just provided a few really elementary functions.[1] Later programming languages come with quite substantial sets of pre-defined functionality,

---

1 Hopper's programming languages did not yet have a standard library in the modern sense, but the two issues of a collection of functions and the language to call them already emerge here. The introduction of the notion of program libraries is usually credited to a book from 1951 by Wilkes, Wheeler, and Gill (1982).

systematically covering issues of input and output (files, networking, user in-terfaces), mathematical operations, manipulations of text (search, replace, etc.), and more. While such a standard library is technically not part of the language proper and programmers can define their own functions instead of using those provided, often the success of a language depends on the library and its capabilities.

In consequence, as soon as programming becomes more than the most basic listing of machine code, it depends on algorithms in a two-fold manner: First, writing code is not just programming algorithms but most often calling other algorithms that are readily available in programming libraries. Second, code needs to be processed by specific algorithms, such as compilers, before it can execute the algorithm it "implements."

Many textbooks from computer science describe this manifold transfor-mation of code by other algorithms as a set of translations where an abstract mathematical algorithm is implemented in code which is in turn translated into machine instructions (Dourish 2016). This implies a platonic idea of an algorithm that stays the same throughout its different materializations as mathematical notation, program code, and machine operations. It resonates strongly with the cybernetic conviction that information processing is deci-sive, not the carrier of information (Hayles 1999).

Such a view has been challenged by authors working under the rubrics of software studies or critical code studies (Fuller 2008; Kitchin 2017; Seaver 2017). They show that the environment in which code is created is important, but also that code itself is not a neutral medium in which arbitrary algorithms can be expressed. To begin, the mathematical world of infinite storage and infinite precision is replaced with discrete values, rounding errors, formal and technical constraints, material factors (see Chapter 4, p. 57), etc. Furthermore, as will be discussed in detail below, the way code is written and organized influences what is written. However, while this means that the first link in this chain of translations, between an abstract algorithm and code, has been critically reworked, many still consider the relation of code to machine operations as purely "technical" (Galloway 2006b, 321). While no one denies the socio-culturally defined access to the code, its essence is seen in its ex-ecutability. E.g. Galloway writes: "Code essentially has no other reason of being than instructing some machine in how to act" (Galloway 2006b, 321) or similarly Hayles: "code causes changes in machinic behavior" (Hayles 1999). This view has been critized by Chun as considering "code as fetish," which mainly is based on a tendency to "forget or trivialize execution" (Chun 2008, 304). She shows that the "translation" a compiler does is a complex re-working, introducing all kinds of adaptations to the specifics of the machine. Chun suspects that this complex process can be easily ignored also because of the genealogy of computing, where this "dull labor" was often relegated to "girls" under the command of male engineers (Chun 2004). This gendered distribution of labor precluded the recognition of the "girls'" labor as a contribution in its own to the process of computing. Chun contrasts this view with a more performative account where "source code thus only becomes source after the fact" (Chun 2008, 307).

> Source code is more accurately a re-source, rather than a source. Source code becomes a source when it becomes integrated with logic gates (and at an even lower level, with the transistors that comprise these gates); when it expands to include software libraries, when it merges with code burned into silicon chips; and when all these signals are carefully monitored, timed, and rectified.
>
> (Chun 2008, 307)

I discuss in Chapter 4 that the relation of hardware and algorithms is itself a complex co-constitution. Integrating code only in this relation would, however, ignore the manifold ways in which algorithms contribute to the performance of code as "code after the fact." Algorithms are called in libraries, other algorithms turn code into something that eventually can run on hardware, and yet another set of algorithms structures and organizes programming. All these algorithms have been created in different contexts, in different languages, by different people, with different intentions, etc. Thus, the influence of algorithms on code happens in manifold co-constitutive relations. Ignoring this plurality of relations would also ignore many socio-cultural factors that are imported into the code via these algorithms.

Vice versa, code also influences the algorithms it purportedly just "implements." Such concerns can already be seen regarding the second element that emerges with Hopper's work: not just a collection of algorithms but a language to call them. This language immediately was a matter of dispute. At that time Hopper worked for the Eckert-Mauchly Computer Corporation and later Remington Rand who wanted to bring computers to a civil market. For this market, she argued, the programming language should neither refer to the basic operations of computers nor to mathematical formulae. She suggested to develop a programming language based on English words. To make that suggestion more attractive to her management, she proposed that such a language could be easily adapted to other markets, for example using French or German instead of English. She recounts the reactions in a keynote for the Association of Computing Machinery:

> That hit the fan!! It was absolutely obvious that a respectable American computer, built in Philadelphia, Pennsylvania, could not possibly understand French or German! And it took us four months to say no, no, no, no! We wouldn't think of programming it in anything but English.
>
> (Hopper 1978, 17)

In the keynote address, Hopper makes fun of that reaction, because for her it does not matter which language is used: all the words are essentially just "bit patterns" that are compared by the compiler to be substituted with the appropriate machine commands (Hopper 1978, 16). What these patterns mean to humans is not important for Hopper who was still trained to work with the machines directly. Yet, for the success of programming via code, of course, such things do make a difference. They determine what can be programmed by particular, situated people in specific contexts and for specific tasks – not in (mathematical) principle. From an abstract view, all algorithms that can be written in one language can be written in the other. Yet, from many practical points of view, they are only written in particular languages. Hopper already had developed a language based on mathematics in addition to the English-based language. This was only the beginning of an immense differentiation and specialization of different forms of code. In such a practical, situated perspective, code itself is not a free expressive medium, but from the beginning geared toward particular algorithms.

Thus, algorithms in many forms contribute to code – in particular, if it is considered to be "code after the fact." Vice versa, code influences in many ways the algorithms that are written – and not just implemented.

Technicity of algorithms

Before elaborating on this co-constitutive relation, I want to consider Bernhard Rieder's somewhat opposing claim that algorithms – or more precisely what he calls "algorithmic techniques" – are a specific form of technicity independent of code or implementations. His approach is noteworthy because he does not define technicity regarding computability in principle or the theoretical interchangeability of programming languages. Rather, Rieder finds technicity in concrete practices; arguing that the "incessant evocations of Turing, Shannon, and von Neumann" in a lot of theoretical literature on computers, algorithms, and digital media are of limited help to understand the complex field that they have become today (Rieder 2020, 88). Yet, he wants to approach algorithms, that is "some of the most complex techniques in computing from a humanistic perspective with regard to their technicity and not just their social effects and entanglements" (Rieder 2020, 102). To that aim, Rieder transfers Simondon's philosophy of technology to algorithms.

For Simondon, technology admits different configurations, it admits a genealogy. Yet, both – different configurations and genealogy – are specific to technical objects. Simondon thinks that each "lineage" of technical objects, as he states it in his biologistic language, is characterized by the invention of a technical essence that remains stable throughout further developments. His examples of such essences include asymmetric conductance (which is relevant for electron tubes and also later successors such as transistors) or combustion engines. Such inventions entail the "translation into matter of a set of notions and scientific principles" or more general of "an intellectual system" (Simondon 2016, 49). They contextualize these principles in a way that makes the technological essence work in a particular object, in a specific situation. That needs a lot of engineering knowledge and innovation. Yet, the process does not stop there. Simondon devotes long and detailed studies to the way in which technical objects evolve. This happens mainly by integration. For example, the first combustion motors translated each physical task into an object: there was a cylinder to create and contain the pressure of combustion, and there were cooling elements attached to the cylinder for cooling. In later engines, particular shapes of cylinders were developed that integrated these two functions of cooling and containment. This integration, however, is not an additional translation. Rather, it realizes a technical potential that is already present in the technical object. It maintains the function it had as a combination of different elements and integrates that into one element that can provide the same or even better function. Thus, the integration is itself technical.

Such adaptations always relate to the "milieu" of the technical object, thus it is a contextualized adaptation. An example from Simondon's book are electrical grids with specific voltage and frequency without which some applications just will not work properly, while other, less adapted objects can work with all kinds of voltage and frequency (Simondon 2016, 56). In the long run, technical evolution does not just react to but will eventually also change the milieu. Thus, there is a second sense in which technical evolution is properly technical. It is not only based on a potential in the technical object but also reacts to a milieu that is itself increasingly technical. Simondon introduces a co-constitutive relation himself: "a milieu that the technical object creates around itself and that conditions it, just as it is conditioned by it" (Simondon 2016, 59).

Rieder considers algorithmic techniques as "elements" in Simondonian terms. Thus, these techniques have their own history and need to be understood as a constantly evolving practice with respect to a corresponding milieu. In order to function, they still need to be combined time and again into "ensembles" (e.g. with hardware).[2] Such combining is what software engineering does. Yet, the algorithmic techniques carry the evolving technical essence.

That way, Rieder clearly opposes a reductionist logic and knows that use and culture are important. Still, in his view, they are separate areas of concern. Rieder considers algorithmic techniques as cultural techniques in the sense of

---

2 Malaspina and Rogove translate "ensemble" as "whole" in the English edition *of On the mode of existence of technical objects*. I retain the original French use of "ensemble," which also works in English, connoting not only wholeness but also a specific, structured togetherness.

Siegert (2015). This line of thought provides him with reasons to repudiate a reductionism to hardware or artefacts, since it clearly focuses on practices. Yet, it still has not given up the search for an "a-priori" of culture, and in consequence, Rieder tends to give algorithmic techniques an a-priori status in relation to both programming and using computers (Rieder 2020, 84).[3]

Understanding algorithms, Rieder argues, does not mean an under-standing of the fundamental possibilities of programming (as explored by Turing, etc.); neither does it suffice to just follow code line by line. Knowing algorithms is to know a lot of specific algorithms for specific tasks, their relationships and differences, caveats and potentials. He illustrates this with regard to Donald Knuth's (1997) famous four-volume collection on *The art of computer programming*, which essentially is a huge collection of algo-rithms for all kinds of tasks from sorting to arithmetic to random number generation. Knowing how to program, Rieder argues, is proficiency with the many algorithms that span the hundreds of pages of Knuth's books. Importantly, these algorithms do not exist independent of both coding and formal notation. Algorithmic techniques evolve, are communicated and learned, discussed and evaluated while programming or while reflecting al-gorithms using their abstract notations as it is used in Knuth's book. Yet, according to Rieder, they are technical in Simondon's sense: the possibility to solve particular problems with particular approaches (Rieder 2020, 98). In consequence, not only on the level of concrete software products but also on the level of algorithmic techniques an evolution takes place. This evolution happens similarly to the way it is described by Simondon, such as the adaptation to a specific milieu. For example, Rieder describes the develop-ment of QuickSort, a by-now canonical algorithm for sorting numbers. It was invented at the end of the 1950ies in a quite specific setting, where particular building blocks of the algorithm were easily available in a pro-gramming language, but which was also confronted with specific technical

---

3 This entails removing Simondon's thought on technicity from his wider theoretical approach, since for Simondon culture is a synthetic achievement that needs to integrate technicity, rather than depending on it a-priori. For Simondon, "[T]echnicity is one of the two fundamental phases of the mode of existence of the whole constituted by man and the world." This phase of technicity emerged out of a "unique, central, and original mode of being in the world: the magical mode" which split into the two phases of technicity and religion balancing each other (Simondon 2016, 173–74). Simondon's more general aim is to integrate technicity into cul-ture in order to eventually enable philosophical thought to make these different phases converge again (Simondon 2016, 171). This illustrates that everything in Simondon's thought needs to be understood as part of a circumspect, dynamic evolution that still works in big oppositions (nature vs. technology, human vs. the world). Even if they are moments or phases in a dynamic development, they are always located in a specific moment of a general genesis. Simondon does not deal with situatedness in the radical way that I have developed in Chapter 2.

problems such as "particular challenges of sequential tape storage and the small working memory available at the time" (Rieder 2020, 67).

The perspective of an algorithmic technique, that is a praxis, and its adaption to changing milieus cuts across the common distinction between an abstract algorithm and its implementation in code. Yet, as I have described at the beginning of this section, Rieder still considers algorithmic techniques as elements in Simondon's sense. That is they offer a specific, and *specifically technical* potential. Certainly, that potential needs to be integrated with other elements to form a stable technical object. Programming is one important step in this integration, another one is execution on hardware. However, this does not underrun the inherent technicity that Rieder wants to maintain. As in Simondon, the problems encountered during the integration between the object and milieu lead to the refinement of the object. The element of algorithmic techniques then marks one spot where technicity manifests itself.

Yet, it is important to note that nothing of what has been discussed so far is purely technical. I will use one of Rieder's many very detailed and very helpful studies from the practice of programming to explain this. He also refers to standard libraries that enable programmers to use all kinds of functionality without caring about their details. His example is a call to a function of the standard library of PHP, a language used for a lot of web programming. Rieder interprets this call of a library function using Simondon's idea of technicity:

> This is how technical elements in software can be seen as both means of injecting existing technicity into a new program and carriers of objectified knowledge.
>
> (Rieder 2020, 110)

> [H]ow such functions are packaged, distributed, and rendered accessible to programmers is less important than to recognize that this allows for techniques of all levels of complexity and sophistication to become elements in larger systems of functioning, without actually having to be understood in any substantial way by the programmer.
>
> (Rieder 2020, 111)

The technicity, in this case, would be an evolved state of libraries for internet communication that are available to programmers. Yet, it provides not just technicity or objectified knowledge. The programmer is no longer proficient in Knuth's collection of algorithms, but in the PHP standard library, which is in turn structured by all kinds of concerns on software engineering that forms its code and the code that is written with it and thus fully saturated with the co-constitutive relations of code and algorithms mentioned above.

Such a library is not just a functional a-priori for a culture, it is part of a (coding) culture itself, with its own concerns, a community, etc. that is structured quite differently than the coding culture Knuth addressed with his book. In the case of PHP, this community is closely related to spread of the internet to private users and the according requirements of easy integration of programming with the design of web pages and with ever more complex websites (such as e-commerce functions) being demanded starting in the later 1990s.

Rieder discusses these communities and the many tools and practices they develop as well. He also distinguishes commercial forms of software engineering from more crafty and personal open-source programming. He mentions the "work of consultants, analysts, modelers, optimizers, or rationalizers specialized in capturing practices into technical form" (Rieder 2020, 91). Yet, for him, all of this hinges on technicity:

> [U]ltimately, there is a technical substance, an internal or objective technicity, that demarcates a space of possibilities and limitations that the methods and practices dedicated to external or objectal aspects are ultimately bound to.
>
> (Rieder 2020, 91)

This technical substance, that enables both the work of the programmer and the consultants, analysts, etc. is Rieder's answer to the question: "what can be programmed" (Rieder 2020, 92). Simondon, despite all attention on evolution and co-constitution with milieus, still attempts a universal trajectory of technicity as a phase of humanity (Simondon 2016, 173). Here, clear traces of this show in Rieder's thought. What can be programmed, for him, is the universal current state of programmability.

However, what can be programmed is a question that gets a different answer depending on the context, that is dependent on concrete possibilities in a concrete situation that is in important aspects co-constituted by code. If algorithms can appear as the technical substance that can be – even if just analytically – subtracted from code, this is to a large extent an achievement of code itself. As I show below, the possibility of using an algorithm "without actually having to be understood in any substantial way by the programmer" has been a prime concern in the development of programming languages. Thus, again this is co-produced by particular forms of code and practices of coding, not the technical self-sufficiency of algorithms.

More generally speaking, on the level of situated practices, code is not just a milieu in which algorithms can evolve – but still remain separate. Code is not just what programmers do when they use algorithmic techniques. If a situated perspective is taken seriously, code, which includes how functions are "packaged, distributed, and rendered accessible to programmers" (Rieder 2020, 111), co-determines what can be done with algorithms in the first place.

Thus, it is no surprise that such features of code have become a central issue of both practical and academic concerns in software engineering.

The structure and organization of code

To consider an academic perspective, Edsger Dijkstra in a famous text from 1968 demanded to "shorten the conceptual gap between static program and dynamic process, to make the correspondence between the program (spread out in text space) and the process (spread out in time) as trivial as possible" (Dijkstra 1968, 0). He argued for a reduction of complexity in coding that pertains to the organization of code as a problem of its own, independent of its compilation and execution later on. In my words, he demands that the relation of code and algorithms be considered as important as the relation of hardware and algorithms. This debate, in which Dijstra took part with his text, is an example of an entire development within mathematics and computer science to deal with code itself. While this clearly emphasizes the influence of code on algorithms, it also frames this influence as a problem to solve or optimize. With this framing, a lot of the socio-economic factors that structure this "problem" are ignored or just accepted as a given condition.

Here, we begin to see the particular situatedness that a specific form of code entails. It does not just reflect but creates – and is intended to create – particular possibilities for using or working with algorithms, while foreclosing others. This situatedness can be quite different, depending on time and setting, relating to different social, economic, and political factors.

Let me just quote the fact that the term "software engineering" rose in popularity due to the "NATO software engineering conference," whose organizers stated that the "phrase 'software engineering' was deliberately chosen as being provocative, in implying the need for software manufacture to be based on the types of theoretical foundations and practical disciplines that are traditional in the established branches of engineering" (Naur and Randell 1969, 8).

The conference already covered most aspects of software engineering that this field comprises today: how to introduce the user requirements (who usually are not computer experts) into the design, how to split design from implementation and make both interoperate, how to manage software development in teams, how to evaluate and test software, how to organize releases and maintenance as well as pricing, i.e. software as commodity (Naur and Randell 1969).

Around the same time, software became a matter of academic concern. In a classic paper, Böhm and Jacopini (1966) proved that any computable function can be computed by a program that consists of only three types of control structures:

- a sequence of commands

- a selection of sequences depending on a given condition: if it is true one sequence is executed, if is false, another
- the iteration of a sequence; i.e. its repeated execution as long as a given condition is true

It gave a new perspective on computing the formal, rigorous background that the computer scientists of the day considered essential. Software engineers dealt with the relation of what the program should do and the best way to write it down into code – thus with the relation of algorithm and code – and not the relation of code and what the machine should do. In his *Notes on structured programming*, Dijkstra argued for a hierarchical organization of software that could be distributed to many programmers. Each programmer should be able to program as if there were a special "machine" for his section of code – even if the functions of this "machine" are really provided by the code of other programmers (Dijkstra 1970, 86). In the same vein, a few years later Niklaus Wirth described programming languages as an "abstract computer" (Wirth 1976, 3). In consequence, code is no longer just giving commands to machines but rather to other algorithms, programmed by other programmers in yet another form of code. This repeated interplay of code and algorithms replaces the original concern of how to give commands to machines efficiently mainly due to economic and pragmatic reasons.

Dijkstra's and Wirth's idea of a hierarchical distribution of code to different, independent programmers clearly reflects programming becoming a professional occupation organized in large enterprises. In fact, the development of programming paradigms and the economic organization of software engineering has developed in close interaction (Neubert 2015). Berry notes that while programming has inspired a lot of thought about immaterial labor, still many "Taylorist techniques, like time-and-motion studies, peer review programming, software libraries, modularity, and so forth" (Berry 2011, 40) are employed. In fact, part of today's form of organizing code is to transport these Taylorist methods out of controlled work environments and to remain effective even if the programmer can sit in a fancy café with a latte and a vegan dish at hand.

The free and open-source movements were a reaction to the starting commodification of software, arguing that programs should be treated like scientific or mathematical insight, which no one can possess (Stallman 2015). They developed into complex social formations, with their particular ways of organizing programming, distributing labor, and their own preferred forms of code (Coleman 2012). In particular, the free software movement emphasizes that this is not just about having to pay for software – although this is one major issue in access. It is also an issue of being able to study and modify it, to adapt it to one's own needs. All of this not only depends on the question of whether the code is accessible, but also how, and in which form of organization, language, documentation. While open-source code is often heralded as a means to transparent algorithms, their effective transparency is mediated by the features of code, and how it is organized and documented. As I will argue in the next section, this may also include understanding how a particular community works – also through the code it produces. In consequence, the co-constitutive relation of code and algorithms does not only concern programming before algorithms are used. Rather it extends to issues of oversight, regulation, and modification.

Code as a claim to community

Even among those arguing for an engineering approach to programming, there were huge debates what that should mean. Roughly a decade after the NATO conference and Dijkstra's paper, John Backus used the prestigious Turing award lecture to promote a different alternative: functional programming. Backus noted that many so-called "high level" programming languages had been established with formal specification of their semantics that no longer relied on tying them to the machine instructions they would eventually be resolved to. Yet, he argued, they still were based on an abstract machine as advocated by Dijkstra or Wirth. In contrast, he proposed to disentangle programming even from these abstract computers and to use mathematical functions as the basic building block of programs. These, he argued would be easier to understand because they came in the form mathematicians knew and did not need a mental execution of a program in order to understand what it did (Backus 1978, 615).

This is just one of many proposals for programming paradigms that have been made. I mention it because it allows to show that code is performative beyond the concern of creating software in a narrow sense. Dijkstra, proponent of the criticized "high level languages" wrote a ravaging, ad hominem critique of Backus' lecture, doubting his thorough understanding of the matter. In a series of letters[4] exchanged afterward, Backus complains to Dijsktra and the latter responds: "I make a great difference between 'your work' and 'your Turing lecture [.]' I regard – and continue to regard – your work (as I wrote) as 'a valid research effort'" (Jiahao 2016, letter 24 April 1979). What had upset Dijkstra was that "Backus presented his thing by way of Turing lecture, the glamour of which immediately caused the significance of functional programming to be overrated beyond justification." Thus, his review was

---

4 Many thanks to Jiahao Chen for digitalizing them at the Library of Congress and making them widely available for discussion (Jiahao 2016).

a political pamphlet where a political pamphlet seemed needed, a need that, I hope unintentionally, you yourself [Backus] had created. My guess is that, had you fully realized the glamour of the Turing Lecture – and the lack of independent judgement of most of its audience – you had made more sober use of your eloquence.

(Jiahao 2016, letter 5 April 1979)

Backus replied that political pamphlets for an audience that Dijkstra presumed to be "ninnies" were usually not the business of scientists (Jiahao 2016, letter 18 April 1979). The latter justified his "pamphlet":

The sad fact is that ninnies do have influence, for instance in the process of assigning research budgets. Not the opinion of ninnies, but the possible consequences of their opinions is what matters: by diverting research opportunities they can easily retard progress very much.

(Jiahao 2016, letter 24 April 1979)

The immense arrogance that speaks from Dijkstra's implication that Backus should accept his judgment of the latter's work as a "valid research effort" over which they could have an academic debate is one thing. Yet, the character of famous computer scientists is not my concern here. What I am interested in is Dijsktra obviously talking from experience that coding paradigms have connotations beyond the concerns of programming code itself – here in the form of funding. These issues that Dijstra tellingly calls "politics" are for him a matter of dealing with "ninnies."

I have already mentioned with regard to Hopper that specific forms of code are geared toward particular algorithms. While a theoretical computer scientist could argue that all algorithms in all programming languages could be reduced to a Turing machine and thus show their theoretical equivalence, already in the 1970s there are two Turing award laureates arguing in the risk of their personal friendship that they are all but equal. Like Hopper, they are not concerned with fundamental theoretical possibilities. They are concerned with software engineering becoming an institutionalized activity in quite different contexts, military, businesses, and universities. They are concerned with the concrete, situated task of writing code – that requires funding.

In consequence, Hopper as well as Dijkstra and Backus are also concerned with code as mediating the relation to an "outside" of programming. Yet, an outside as seen from the situatedness of code: Hopper's "management" that would only accept an English computer and Dikstra's "ninnies" whom he fears could direct funding to the wrong people (i.e. not him). All portray those involved with such issues as an outside that do not really understand what is going on in code. In Hopper's case, the management does not get that all languages are just "bit patterns," and they are, "ninnies with influence" that are too easily impressed by the "glamour" of a lecture rather than the qualities of code in the case of Dijkstra.

Given the reflections collected here so far, this is no surprise. Coding, as any practice, is a claim to a community (as discussed in Chapter 3, p. 49). Yet, here this community is quite explicitly felt and addressed. Part of this explicit nature is that code itself contributes to how these communities distinguish themselves and create their respective outside. In my words, code is not just what happens on the inside, that is "behind" the interfaces. Rather code is a relation to the outside of the situatedness of programmers. The way in which programmers considered management or others as outsiders, is the way how that outside looks from inside, mediated by code – rather than being enabled by code as a privileged form of access to computing. That is, code addresses other programmers, not just machines, and in a way that signals that they are part of a community that is distinguished from others. As Chun and others rightly criticize, this immunizing gesture that has been repeated in a lot of media theories (Chun 2008; Seaver 2017).

To sustain these communities of programmers, programming code quite literally becomes social code. The fact that the choice of the natural language from which programming languages take their words was indeed an issue at the very beginning of programming but turned quickly into a matter of course acceptance of English that up until today is only challenged by nerd projects[5] and artistic interventions[6] is an impressive illustration how code can transport such decisions quite tacitly. Only on the Eastern side of the iron curtain, these politics were made explicit. For example, the earlier Soviet computers called MIR were programmed in a Russian-based language called Аналитик (Husberg and Seppänen 1974). The German Democratic Republic saw a German version of BASIC called DIWA.[7] Yet, even in these countries in the long term, the Anglophone languages prevailed.

Although in many regards thought of as opposition to commercial software development, also the free and open-source communities very much rely on such a distinction between inside and outside. There even exists a codebook for all the group talk and inside jokes, the "jargon file" (Raymond 2004b), which was started at MIT already in 1975 and lives on the internet even today. Generally, the makeup of the community and its outsides is particularly salient in the free and open-source movements. Academic and commercial coders usually go through some kind of recruitment and formal

---

5 See for example the programming language Whitespace that only uses non-printing characters tab, space, and line-feed for its statements.
6 See for example the Arabic programming language قلب, including left-to-right printing, an attempt to highlight the Anglophone bias in programming. https://nas.sr/ قلب/
7 https://www.robotrontechnik.de/index.htm?/html/software/sprachen.htm

training which gives the transition from the outside to the inside an institutional correspondence – even though the respective communities form in fact much more through everyday practices and tacit assumptions – and code. In contrast, the basic ethic of free and open-source software centers on participation and is often explicitly critical of the institutionalized demands of commercial (and sometimes also academic) programming. Yet, a lot of communities within these movements are notorious for being socially inaccessible (Coleman 2012, 110) with constant denigration of "newbies." Using the wrong formatting of code can suffice to provoke harsh reactions. Coleman describes that the direct criticism and self-congratulatory gestures that are usual in many such communities – and contribute to making it inaccessible – do not just concern forum discussions or chatrooms. They are literally done in code, through comments and variable names (Coleman 2012, 112). Vice versa, often the conventions of code are ironically used in discussions, such as the diagnosis that one deals with an "ID 10T" error, which is easily read as having to deal with an "idiot" (Raymond 2004a). Coleman reads this primarily as face work in the sense of Goffman (Coleman 2012, 113).

At the same time, these processes guarantee the stability of the group. The free and open software movements are driven by strong political views that bring many people to commit a lot of time and energy to these projects. Thus, one of the main necessities of such communities is to perpetuate and uphold these values. Without enough ethically committed people, they would simply vanish. However, that necessity is rarely explicitly addressed – in contrast for example to NGOs or political parties that equally rely on voluntary work but where recruiting new members is a central strategic aim. For free and open-source or hacker communities, the harsh reactions to those from the "outside" is both a test of their commitment and a challenge to build it. People not driven by the *same values* and people not *driven* by these values would simply not bother to deal with these barriers. Many algorithms that became accessible to many people thanks to hackers and free software – from encryption to operating systems – thus paradoxically derive from a socially uniform and quite inaccessible way of organizing coding. Of course, this way of maintaining a community still excludes many – those who cannot or do not want to invest the resources to teach themselves enough to take up the challenge; and those who want to collaborate in a less individualized and less meritocratic manner. In consequence, things change. When I was planning my first trip to a Chaos Communication Congress – by now one of the largest hacker conferences in the world – in the early 2000s, I would have never even thought of bringing a computer running Microsoft Windows to the venue; out of fear to be hacked and shamed. At the last conference in 2019 with more than 17,000 people, participants from all parts of society attended and brought in all kinds of devices without even thinking about them. Also, in the last decade, all big communities and free and open-source projects had their debates on inclusion, style of communication, and more. The challenge remains how to maintain a value-driven community without such harsh, exlusionary boundaries.

Such communities, however, also form in commercial settings. Berry analyzes a rare moment, when a leak gave insights into the code of a major software company, in this case, Microsoft Windows. This code does not just express the way in which labor is organized at Microsoft. It also contains inside jokes and comments using which programmers communicate with each other via the code they write. They comment on the quality of the code: "TERRIBLE HORRIBLE NO GOOD VERY BAD HACK," express juicy opinions on other Microsoft products: "We have to do this only because Exchange is a moron" and of course on their colleagues' performance: "should be fixed in the apps themselves. Morons!," yet also not sparing themselves: "We are morons" (Berry 2011, 70–71). In this code, we see a manifestation of a particular self-understanding of a group, including its chummy but exacting form of commenting work and an odd preference for an ableist insult. We see a way to collaborate and to communicate. Code does not only reflect but is itself a part of this collaboration and communication.

The way in which code structures and situates communities of programmers of course influences the code they write. This factor is often overlooked in discussing the politics of algorithms. In particular, the demographic composition of programming teams has recently been discussed as an influential factor. For example, the AI Now institute demands not only to include legal experts and social scientists in programming teams but also more "diversity within the fields building these systems [that] will help ensure that they reflect a broader variety of viewpoints" (Campolo et al. 2017, 17). Of course, the demand for more diversity in the tech industries is important for many reasons: equal opportunities, challenging the perception of tech as a white and male thing, encouraging more emancipatory uses of technology, and more. Yet, as a measure against biased algorithms, there are some problems with such demands. Quite generally, they tend to imply a strategy that runs counter to a long line of work in critical theories that emphasize that the responsibility to counter discrimination and injustice should lie with those causing or profiting from it and not with the victims (Alcoff 2015; Dyer 1997). It also tends to ignore the complications that intersectional thought has shown to be necessary (Crenshaw 1995).

Regarding the discussion on code, such proposals also underestimate the technical nature of situatedness, more precisely the way code situates programming. Code is not just the medium that transports the programmers' biases into the algorithms they create. Code also contributes to shaping this community in the first place. Who is present, and which biases are present also depends on code. This influence, though, happens on a smaller scale than social categories such as race or gender. Code is geared toward a group with a specific understanding of itself and its purpose, reflected also on who is considered an outsider (management, "ninnies"). This does not mean that demographic factors have no importance. Yet, they intersect with the way the community works. Programmers are not just situated regarding race, gender, class, and other factors that track their lives beyond their workplace or spare-time projects. They are raced, classed, gendered, ... *programmers.* As I have shown being a programmer means, among many other things, to perform a certain form of face work via code.[8] It means to be part of a community that is structured by a self-understanding to have a privileged insight respective to an outside. This boundary is again drawn by code – forms of using it, possibilities to access it, and ways of comprehending it. In fact, for those who make it to the inside, these structures can superficially cover the differences that derive from race, class, gender, or other circumspect identities. One shares the same inside jokes, and fights the same "holy wars" over what appears to be marginal details to "outsiders." Whenever I visited large tech companies in the last decade, especially in Silicon Valley, everyone I met regardless of origin, gender, or skin color, shared a success story: they made it "inside," and they are part of one of the best tech firms in the world – many after having worked very hard to get a degree from a prestigious university in the US or Europe. Again, this does not make discrimination and injustices go away. Yet, the situatedness in which these factors play out changes and with that certainly also the potential to reflect "a broader variety of viewpoints."

A related point concerns the epistemic situatedness of programmers regarding code. As I have shown and will continue to discuss below, a central feature of code in most scenarios is that it is distributed among many programmers and contributes to organizing this distribution. Almost from the very beginning of structuring code into rather self-contained parts that can be assigned to different persons or be re-used later on, the central approach was to hide the functionality – or at least make it unnecessary to know it. One should be able to use other parts of a program, as Dijskstra wrote, as if it were a special computer for the own task. Thus, contrary to the implications of a lot of efforts in fairness and transparency, programmers (at least in commercial settings) are not inside the "black box." On the contrary, they need to have a lot of stuff blackboxed in order to work efficiently. This entails that internal to software companies, there are group politics mediated by code, many of which reflect the socio-economic setting of coding. This setting, which might for example demand quick and efficient development under the constant pressure of a high-achiever environment, with re-using a

8 See also the discussion in Chapter 7.

lot of code from libraries might dim down a lot of the potential positive effects even a highly diverse programming team could have. If they to a large part rely on existing code, uncovering the politics and structural decisions it embeds is very difficult – particularly if it is meant to happen as a side effect of the teams' composition rather than a deliberate effort, which I discuss in Chapter 7, p. 147.

The complexity of code and the trustworthiness of algorithms

In today's world of computing, the co-constitutive relations of algorithms and code have intensified and become more dynamic. Often, a programmer is much more collocating or orchestrating components rather than writing code that provides new functions. These developments are not limited to libraries that programmers use to compose their own programs. Huge, mostly commercial platforms, so-called "middleware," do not just provide an immense range of functionality to individual programs. They also change how programs interact. Operating systems usually provide two ways for programs to exchange information: files and network adapters. One program has to format the information in an appropriate file or network package and write it out to the disk or network adapter. The other program has to read from the file or network, decode it from the file or networking format, and then can use the information. Via the mentioned middleware, one program can simply call functions or use objects from other programs, very much as if they were part of its own program, without dealing with the specifics of files and networks anymore.

In practice, code coordinates many libraries, as well as services and functions provided by complex frameworks such as middleware. This has far-reaching consequences, for it makes it practically impossible for the programmer to trace the functionality that is involved in the routines they are calling for their own program. During the time I have been writing this book, a security vulnerability called "Log4Shell" was discovered. Experts have called it the most severe vulnerability "ever" (Hunter and De Vynck 2021). It allowed attackers to execute arbitrary programs on any machine that ran a program with the vulnerability. Despite this huge risk, this issue had been existing unnoticed since 2013 on millions of servers on the internet.

Log4Shell affects Log4J, a logging framework for the programming language Java. Logging is part of most applications that run on servers. It allows to store usage statistics, errors, and everything else the programmers deem noteworthy or the law requires, e.g. through data retention directives. Log4J provides programmers with logging functionality in a very circumspect manner. Part of the Log4J functionality is the ability to call the so-called Java Naming and Directory Interface (JNDI). This service is part of the interoperability I have described above. It provides programmers with a directory, in which they can look up all kinds of objects they might want to use. One of the functionalities that can be accessed via JNDI in turn is to look up things on the internet via the so-called Lightweight Directory Access Protocol (LDAP). This is a system-independent protocol for all kinds of structured records. If part of the logging means to access a structured record, e.g. to resolve a user name to an address, the programmer might tell Log4J to use JNDI to look up that data on a server that is available via LDAP. This means that one simple logging operation means calling one complex service (Log4J) calling another complex service that provides the JNDI programming interface which in turn accesses a server somewhere on the internet running yet another service: LDAP. An error in the way in which information was passed from one service to the next allowed attackers to trick the program into loading arbitrary program code from any address on the internet.

Confused? Apparently, even daily users did not notice that error in the depths of this chain of execution. This is commonplace software development – no complex data-driven AI algorithms that are discussed as inherently inscrutable (see Chapter 6, p. 129). Still, this provided a situation that frustrates any expectations of transparency and oversight as a political tool for software development. Log4J, particularly, is open-source software, so in theory, anyone using it – and not just its programmers – could have discovered the vulnerability. Yet, no one did, which again illustrates that it is not very helpful to understand algorithms via fundamental possibilities – even if they are fundamental possibilities of code.

The sheer complexity of dynamically interacting services is just one reason why the error went unnoticed. Another reason is the economics of programming where using a library or service is based on the very idea of not having to deal with functionality. Using such a library does not only distribute the labor of programming but also the responsibility of error checking, maintenance, etc. This turns using such code by others at least implicitly into a matter of trust – which directly affects the trustworthiness of the algorithms that eventually run.

The trustworthiness of frameworks, libraries, and services hinges on a complex form of mediation. In the commercial setting, this can involve legal regulations concerning the liability for software products and services. It can also rely on the reputation of the issuer. In the case of Log4J, this is the Apache Software Foundation, a US-American nonprofit corporation that provides the most widely used software for internet servers, development tools, and more. Individual programmers, which are often seen as authors or responsible agents in many discussions of software and code, rarely figure in such mediations. If at all, this happens in open-source projects, which are either small enough to be maintained by a single person or where a single person has considerable influence over the work of all contributors. Linus Torvald's persisting – but also debated – control of the Linux kernel development is an example for the latter case (Sharwood 2015).

Louise Amoore invokes Foucault's notion of the "author function," which highlights that the author is not a feature of a text, but a production of the text and its surrounding contexts and institutions (Amoore 2020, 94). Talking of the author function of code allows one to unite several issues under one term. First of all, it reminds us that even a programmer working alone, who might seem rather free from many of the influences of code on algorithms that I have discussed here, depends on the language and libraries they use. In Foucauldian terms, any author can only say what their language makes sayable. The author, however, remains important as a mediator of trust or quality. The notion of the author function shows that establishing an author is itself one of the functions of code. In the case of Jog4J, the Apache Software Foundation is a trustworthy "author" because of the quality of the code that it has produced over the years, because of the specific open-source style of organizing and writing code, and because of its usability for others, including many of their products being quasi standards for developing web services. Even many approaches for explainable algorithms or explainable AI very much focus on properties of code and programs, rather than on a social or legal process of explanation (Rohlfing et al. 2020).

Code is geared toward a certain function/politics

In Chapter 3, I have introduced the performative distinction of programmers and users based on the work of Lucas Introna. It shows that both have different rather than more or less privileged access to algorithms. However, with the developments discussed in this chapter, the situation of programmers approximates that of users. As I have shown, most algorithms are available for the programmer quite like they are for the user: as a functionality that more or less serves their purposes and not as something that they themselves have to code.

This becomes even more of an issue with so-called software as a service, service-oriented architecture, and other phenomena commonly summarized under the term "cloud computing." Rather than providing libraries or frameworks, which the clients still have to run on their own, companies increasingly sell the execution of algorithms rather than code or libraries. For example, if one wanted to incorporate image recognition into an application, it would be possible to use a pertinent library, even one that comes with a pre-trained model. Yet, a programmer using this library still would call a function on a machine they control, where they have to install and maintain the library and become familiar with its functions. The alternative would be to just send the image to a company that processes it on their own machines and just returns the result of the recognition process. In fact, image recognition services are offered by most major platforms.[9] Via so-called application programming interfaces (APIs), calling these functions is as easy as calling a function in a local library. For a programmer, the code they write does not look much different. Yet, everything happens on someone else's machine, where the programmer has no control over the use of the data, where the functionality that the service provides could change every time, that is dependent on the availability of a service.

These developments have added yet another way in which code constitutes algorithms in computing. There are special forms of code that are only intended to orchestrate or choreograph such services. For example, the Web Services Business Process Execution Language (WS-BPEL) is a standard to formally model, i.e. code, business processes that assumes that every part of this process is available as a web service. Once such a process is formally specified, it can be "run" on another piece of software, e.g. the Apache ODE (Apache Orchestration Director Engine). This "engine" is nothing but a program that communicates with the different web services and processes their information according to the specification in WS-BPEL. Orchestration and choreography – rather than programming – have become terms of the trade, with a prominent choreography language aptly named "let's dance" (Decker, Kopp, and Barros 2008).

Christoph Neubert discusses this as yet another layer of hiding functionality in a virtual machine (Neubert 2015). Many computer scientists would probably agree. Yet, this again introduces a notion of code that is more or less close to the "real thing," that is processes in hardware. In this case, the programming languages that code the services would be closer to the real thing than the orchestration and choreography languages. Instead, this can be understood as adding another way in which code constitutes algorithms. Here code serves the function to mediate algorithms directly with business processes. Usual entities in such languages are "orders," "requests," "invoices," "clients," "customers," etc. While computers have always also been "Industrial Business Machines," here we have in a sense the pure business machine with its appropriate form of code. The algorithms that such orchestrators run can in theory execute any programmable function in Turing' sense, in practice, they cannot do anything else than business. Yet, they can do that quite easily, since the code looks much more like a business model than a programming language.

What a "client" or a "customer" can be for an enterprise using such services is in important regards prefigured by code. Thus, code can be geared to very specific algorithms that reflect a very particular socio-economic

---

9 See Amazon's "Rekogntion," Google's "Cloud Vision," Microsoft's "Image Processing API," or IBM's "Watson Visual Recognition."

situation. This situation becomes so tightly intertwined with the structure of code, or in fact becomes the structure of code, that it would cease to function in a different situation. This structural/functional encoding of particular situations into algorithms is important. It is not just a structural analogy.

Such an argument by analogy has been advanced by Tara McPherson. She rightly criticizes that not only the practitioners in digital media and technology are often disinterested or ignorant of political issues. Also the academic theorists of digital or "new" media, predominantly in the 1990s and 2000s, have rarely taken up these issues. Thus she urges us to "understand the infusion of racial organizing principles into the technological organization of knowledge after World War II" (McPherson 2012) – a question much less prominent at the time the text was written than today. However, she also asks why this happens so rarely and asks "whether there is not something *particular to the very forms* of electronic culture that seems to encourage just such a movement, a movement that partitions race off from the specificity of media forms" (McPherson 2012 emphasis in the original).

She finds an example of this particular form in the modular structure of the UNIX operating system. Very much like code that is organized in a modular fashion to allow the distribution of labor, the parts of UNIX are distributed to many small programs. Each program does ideally just one task, for which it provides a standardized interface and – again as in code – hides the functionality from the users so that it becomes applicable without knowing its inner workings. This concept also assures exchangeability of individual programs. If program one somehow depended on the way program two works and not just on the results it produces there would be path dependencies.

McPherson likens this structure to the "lenticular logic" she has used in earlier works to describe racism in America. The term "lenticular logic" derives from lenticular cards. On these cards, two images are printed, cut into very fine stripes that are laid out in an alternating pattern. "The viewer can rotate the card to see any single image, but the lens itself makes seeing the images *together* very difficult, even as it conjoins them at a structural level (i.e. within the same card)" (McPherson 2012). McPherson argues that the postwar USA is organized by a similar lenticular logic. Problems of racism are structurally present but for the white part of the country very hard to see together with their own situation. She then draws parallels between the lenticular logic of UNIX and that of racism in the USA. For example, she discusses the increasing racial separation of US-American city centers that are in her view "reflecting a different inflection of the programmer's vision of the 'easy removal' or containment of a troubling part" (McPherson 2012). Thus, she links it to the easy exchangeability of parts in the modular structure of Linux. Another parallel she draws is to identity politics as "a mode of partitioning that turned away from the broader forms of alliance-based and globally inflected political practice" (McPherson 2012). McPherson is quite explicit that she is "not arguing that the programmers creating UNIX [...] were *consciously* encoding new modes of racism and racial understanding into digital systems." Yet, she aims at "highlighting the ways in which the organization of information and capital in the 1960s powerfully responds—across many registers—to the struggles for racial justice and democracy that so categorized the United States at the time" (McPherson 2012).

She also links these developments to the (neo-)liberal paradigm that structures the US-American society. The latter is certainly an important factor for explaining why issues of injustice and discrimination rarely figure in computing. As I argue in detail in chapter 7, p. 136, liberal subjectivity is inherently tied to the disavowal of its enabling conditions. As a consequence, racist, sexist, and other asymmetrical power structures become invisible. In this chapter, I have shown that the organization of code in many forms supports this individualist and meritocratic form of subjectivity. Yet, to draw a direct parallel between modularity in code and separation in society, that is a mere structural analogy between code and politics, is too far-fetched, since it leaves out the performative or functional aspects of the relation of algorithms and code. Just on the level of structure, one could as easily draw a parallel between UNIX and militant activist or urban guerilla tactics, where modularity is a central way to achieve security. Each group only knows what it needs to know for the current mission. Should it be arrested, they cannot give away more details about the entire organization or its strategy even under coercion or stress – since they do not know it. To be clear, I do not want to draw that parallel, but rather illustrate that on a too general level of abstraction, analogies both to liberal capitalism and its most militant opponents can be found.

Programmers as users and the politics of platforms

The organization of software certainly has politics. Yet, as the discussion of McPherson shows, the argument needs to either include the subjects – or communities as discussed above – that it co-constitutes or the algorithms that it co-constitutes. In recent years, the big platforms have quite explicitly used the power to influence the performativity of algorithms – and accordingly their politics – through code.

Platforms offer a wide range of APIs that allow developers to use data and services from e.g. social networking sites for their own applications. This can be distinct services such as login and authentication via a platform. Rather than having their own login name and password for each site, users can just log in with their credentials from a platform, such as Google or Facebook. It can also be services that form an integral part of a program. The successful dating app "Tinder" integrates tightly with users' Facebook profiles, using profile information and pictures. Potential dates can present themselves in the app using images from Facebook. All of this information is available for the programmers of Tinder via the Facebook API. Another important set of services that are available via APIs is the functionality that Google and Apple provide for their Android and iOS smartphones respectively. I discuss messaging services in Chapter 4, p. 71. App developers can use other complex functionalities such as payments or location-tracking which would be very hard or even impossible for them to run themselves. Both companies also provide graphical programming tools and accompanying libraries which offer easily usable interface elements. Programming an app can be almost as easy as connecting several pre-existing elements with a couple of clicks – as long as that app conforms to what these tools and APIs suggest. Similar to the code turning computers into business machines, here the code that the platforms provide strongly guides and limits the algorithms that programmers themselves can produce.

This happens on several levels. Van der Vlist et al. (2021) have analyzed the development of the Facebook API. It allows programmers to use Facebook profile data, the social graph (who is "friends" with whom, etc.) but also Facebook's marketing and advertising tools. The authors argue that in this case, the code by Facebook turns into a means of governance, not just influencing but essentially regulating which code the users can produce. Sometimes this is quite explicit, e.g. in cases where Facebook reacted to charges of discriminatory use of their data through changes in the API. In one case it removed the "interested_in" field from the data that could be accessed about a user. In another case Facebook made "housing, employment, and credit ads [...] a 'special ad category' with fewer available targeting options in compliance with US non-discrimination laws" (van der Vlist et al. 2021, 14).

This indicates, that the entire "user" object that the API provides with its changing fields has an impact on how algorithms coded by Facebook's clients constitute a subject as a user for other programmers. Importantly, these are quite different possibilities than Facebook or its owner Meta has. Referring to the discussion on "data doubles" in Chapter 7, p. 71, the "user" that is accessible via the API is most likely not statically stored at Facebook. Rather, it is itself an algorithmic performative, created from the vast repository of data at Facebook at the moment that the API is called. This "user" object will then influence how the application of Facebook's client interacts with its users, creating a doubly mediated form of algorithmic subjectification.

Van der Vlist et al. also analyzes the documentation that comes along with the code. Programmers, in their position similar to users, invoke algorithms that the platform can change at will, and initially did without any notice to the programmers (van der Vlist et al. 2021, 11). This meant that a presumed functionality suddenly stopped and applications broke. This highlights another way in which the relation of code and the commands that are eventually executed is not just purely technical – here the same line of code suddenly can have a different effect; not only due to the contingencies of execution but by deliberate decision – or accidental change – of another coder: Facebook's. While writing code is generally a matter of the affordances of the programming context, documentation attains a more governmental function in such an environment where documents are the only pragmatically viable form in which the stability of the commands that are used in code is constituted.

The influence of APIs and frameworks on the algorithms that can be coded is even stronger on smartphones. Here, the platforms do not only control code that accesses their APIs, they control the entire operating system that is necessary to run *any* program on the phone. While the owner of a smartphone, in theory, has a universally programmable computer in their hands, the actual algorithms it can run are not only determined by programming languages and other features of code discussed so far, but to a great extent by the governance that is executed via the frameworks of Android and iOS. Some of these means of governing code lie beyond the questions of code itself. For example, iOS did not only provide programmers with an easy integration of their payment system, but Apple also forced programmers to use it if they wanted their app to be distributed through the official store until a lawsuit ended this practice (Kwan 2021). In this case, the possibilities of code to be executed are controlled via business terms and other legal means. Yet, there are also strong influences that happen via code itself. In Chapter 4, p. 70, I show that a mobile, distributed, and networked environment such as smartphones only works as a material platform via several algorithms that enable the communication between these elements. In the case of Google, this is for example the Firebase Platform. It incorporates what earlier was called Google Cloud Messaging, a service that enables a server, for example running a chat service, to address each of their clients by a simple identification number, without caring where on the planet in which network the phone currently is located. APIs are the way this algorithmic constitution of material platforms manifests themselves for the programmers. Firebase does more than cloud messaging though. What used to be an independent service is now integrated into a complex platform addressed at programmers that offers all kinds of services: analytics for marketing, A/B testing, storage, authentication via Google accounts, and more (Google 2023). A programmer who may need cloud messaging because running their own server infrastructure is too costly or laborious is enticed or even forced to build their app just by invoking all kinds of algorithms that Google provides via Firebase. One cannot have Cloud Messaging without these other services.

Another case in point is the proximity-based contact tracing apps that emerged in many countries during the Covid-19 pandemic. While all the necessary hardware was long available on an average smartphone, the possibility to measure low-energy Bluetooth signals emitted by other phones as an estimate of proximity was only possible once Google and Apple changed the APIs in which programmers could access the functionality of the phone. In consequence, the policies of these companies and not the necessities of epidemiology determined the possibilities of these apps (Albergotti and Harwell 2020).

This shows that much more than on a laptop or desktop computer, the algorithms that can be evoked by code are controlled via the general framework or platform that runs smartphones. Certainly, these limits can be circumvented, yet this entails that users need to change their phones to allow software that does not arrive via the official channels or even to completely exchange the operating system of their phones. Both involve additional skills, increased security risks, and also economic risks, e.g. often voiding the warranty of the phone.

Digital platforms consist of a complex interplay of technical, cultural, economic, and legal elements (Bucher and Helmond 2017). In the cases I discuss here, code is also used to sustain the economic and legal structure of platforms in particular. The co-constitutive relation of code and algorithms thus also works in the way that code meditates both legal rules and the terms of the platform with algorithms. Similarly, code mediates also the business model of the platform with algorithms. This does not just happen in the way that these rules are implemented via code in the platforms' algorithms – as the phrase "code is law" would have it (Lessig 2006). Rather, code in its form of APIs and services provided to others is organized in a way that forces its users – which are programmers in this case – to conform to them.

In order to use Facebook's API, one needs to be a registered Facebook client. In order to use Firebase, one needs to be a registered developer. This introduces another change in the way code performs. Each call of a function is now parametrized with an authentication element. Only if that element is tied to the appropriate rights is the function executed. Permissions and authentication have early on been a structuring element of the relation between individual programs. Most early computers have been shared by many users and their data and programs had to be shielded from each other. With the developments of code that I have traced here permissions and authentication have moved into program code on the level of individual lines. Whereas a program could be given some access permissions and others not, now it is imaginable that some lines of code have the sufficient permissions while others do not. Furthermore, these permissions do not just depend on the relatively local configuration on one server. They are part of a distributed, networked platform and can remotely be granted and revoked.

This structure does not just add another element in the co-constitutive influence of code on algorithms. It introduces yet another set of algorithms that co-constitute code by authenticating and checking permissions. Since they check platform membership, these algorithms work in an untransparent interplay with algorithms that are meant to control and enforce the rules and terms of the platforms – with all their known problems of overblocking, bias, etc.

Quite generally, the oft-discussed platform effects, the need to subscribe, lock-in effects including high switching costs, etc. (Bucher and Helmond 2017; Helmond, Nieborg, and van der Vlist 2019) also manifest themselves in code. Here the word platform ceases to be a good metaphor since it is not just the platform on which users and programs move. The platforms move "inside" of individual algorithms and permeate their structure to the level of individual lines of code.

6

ALGORITHMS AND DATA

All algorithms process data. Formal definitions from computer science all contain the property that an algorithm deterministically – or at least reliably in the case of probabilistic algorithms – transforms a specified input into a specified output. In fact, that relation between input and output is what the algorithm "does," i.e. what characterizes the algorithm as a sorting algorithm, compression algorithm, search algorithm, etc. Within the established distribution of labor in computer science that is discussed in Chapter 5, the input data are just considered as given in the precise form needed by the algorithm. Algorithm design then focuses on achieving the desired transformation into output data efficiently in terms of memory and processing time and similar issues. Here, computer science still shows its heritage from math, where the input of a problem can be arbitrarily defined. Invoking the canonical "let X ...," X can be whatever it needs to be as long as it is formally defined.

An important issue in critical perspectives on data is to challenge this givenness. Data go through all kinds of processes and are transformed, adapted, and tweaked until they have the specific form that an algorithm can use. That data are made in specific ways rather than given – as their etymology claims – pertains to many applications and cases: from classical statistics over maps or administrative data to machine learning and data science (Rosenberg 2013). Yet, the specific form of how data are made varies substantially among such cases. Thus, in this chapter, the specific interplay between data and algorithms is put into focus. It is an interplay because data are not just prepared and then algorithms take over. Data become data only for specific algorithms, but they only become data through the interpretation of algorithms as well. This interplay is particularly salient in machine

DOI: 10.4324/9781003299851-8

learning, which will be the central focus of this chapter. Yet, a lot of the issues that are discussed hold for algorithms in general.

Machine learning is the main reason why data have become a key element, sometimes even more emphasized than algorithms, in critical discussions of digital technology. Data are particularly important in machine learning because they are no longer just the input of an algorithm once it is programmed. Data are also used to create – or as it is often framed "train" – the algorithm in the first place. Very generally speaking, machine learning can be described using two algorithms instead of one. Rather than programming an algorithm for a task, programmers specify how the task is to be solved but leave specific elements open. I call this the task algorithm. Most of the time, programmers specify that a particular probabilistic model is to be used – such as the infamous artificial neural networks (ANNs) – but leave the parameters of that model unspecified. These parameters are determined by a second algorithm – the training algorithm – that uses training data to find good estimates of these parameters. Thus, the training algorithm completes the elements in the task algorithm that had been left unspecified by the programmers. There are cases where the training is done just once and then the task algorithm is deployed and runs like any other algorithm. Often, though, training is done constantly. That is, both task and training algorithm are deployed and the training algorithm constantly adapts the task algorithm to new incoming data.

Usually, different forms of machine learning are delineated by the way data are used during training. So-called "supervised learning" needs specific training data. That is exemplary input data labeled with the expected output that the task algorithm should produce when it processes that data. For example, to detect faces in images, the training data would be a set of images with the faces already marked. To classify the quality of applications for a job, an algorithm would need a set of applications and some measure of the qualification of each applicant. The training algorithm uses the data to adjust the parameters of the task algorithm so that its output approaches the one determined by the labels in the training data. The problem is that with many machine learning models, the individual parameters have no meaning in terms of the task. It is impossible to say, for example, that one parameter represents a particular aspect of a face or a specific quality of an application. Rather, the training algorithm employs a numerical measure of the performance of the task algorithm, such as the number of classification errors, or the size of the error if the output itself is numerical. Using that measure, the parameters in the task algorithm are adjusted in a purely numerical fashion: if the training algorithm finds, e.g. that a change in a parameter increases the measured performance, it will change that parameter. There are several approaches for such training algorithms (even if the same task algorithm is used) that differ in how they proceed in optimizing the quality of the output. In most cases, it is not guaranteed that the best possible output is found, so repeated training attempts might be necessary.

Supervised learning is the case that is most often discussed as machine learning and of course, a lot of its potential problems derive from the way the training data are created: who selects them, how, who provides the labels, how are they found, how are those doing it instructed, etc. My short description already shows, however, that there are other important choices: how is the task algorithm specified, how is its performance measured, which training algorithm is used, etc.

A second form of machine learning is called unsupervised learning. Here data are used, without labels. Rather, the idea is that the algorithm finds relevant structures or relations in the data that have not been specified before. However, to do so, a specification of how to relate the individual data points is needed. For example, a simple unsupervised algorithm could use the sales statistics of an online shop as training data in order to find recommendations for customers. If it finds that three items are bought together often, it could recommend the third one to customers who already have shown interest in the other two. Here, implicitly, occurring in the same checkout transaction is considered a meaningful relation between data points. Of course, such assumptions are sensible in many cases; although many know the phenomenon that one buys a gift for a friend and consequently receives suggestions based on that item that does not coincide with their own interests.

A third form of machine learning is called reinforcement learning. It works quite similarly to supervised learning in the sense that the training algorithm measures the performance of the task algorithm and changes the parameters accordingly. Yet, reinforcement learning can use data that occur in the usual operation of the task, instead of using labeled training data. The desired output is provided through some kind of metric to judge the performance of the task algorithm. This of course presupposes that such a metric can be specified. In many board games such as chess or go, for example, there are established ways of judging the quality of a position. Thus, the task algorithm could simply start playing and be trained to increase that metric. In contrast, supervised learning would use transcripts of past games labeled with their results as training data. Similarly, if the task is to steer a self-driving car in the middle of the lane, deviations to the left or right from that aim are a simple metric to judge the quality of the task. This can be done without pre-establishing a direct relation between specific input data and output. A car should always stay in the middle of the lane when driving straight, regardless of the current input, whereas a face detection algorithm should only detect a face where one is present. However, this does not mean that reinforcement learning is independent of training data. If a self-driving car is trained only on roads with road markings and suddenly encounters a road without them, it probably will fail. If a chess algorithm only plays against weak players while being trained it will most likely lose against stronger opponents. In consequence, even if it is not necessary to establish what each element of the training data represents item per item, the data used for training in total still needs to be representative of the task at hand, much as in supervised and unsupervised learning.

The requirement of data being representative of the given task is central for all three kinds of machine learning. This is where most ethical or political perspectives on machine learning engage. I will shortly summarize this critique in order to show that it raises important issues – but also misses some when the particular interplay of algorithms and data is not taken into account. As I will show, this will need to move beyond the question of representation toward what I call a performative view of data.[1]

The representational critique

Examples of racist, sexist, classist, or otherwise biased outputs of machine learning abound. The posterchild case was published by ProPublica who found that a recidivism prediction algorithm in the USA underestimated the likelihood of recidivism of whites and overestimated it for non-whites (Angwin and Larson 2016). A hiring algorithm by Amazon was biased against women. A google image classifier labeled two persons of color as "gorillas" (Benjamin 2019, 110). The advertising algorithm of Facebook was found to be skewed by gender in choosing ads for higher-qualified jobs (Imana, Korolova, and Heidemann 2021). A gender detection algorithm was found to work better on lighter than darker faces (Buolamwini and Gebru 2018). The list could fill the entire book and many detailed studies have described such cases in depth (Benjamin 2019; Eubanks 2017; Noble 2018; O'Neil 2017; Sweeney 2013).

In most of these cases, the problems have been diagnosed using the results of algorithms without access to the training process, which the companies that produced the respective software usually keep secret. However, it is quite plausible that all of these and many similar errors derive from the training data. If, for example, a company hires predominantly male employees, it is quite likely that the share of high-performing applicants who are not male in the training data is quite low and thus the algorithm could learn to prefer male applicants. If a face detection algorithm is trained on a dataset that contains more light-skinned faces, its performance on darker-skinned faces will probably drop. This shows that selecting and labeling training data comes

---

1 The coarse structure of this argument can already be found in my texts on using machine learning on surveillance data (Matzner 2016; 2017). Here it is extended to the relation of data and algorithms in general.

with great responsibilities. It also shows the influence of prevailing social norms. For example, critical scholars of race have shown that the relation between white and non-white is not symmetrical. Lewis Gordon calls this asymmetry "white prototypicality": only non-whites "have" a color of skin or what English-speaking countries call "race." Both are considered a deviation from white normalcy and that normalcy includes that being white does not need special concern. Lisa Nakamura has shown that this white proto-typicality – she calls it "default whiteness" – also exists in mediated commu-nication. Absent racial markers, (white) people interacting online just assume the person they interact with was white (Nakamura 2010). As a consequence, a database of predominantly white faces could be considered a database of simply "faces," which would not be the case with a database of non-white faces (Browne 2010).

This example is important for grasping the political impact of training data. Using biased data is not just an oversight that leads to biased algo-rithms in specific cases. Rather, biased training data extends existing social norms and inequalities that structure large parts of societies into the digital realm. Similar effects have been shown for sexism, classism, and other forms of domination or inequality (Eubanks 2017; Noble 2018; O'Neil 2017).

Many such studies, but also computer scientists trying to address this issue as well as the public discourse on artificial intelligence and machine learning address this impact of training data via representation: the data represents something wrong or biased. However, the examples I have given already allow to see some problems with that perspective. They derive from the question: if the data represent something wrong or biased, what should they represent instead? If, for example, a hiring algorithm is biased in favor of men, it is quite conceivable that the training algorithm actually did its job in finding a good representation for the input data – which are skewed toward men, too. More generally, if data stem from an unjust society, the data will be probably biased as well. In consequence, the task would be to find training data that does not represent society as it is but as it should be. First of all, this is a frustration for all hopes that the aim would be to find unbiased data because that does not exist. Altering the training set, for ex-ample, to include as many women as men could be a way to go. Yet, this would not mean a neutral data set but one conforming to a particular emancipatory political decision, including for example a clear emphasis on substantive rather than formal equality (Fredman 2016) but also its binary gender logic. In general, the alternative to biased data from the current society is not neutral data but data based on a political decision on what society should be like – which people of course have quite differing opinions about. If that was not big enough a question, a second problem is to determine how training data should look like that conforms to the desired political views. As several authors have shown, it is not possible to simply formalize views and concepts from political theory into data or formulas (Binns 2017). A telling case is the aforementioned analysis of recidivism prediction software as biased against non-whites. After the report was published, the company selling the software reacted arguing that the algorithm was not biased and did its assigned task quite well. Kleinberg et al. have shown that in a sense both are right because they employ different ideas of what algorithmic fairness means. The company referred to what Kleinberg et al. call well-calibrated: "if the algorithm identifies a set of people as having a probability z of constituting positive instances, then approximately a z fraction of this set should indeed be positive instances." In contrast, ProPublica used a different intuition: "the average score received by people constituting positive instances should be the same in each group" or in other words "the chance of making a mistake on them should not depend on which group they belong to" (Kleinberg, Mullainathan, and Raghavan 2016, 2). Both are perfectly reasonable requirements. Yet, as the authors show, both are incompatible when formalized. In consequence, the question of what training data should represent hinges on complex political or ethical decisions that cannot be easily translated to the formal level of a concrete data set.

There is another group of problems with a perspective that focuses on representation. The discussion so far only focuses on data and leaves both the training algorithm and the parts of the task algorithm that are specified beforehand out of the picture. In particular, the training algorithm is implicitly reduced to a kind of neutral channel that transports any bias found in the training data into the task algorithm. A lot of their programming depends on the interplay of code and algorithms that has been discussed in Chapter 4. Regarding machine learning, there is the additional problem that training data cannot be assessed independently of the algorithms that are used. As explained above, the performance of the task algorithm can only be measured on data. Training and task algorithms implement a specific form of situated epistemology and only regarding that can even something like bias be assessed. One reason to go beyond bias as a perspective is this very need in conforming to the algorithmic epistemology – or rather the problems that derive from that.

One of the aforementioned studies is a great case in point. Buolamwini and Gebru (2018) have analyzed an algorithm that is meant to identify the gender of a person based on a picture. They could show that the error rate increases when the skin on the images is darker. However, to measure the error rate, the researchers needed a data set that has the correct answers that the algorithm is supposed to give. In this case, this means the gender of the person in each picture. In my words, they had to conform to the epistemology of this specific algorithm. It entails that first, each person has a binary gender, and second that this gender can be derived from the looks of the face. Both of these elements have been at the center of feminist and queer critique for decades (Butler 1993). The authors make that requirement explicit:

An evaluation of gender classification performance currently requires reducing the construct of gender into defined classes. In this work we use the sex labels of "male" and "female" to define gender classes since the evaluated benchmarks and classification systems use these binary labels.

(Buolamwini and Gebru 2018, 3)

Without that reduction, a higher error rate for darker skin cannot be attained because the outcome only makes sense within this reductionist epistemology. Similarly, the authors write about having to turn race into something measurable:

Since race and ethnic labels are unstable, we decided to use skin type as a more visually precise label to measure dataset diversity. Skin type is one phenotypic attribute that can be used to more objectively characterize datasets along with eye and nose shapes.

(Buolamwini and Gebru 2018, 4)

We begin to see two divergent forms of critique here. One, as Buolamwini and Gebru, needs to conform with the algorithmic epistemology to detect biases in the output; and a second one that I will detail in what follows that takes issue with this algorithmic epistemology *per se*. In this case, such a critique would engage with the fact that the algorithm continues highly criticized practices: assuming a binary gender and fixed race categories that are both considered as something that can be read of biological or bodily features (Browne 2010).

Importantly, both forms of critique depend on the data and the algorithm in their interplay. The first form of critique clearly depends on the algorithm, because the way the task algorithm is designed, here using a model that produces a binary output, prescribes the categories that can be used to analyze bias in the training or test data. Thus, in this form of critique, a dataset is only biased relative to a specific algorithm.

The second form of critique depends on both the algorithm and the data because only in their interplay does the specific epistemology that is implied take shape. This is the reason why I will call this perspective performative later on: the question is no longer if something is represented correctly but what the algorithm in complementary relation to data does – e.g. sustain a binary gender norm or racial categories.

The performance-based epistemology of algorithms

The two divergent forms of critique are not only relevant if the algorithmic epistemology is ethically or politically questionable. They follow from an epistemic difference that structures all algorithmic processing of data. In order to illustrate that difference, I will revisit a moment in the early history of AI that is often cited to this very day in introductions as well as critical texts.[2] This entails the problem of defining contemporary technology by its origin that is discussed in Chapters 4 and 5 – particularly because in machine learning circles this moment has become a bit of a heroic tale. Yet, it is a moment where the specific difference that I discuss here was still a matter of debate. I refer to the work of the Continuous Speech Recognition (CSR) group at IBM Research, starting in the 1970ies. The group developed one of the first successful statistical approaches to machine learning for speech recognition. At the time, the dominant attempts in speech recognition tried to translate grammar or other linguistic formalisms into algorithms. In contrast, the CSR group at IBM used an approach that, they claimed, did not rely on knowledge about language at all (Jelinek 2005).

In particular, the CSR group used so-called "Hidden Markov Models" (HMMs). They are mathematical models that consist of a series of states that are unobservable, and each state produces a certain observable output that is statistically distributed. Using dedicated algorithms, the sequence of hidden states can be approximated just by observing its output. A common example is the attempt of a person in a windowless room estimating the weather outside by observing visitors. While the weather itself cannot be observed from the room (hidden state), it changes the probability of certain observable phenomena such as visitors carrying umbrellas or wearing shorts (the output of the hidden state). Of course, the person in the room uses common knowledge to approximate the relationship between their observation and the weather. HMMS allow to do the same without any such knowledge. They can be built just by using a lot of data about observations where the hidden state is known: training data. Leonard E. Baum and Lloyd R. Welch had developed the algorithm for estimating the parameters of HMMs from training data while working at a think tank called "Institute of Defense Analysis" in the 1960ies. They published their algorithms in mathematical journals without naming a particular application, just describing pure mathematics (Baum et al. 1970; Welch 2003).[3]

The IBM CSR group applied these models to speech. The hidden sequence of states was a series of phonemes that make up a word and the observable output were the corresponding sounds if the phonemes are pronounced. Since these models are designed for arbitrary statistical processes, they could be built in a purely data-driven fashion. Using training data, that is precisely

2 I thank Amira Möding for the invaluable discussions on this topic from which this section has benefitted a lot.
3 Which question led to their results is not publicly known – at least I could not find that information anywhere.

transcribed speech recordings, the Baum-Welch algorithm (the training algorithm in this case) found parameters for HMMs so that the likelihood that the model produced the observations known from the training data was maximized. In that sense, nothing needed to be known about pronunciation, just the statistical relationships of sounds and their transcriptions needed to be observed and implemented in the model using the training algorithm. While the pronunciation was modeled using the rather complex HMMs, "grammar," that is the sequence of words was approximated even more simply. The team just counted occurrences of so-called n-grams, which are basically all combinations of n-words. Using trigrams, for example, one can estimate the probability of the following word, given the two preceding words by simply counting all trigrams that start with those two words. Thus, given the sequence "I am," the continuation "I am right" is considered more probable than "I am write" because the latter is much less frequent in the training data. These counts were amended by a simple categorization of words into different "content classes" such as "determiner," "noun," "verb," or "adjective" (Jelinek, Bahl, and Mercer 1975, 252).

Those two components, one for modeling the pronunciation of words, the other for modeling the sequence of words provided the core of a successful speech recognition program. Both components were created in a completely data-driven manner from transcribed speech. Linguistic knowledge, rules, etc. no longer played a role. Xiaochang Li in her detailed history of speech recognition at IBM summarizes this development:

> The turn towards statistical methods in speech recognition thus entailed more than simply the introduction of statistical techniques as a means to represent speech and linguistic knowledge. It required the radical reduction of speech to merely data, which could be modeled and interpreted with in the absence of linguistic knowledge or understanding. Speech as such ceased to matter.
>
> (Li 2017, 89)

Here, Li quite forcefully points out the epistemic difference that is at issue here. The algorithm does not just solve the task of language recognition differently, it turns it into a different task. It deals with language neither as the daily practice of speakers nor as the object of scientific analyses (as in linguistics, psychology, philosophy, etc.) Rather it turns the task into estimating statistical patterns in data. It is, however, important not to overstate that difference. The CSR group did not reduce speech recognition entirely to a generic statistical task – even if that is what their proponents claim (Jelinek, Bahl, and Mercer 1975). Rather, they tweaked a statistical model to the specifics of *speech* data. Thus, speech as understood by both linguists and quotidian speakers, ceased to matter, but not speech "as such." The choice of HMMs as a model that deals well with dynamic processes, and the reduction of grammar to n-grams, all of this reflect specific features of language data, but also the availability of language data. For example, Jelinek, head of the CSR group, recounts that they had to approximate many n-grams because they just did not have enough data to provide all the necessary counts. When I was studying computer science with a focus on speech recognition in the early 2000s, the basic technology that the IBM group had pioneered was still in use. Yet, the task was to tweak the models to speech-specific challenges: people repeating words slowly and overpronounced when they are not understood the first time, people with accents and non-native speakers, etc.

All of this meant finding training data to represent these problems. Since all the parameters are data-driven, one can only change them through data – and check them through data. This is an important qualification, also emphasized by Li, for the way in which the CSR group used the word statistical. They did not use "statistical techniques as a means to represent speech and linguistic knowledge" (Li 2017, 89) as many linguists do. They used a model of speech that could be parametrized based on probabilities in the training data. Yet, that model itself does not have any explanatory or scientific value. Its only task is to make the recognizer work and its only form of evaluation is the quality of recognition. As an illustration, Fred Jelinek was bragging about an early peer-review rejection of his method, judging that "[t]he crude force of computers is not science" (Jelinek 2009, 493). No one would have argued that conventional statistics was not science in the 1970ies.

Quite generally, while there are not too many approaches in machine learning, the process of adopting them to a specific task, which always means not the task per se but the task as it is represented in data, is complex and needs a lot of testing, tweaking, and kludging. It also means that specific training data for the current algorithm need to be found or created – and as Li recounts, this has been a major problem of the CSR group. Their approach was speaker dependent which meant that people had to record a lot of preselected text. These recordings, in turn, had to be processed into the particular features that the algorithm could work with. In this case, this meant a spectral analysis, in which certain frequencies were identified. Quite generally, such feature engineering, that is transforming data into the specific form that the task algorithm can process, is a fundamental step in any form of machine learning and the respective textbooks devote entire chapters to it (Bishop 2006; Mitchell 1997; Russell and Norvig 2016). As Florian Cramer quips: "Since analytics is dumb, society must make itself computer readable" (Cramer 2018, 38).

These observations are important to render more precisely the epistemic difference of machine learning algorithms. They do not just work on a different task (like in the difference between linguistic rules and statistics). This task is also highly specific: it is a particular model, adapted to concrete training data that was selected to introduce features of the specific challenges that the developers currently face. This model need not have an explanatory value or meaning in terms of the task – by design. It is supposed to work in the absence of any complex knowledge, just by using training data. In consequence, the only way to test the quality of the trained algorithm is *to run it* on so-called test data, which needs to have the exact same features as the training data (most often it is just a part of the training data set to one side for later testing.) There is no external point of view that can check whether the algorithm has "learned" something correctly, other than its performance. It is this requirement that forces Buolamwini and Gebru to prepare data that conforms to norms they most probably oppose. More generally, the epistemic shift that is introduced via machine learning poses a problem to all forms of representative critique, because they only work if representation is understood in terms of the specific process that hinges on the interplay of training algorithm, task algorithm (including the models it contains) and data that are the results of a particular process of feature engineering. All forms of bias in the output, for example, can only be found if the algorithm is observed while producing output. Thus, bias can only be attained regarding data in the specific form required by the algorithm.

In consequence, algorithms and training data mutually complement each other. Data is only training data if it is crafted toward the specific needs of the algorithm. However, whether it really is *training* data only can be discerned through the algorithm. There is nothing beyond the performance of the algorithm to judge the quality of the data. In consequence, the algorithm is neither just a neutral channel of information – or bias – that is already contained in the data; nor does the algorithm read meaning into raw or given data. Only the interplay of algorithm and data creates the information that a particular instance of algorithmic data processing yields. Vice versa, the algorithm is only complemented through the training process, without which it could not perform anything.

Beyond interpretation and representation

The last section has shown the necessity to find a perspective that takes the co-constitutive relation of algorithms and data seriously. In turn, that entire relation needs to be scrutinized regarding socio-political issues such as discrimination, and not just one element that occurs within that relation such as a classification error.

Florian Cramer points in such a direction when he urges to understand any output of data analytics as an "interpretation." He picks up the work of Johanna Drucker, who emphasized that data is "qualitative, co-dependently constituted" (Drucker 2011). Her writing is mainly directed against the purported neutrality of data analytics that "extract" information – as if it was already there and just needed to be laid bare. However, her counterpoint is to emphasize insights from the humanities about interpretation: "By definition, a humanistic approach is centered in the experiential, subjective conditions of interpretation" (Drucker 2011). Thus, she urges us to find these "experiential, subjective conditions" in all uses of data.

This view motivates a lot of critical studies that focus on the process of data creation. As has become clear in the last section, data need to be painstakingly prepared, particularly for machine learning. While early attempts at machine learning still worked on relatively small data sets, they could hire people for preparing the data. Even that, however, continued the gendered distribution of highly esteemed scientific and engineering work and the denigrated work on keypunches (Li 2017, 149). For today's data sizes, even badly paid dedicated staff is too expensive. ImageNet, one of the biggest data sets for image recognition that became a kind of benchmark – and thus a driver of image recognition development – was created using a micro-labor platform called "Amazon Mechanical Turk" (Deng et al. 2009). The same platform has become a routine instrument for the creation of training data – but also the collection of qualitative and quantitative research data more generally. All big AI conferences feature papers, workshops, and debates on how to do research on the platform and how to control its quality. Respective searches on Google Scholar will return tens of thousands of results. Amazon Mechanical Turk (AMT) allows to post tasks that usually involve many small steps – such as assigning a label from a given list to thousands of images. These tasks are often paid in very low amounts per item. Registered workers can complete the job to gather the fee. The demography of the workers on the platform is quite heterogeneous. As one might expect, many are from countries where the cheap pay still is better than many alternatives – predominantly India. Yet, a large part of the workers uses the platform as a second or even third job. Thus, there is also a substantial group from Western countries, with a huge majority in the US, with bad income who resort to this form of platform labor (Naderi 2018; Ross et al. 2010).

There are all kinds of issues to discuss, particularly the reliance of both prestigious research institutions and the billion-dollar tech economy on underpaid labor. Similar conditions exist for content moderation (Gillespie 2018). The questions of labor, injustice, exploitation, etc. in the IT sector are its own matter of debate (Casilli 2017; Fuchs 2022). Yet, they also figure in problematizing data creation as interpretation.

Returning to Drucker's view, each of these many workers brings their own "experiential, subjective conditions" to the data. Preparing data for little money, maybe due to economic pressure certainly is part of these circumstances. Their respective culture, age, education, biography, working conditions, and many more factors, are too. What that means, however, is not easily answered. It is difficult not to fall for orientalist or classist assumptions – or at least suggestions in the subtext – that work done by badly paid persons or in non-Western countries is of low quality. One might be surprised to learn, for example, that the majority of workers on Mechanical Turk have a university or college education (Naderi 2018). Assuring the quality of the results gathered on AMT has become a research topic on its own. They discuss the problem of an "inexpert" workforce, but also the subjective character of the individual results (Mitra, Hutto, and Gilbert 2015). Such issues are particularly salient in applications for qualitative research, where training coders particularly to mitigate individual predispositions is a central methodical problem. A lot of existing methodologies for measuring coder reliability are ported to AMT. They are complemented by specific measures, e.g. for estimating the bias of individual workers (Ipeirotis, Provost, and Wang 2010). These work by either giving the same task to many different workers and analyzing the result statistically, or using pre-labeled data for a screening phase that the workers have to complete. Generally, they all work within the algorithmic epistemology discussed above in that they try to measure deviation from an assumed correct result. Based on these measures, workers – or some of their results – are either singled out or given additional instructions that are usually tied to exercise tasks that need to be completed before being able to gather a fee (Mitra, Hutto, and Gilbert 2015). Other measures that aim at "data quality" aim at the motivation of the workers. There are quite some methods proposed to prevent "opportunistic exploitation/gaming" (Mitra, Hutto, and Gilbert 2015, 2). They involve questions that detect inattentive workers (e.g. by throwing in a riddle or math question). Regarding the motivation, both the framing of the task in the description as well as methods for gauging the right monetary incentives are discussed (Mitra, Hutto, and Gilbert 2015; Naderi 2018).

Different cultural and social frames of interpretation are rarely discussed in papers focusing on Amazon Mechanical Turk (and neither is its orientalist name). They do figure in the subtext, though. It is a common practice to block workers based on IP region, or self-reported region. Cultural assumptions are also woven into tests to screen workers. As Lilly Irani recounts from her ethnographic work among programmers using the platform to solicit data workers:

"At one meetup, for example, a group of young engineers requiring workers for marketing experiments joked that they would block any workers who correctly answered a question about the sport cricket; although workers might misreport their location to access jobs, those familiar with India's most popular sport would be caught".

(Irani 2015, 725)

Here, the engineers exhibit a certain consideration for "experiential, subjective conditions," yet reduce it to a too-easy view of clearly discernible cultures. This turns the problem into a simple question of matching a task with the "right" culture for the respective context of the application. The media artist Sebastian Schmieg takes this view to a revolutionary-romantic extreme in an animation film satire where all the data workers of the world unite to provide manipulated data that will make the algorithms of the powerful platforms work on their behalf (Schmieg 2017).

A lot of work on hermeneutics and interpretation in the humanities discusses that the relation of individual perspectives and its socio-cultural context is way more complex. The many attempts of managing quality on AMT are an example of the problems of framing data as subjective interpretation. The workers on AMT do not just get data for their individual consideration. The data, the instructions, and the specific additional tasks that are needed to be completed are all selected to narrow down the individual contribution to one particular aspect. All of this is driven by algorithmic measures and selections working in the background. In consequence, the entire process of gathering data for algorithms is itself deeply algorithmically structured. Rather than constituting a populace of workers, who each individually can bring their interpretation to the data, they are part of a complex, algorithmically constituted arrangement to "capture" (Agre 1994; Mühlhoff 2020) a specific form of human contribution. Importantly, these measures do not work as deterministically as desired by the engineers. The subjectivity of the individual cannot be completely algorithmically restrained (more on this relation in Chapter 7). Yet, what they do certainly is not an interpretation as theorized by Drucker's "humanistic approach" (Drucker 2011) because "the experiential, subjective conditions" in this case are deeply restricted by technology.

This algorithmic situatedness continues in the way AMT is used by its contractors. Luis van Ahn, the founder of the crowdsourcing company reCAPTCHA which was later acquired by Google, spoke of "wasted human cycles" when presenting the logics of crowdsourcing in 2006 (Mühlhoff 2020, 1871). He thus likens the human to a central processing unit, in which the completion of one elementary processing step is called a cycle. This reduction is continued – but also algorithmically created – in a talk by Jeff Bezos in the same year, presenting AMT. On a presentation slide titled "Put The Human In The Loop," he used source code that contains a programming command "CallMechanicalTurk" as if there was no difference of giving a command to the computer and a worker on AMT.

This idea was later put into practice by researchers at MIT, who released the programming toolkit TurKit that allows seamless integration of giving tasks to AMT into regular programming. In their paper, they even use a staple of programming introductions, a simple sort algorithm as an illustration.

```
quicksort(A)
  if A.length > 0
    pivot ← A.remove(A.randomIndex())
    left ← new array
    right ← new array
    for x in A
      if compare(x, pivot)
        left.add(x)
      else
        right.add(x)
    quicksort(left)
    quicksort(right)
    A.set(left + pivot + right)

compare(a, b)
  hitId ← createHIT(… a … b … )
  result ← getHITResult(hitId)
  return (result says a < b)
```

Code to access Amazon Mechanical Turk via programming commands. Example used in (Little et al. 2010).

Here the simple function "compare," which compares two numbers, is delegated to AMT via two other programming commands "createHIT," "getHITResult." They look like just normal lines of code, but instead of being processed by the computer alone, they create a task on AMT to be solved by human workers. Of course, it makes no sense to delegate such a simple comparison operation to AMT. Yet, by using the TurKit toolkit in a common example that is used for introducing computer scientists to the logic of computation, one that they will all remember from their training, the authors of TurKit emphasize how much human work can be assimilated into that logic. Yet, of course, it is a different logic. It is another example of the way that code creates an outside that is only mediated through the situatedness created by code itself that I discuss in Chapter 5, p. 91.

In sum, the entire process of human data creation through platform labor is deeply co-constituted by algorithmic processes. A similar argument can be made for an even cheaper source of training data: the users of a platform. In fact, the key factor for the fast development of machine learning in the last two decades is the huge amounts of data that would be impossible without the internet, the wide distribution of smartphones, and the rise of platforms for anything from social networking to housing, rides, and dating (Mühlhoff 2020). In light of the considerations already made, the suggestion of a resource that already exists and needs to be mined is wrong. As in the case of AMT, the situations in which user data is created is algorithmically co-constituted. This is necessary to get the specific data needed for a machine-learning task. Mühlhoff even argues that any "viable [deep learning] problem today is translated into a corresponding problem in [human-computer interaction]. This problem is: How can a use case and a [user experience] world be constructed so that the data that is needed as training data can be obtained as behavioral data from the 'free labor' of a general audience of users" (Mühlhoff 2020, 1874). He compares several forms in which this problem can be solved.[4] To a limited extent, it is indeed possible to just use the data that accrues anyway in providing a service. For example, a search engine such as Google can use the search terms that users have to provide to train an algorithm that provides search suggestions. However, platforms rarely constrain their data collection to such necessary data. In the case of Google, the platform tracks which of the search results a user follows and nudges users to log in, which promises better personalization but also allows to combine the tracking of searching with e-mail, calendars, and the many other services that Google provides. This is the second form of motivating the creation of user data: promising additional services or functions that however yield more data. Other examples are games or other fun applications that are designed with the aim of capturing data. The third form is forcing users to do something in order to get something else. A classic case would be the reCAPTCHA puzzles that need to be solved in order to "prove" that one is a human when logging in to a service – but that also provides training data, currently for image recognition. A fourth form uses an established social form of interaction – or creates a new one – in order to create data. For example, tagging people in a picture, liking or commenting on their social media posts, and similar actions are expressions of certain forms of social relations. Doing so – or doing so in an appropriate way – is something that is socially demanded (Cover 2012). It is, however, also suggested by the interfaces of apps such as making liking on Instagram the matter of a simple touch of an image. Such design decisions are supported by prompts – see what your friends are doing, see what's new – that the platforms send out. A final form is economic incentives – not through explicit fees as in AMT – but for example through discounts in health insurance in exchange for using a particular fitness tracking app. All of these cases would warrant an in-depth discussion. Yet, for the question here discussed, the situatedness of creating training data, they all share a common structure.

Mühlhoff (2019) argues that each of the different forms of creating user data corresponds to a particular form of power relation. Sometimes it is the power of the platform itself; often it taps into social power and dependencies or economic power. All of them, however, are algorithmically transformed. This is particularly the case in the majority of applications, where training

---

4 For the following, see Mühlhoff (2020, 1875 et. seqq.)

the machine learning models is a continuous process. For example, social media feeds are designed to make users react to the content. That reaction, in turn, is gathered as training data to optimize the feed by predicting which content might provoke even more reactions. The content that is selected using this model is displayed to users for the next round of data gathering. This is the reason why Mühlhoff speaks of "cybernetic AI" that is implicated in a continuous feedback loop (Mühlhoff 2020, 1879). While this intuition points in the right direction, one should not speak of cybernetics here, because the cybernetic idea of feedback is driven by a platonic idea of information that can pass without dependence on its "carrier" (Hayles 1999) from one system to the other. Or as its founding figure claimed in the title of his defining book, there is no huge difference between "control and communication" in the "animal and the machine" where the human is yet another animal (Wiener 2019). In the case of machine learning, however, the information constantly has to pass the threshold of double epistemic situatedness: algorithms only ever can estimate their users with their models while users have an "imaginary" understanding of what goes on in the algorithm. Both influence the other, yet by their very own situated form of praxis (Schulz 2022). Whether the pass over this threshold is successful depends very much on the way in which the cultural practices of the users can be turned into an application, their worries of privacy can be diluted, their economic situation be operationalized, etc.

These last considerations make clear that the discussion of data creation cannot be led independently of the later use of the data and needs to be continued through its use in training and task algorithms to the situation of its application, which will be a matter of the following section. The question of power relations in the situations of data creation is a first glimpse of the theoretical perspective that will be used to do so in a way that does justice to the inherent ties of epistemology and politics laid out in Chapter 3. This perspective leaves both the question of whether the data are a good representation of a given "ground truth" and the question of whose interpretation the data are behind and asks how power structures what can become apparent in data, what needs to be there, and why, etc. This perspective is part of a group of theories that I call performative views of data.

Data as performative

Florian Cramer forms a critique of the entire process of "data analytics," that is data creation, algorithmic evaluation, and application of its results, by calling it an interpretation. Picking up Drucker's intuition, his critique is mainly directed against what he calls "positivist" tendencies in the use of data. Thus, rather than discovering, observing, or extracting, the entire setup "involves a priori choices and decisions as well as unacknowledged biases, etc.

Interpretation hence constitutes the setup, while at the same time being disclaimed by the analysts. Hermeneutics, in other words, is always at work in analytics, though it is rarely acknowledged as such" (Cramer 2018, 34). Even more, it is a particular form of interpretation namely one that denies that it interprets and thus leaves the possibility of a "thorough critical interpretation"(Cramer 2018, 33) behind. While I agree with the general intuition, the last section has shown for the creation of training data that calling analytics "hermeneutical" does not go far enough in a sense. The argument can be extended to the other steps in "data analytics." Hermeneutics, or interpretations connote that there are different perspectives on the same thing – a text, an experience, etc. In fact, Cramer writes: "Operators are interpreters. Though the interpretation of data – or interpretation of sheet music by a musician – may be more confined than, for example, the interpretative reading of a novel, they are structurally no less hermeneutic"(Cramer 2018, 34). He uses this connotation to emphasize that data analytics is just one of these many different possible perspectives, thus emphasizing difference. Yet, the implication of these being different perspective on the *same thing* is not given. As discussed in the last section, the data that are processed are not a given that can then be interpreted. They are in many socio-technical forms geared just toward that specific algorithm and its application that they are meant to train.

A similar argument can be made for its output. The label of positivism or neo-positivism is not unusual in discussions of algorithms and AI (Kitchin 2014). There is in fact a lot of neo-positivist rhetoric used by advocates of AI – often by their more extreme or prophetic representatives such as Alex Pentland who dreams of a "Social Physics" (Pentland 2014) – indeed a very positivist dream. Against those, critiques such as Cramer's and Kitchin's are indeed helpful. Yet, most of the research and applications in AI follow the path discussed above using IBM's CSR group as an example. With a grain of salt, one could say they are not even positivist, because positivism still is about knowledge about the world. Yet, as the CSR engineers clearly stated, they were not trying to replace linguistic knowledge with another form of (statistical) knowledge about language. They were just trying to build a recognizer that works. As has been shown, this leads to the particular epistemics where the only way to test the algorithm is to run it. The aim is not knowledge but the quality of output. This is mirrored in computer science research. In the beginning of computer science, papers looked a lot like publications in mathematics and culminated in the formula of an algorithm; often accompanied by a formal proof. Today, at least in the field of machine learning but also in many others, a paper culminates in the results of a benchmark. These are specific test data sets created to compare algorithms for a specific task. While positivists believe that their knowledge derives from and can be tested against observations of the world, algorithms can only be tested against each other; and even that is only possible by rendering them comparable with specifically created data sets.

Based on similar reflections, Louise Amoore proposes to engage with the algorithmic epistemology per se through a performative view. The things an algorithm presumably detects "do not prexist [...] but are written into being" (Amoore 2020, 97). She takes recourse to literary theory, where deconstruction has moved away from a focus on the author to the productivity of the text itself. Similarly, she argues, searching for the decisive element in the author of the source code – or we might add the creator of the training data – is insufficient. Rather, what the text – or the output of the algorithm – does is decisive. For Amoore, this does not mean that the results of algorithms are *particularly* insecure, fragile, or speculative. They are, but only because any act of writing is. "All languages and codes, then, signify through differential traces, where a trace makes present something not present in the past. In common with all languages and codes, the algorithm writes to make present something that is not merely in the past data" (Amoore 2020, 103). Thus, "algorithms [...] arrange differentially signifying traces to generate an output" without that arranging being determined by source code – or we should add: training data (Amoore 2020, 104). Amoore's theoretical perspective is provided by Derrida (and to an extent Deleuze). In this view, the act of bringing something into being through language does not depend on the subject that speaks. This is in contrast to the famous speech act theory, where the speech of particular subjects – a judge that sentences, a priest that baptizes, etc. – change reality (Amoore 2020, 104). In contrast, for Derrida, meaning is only produced when what is written forms a relation with other things that have been written and read. This relation with text that already exists, e.g. using the same words, manners of speech, etc. is the source of meaning. However, it will never be the same meaning because it is a new relation to a new context that is added. The meaning thus only can be followed along this trace of differential relations, but it is impossible to "catch up" with it. Every form of explaining the meaning forms yet new relations, extending the trace. Amoore applies this general theory of meaning to algorithms, because algorithms, much as other forms of writing can form such new relations – or in Derridean language are "differentially signifying traces to generate an output."

In consequence, the problem for Amoore is the tendency in applications of algorithms to close this fundamental nonclosure of meaning. "Writing always exceeds its context as it travels, iterating and entering into new relations and new contexts. To conceive of algorithms in terms of the nonclosure of context is to resist rather directly the algorithm's determination to reduce the output signal to a single probability, to close the context" (Amoore 2020, 104). For example, she writes about "forking paths, from the branches and leaves of decision trees to the differential paths through the neural network. [... For] the writing of algorithms the fork is a weighing or adjustment of probabilities and likelihood. What could be made to matter, in terms of the ethicopolitical response to algorithms in society, is to trace these branching points: not as a means of securing the knowable source, but precisely to confront the profound contingency of the path" (Amoore 2020, 99).

Similarly, to Cramer and Drucker, Amoore emphasizes the possibility of a different meaning against the purported facticity or objectivity of algorithms. Yet, she does so without a subject as the source of that difference – in contrast to Cramer's and Drucker's invocation of hermeneutics. It is just a difference that is possible in any form of writing.

An ethics for algorithms, in consequence, means primarily to acknowledge this unescapable nonclosure, to care for the "unattributable" as Amoore calls it. This does not mean that an ethical critic can fix that meaning left open by the algorithm. As Amoore puts it, if "the fabulation of the algorithm involves a form of iterative writing, [...] the methodology of a critical cloud ethics must also fabulate" (Amoore 2020, 158). Yet, it must fabulate to open up differences.

Amoore's ethics, in a sense, proposes a similar argument to Barad's that I discuss in Chapter 3, p. 42, yet with a deconstructive rather than ontological gist. Both emphasize a general possibility for change or difference. As argued in detail in Chapter 3, it is necessary to leave that general level and inquire about the structure of the particular situation from a political perspective.

Performativity in the co-constitutive relation of data and algorithms

The view of the complementary relation of data and algorithms that I present here is inspired by a theory that builds on similar intuitions as Amoore's but fuses them with a thorough theorizing of power: the concept of performativity as it is found in the work of Judith Butler. I write "inspired" because what I present is a highly selective reading – after all Butler writes about queer subjectivity and I algorithms, which are quite different subjects. Yet, some aspects of the general way she understands performativity are suitable to be extended to the outputs of algorithms. Others, in particular her entire discussion of psychoanalysis, are left out.

Butler builds on Derrida's concept of signification as relational. Yet, her focus is not on relations between texts. Rather, she describes relations as actualized with every performative act. In particular, they are no stable structure. Butler describes these relations with Derrida's term: "citation." Like a citation, any performative connects to prior uses but puts them into a new context. With that new context, also the meaning of that which is "cited" shifts. Thus, the citation is never only a representation of a prior action but re-creates its meaning as an "iteration," which is something that is based on the prior act but also changes.

Like Amoore and Derrida, Butler emphasizes that no subject is necessary as a source of a performative. In contrast, subjectification is a consequence of performatives – not its presupposition. Of course, this is Butler's focus of interest; a topic that is revisited in Chapter 7, p. 32.

> If a performative provisionally succeeds (and I will suggest that "success" is always and only provisional), then it is not because an intention successfully governs the action of speech, but only because that action echoes prior actions, and accumulates the force of authority through the repetition or citation of a prior, authoritative set of practices.
>
> (Butler 1993, 228)

The important difference between Derrida and Amoore becomes salient in this citation: each performative is structured by power. What is cited is not just a pre-existing meaning but an "authoritative set of practices." Thus, it is not just a contingent actualization of one of many possibilities. Not any relation is sanctioned as a successful citation. Both the present performative signification and the alternatives are structured by power. Power here is understood similarly to Foucault, where it both enables the meaning of a performative (through the authoritative set of practices that are cited) but at the same time precludes others. Thus, it is not an individualized power held by a subject. Rather, it is the power that can be felt in phrases like "Boys don't cry" or "This is not proper for a girl." No one is in power to define such things, but the existing social norms clearly bestow power on those using such phrases. It is much easier to conform to – or cite – these norms than to oppose them.

Performativity is in consequence a situated practice in the sense explained in Chapter 3, p. 35 using Wittgenstein's image of a riverbed (Wittgenstein 1969 §97). While from a general perspective, the conditions of a situation are nothing but something that is enacted in practice (the water forms the riverbed), from within a particular situated perspective, they can be quite constraining (in the riverbed it guides the water). As Butler puts it: "Neither power nor discourse is rendered anew at every moment; they are not as weightless as the utopics of radical resignification might imply" (Butler 1993, 224). While every citation can contest the meaning of what is cited, it still needs to cite enough of the respective practice to count as a contestation of that praxis. In consequence, if contestation succeeds, it needs to be politically directed, that is, it needs to engage with the prevailing power structures (Butler 1993, 228).

The complementary relationship of data and algorithms can be described based on this notion of citational performativity. As I have described in this chapter, data do not speak for themselves but are geared toward an algorithm and are evaluated only by the performance of this algorithm. In this sense, data become data only through the execution of the algorithm.

However, this does not mean that only the algorithm performs, as some have claimed (de Laat 2019), and thus bestows meaning onto data. This, again would make the algorithm the source of meaning (for example, as one of many possible interpretations as discussed by Drucker and Cramer). Rather, the algorithm has to cite a set of authoritative practices. An algorithm connects to such practices through training data. To return to the example of a gender classifying algorithm, the algorithm uses data that someone has labeled regarding the prevailing gender norm in society as binary male and female. The output of the algorithm has to cite this norm, in the sense that its output has to approximate the given labels. In this sense, the data in important regards constitute the algorithm. Taken together, neither the meaning of the training data nor of the output of the algorithm precedes the citation co-constituted by the algorithm and data.

However, citation means not only to continue aspects of the authoritative practice but also to recontextualize them. As I have discussed at the beginning of this chapter, in the algorithm the social norm of a binary gender that is cited solidifies into an epistemology that knows nothing else than the probability of being male or female. Researchers who want to engage with the algorithm – be it simple application or critical scrutiny – have to engage with this algorithmic norm, in turn.

All of this pertains to the normal operation of the algorithm, not to errors or biases that also its creators would detect. To function entails to cite, that is to both continue and re-contextualize prevailing norms.

Generally speaking, an algorithm needs to cite the practices that it connects to through data: searching, using social networks, rating applications, detecting faces, etc. Without such a citation of the "authoritative practices" its output would not have a meaning. Yet, algorithms re-contextualize these practices in their specific epistemology. The sustained execution of algorithms stabilizes and perpetuates these "cited" meanings, turning them into authoritative practices themselves.

The practices in which training data are gathered are not the only set of authoritative practices that an algorithm needs to "cite." It also needs to connect to the practices in the context of its application. Amoore discusses the example of an algorithm for evaluating DNA evidence (Amoore 2020, 95). In my words, the algorithm needs to both make sense as processing DNA, citing practices of biology and forensic medicine, and as something that can be used as evidence in court, citing practices of law and jurisprudence. In consequence, training data is *one, albeit important,* way in which the algorithm connects to prior enactments of a practice.

Through this structure, algorithms connect differently situated contexts: those in which data is gathered and those in which the algorithm is applied. This does not only change the context of the application. It also changes the context in which data is generated.

For example, data-based surveillance gives secret services and law-enforcement far-reaching access to social media data in many countries (Arora 2019; Greenwald 2014; Mateescu et al. 2015). As explained, the algorithms used by these agencies cite established patterns of suspicion but re-contextualize them into new, data-based forms of suspicion. This co-constitutive interplay of data and algorithms adds a new meaning to the context in which the data are gathered, in this case, the potential to make someone suspicious is added to using social media (Matzner 2016). Again, it is necessary to reflect on the situated character of these practices, where the risk of becoming suspicious is much higher in some forms of situatedness than in others.

A political critique of data

A critical evaluation of such consequences does not necessarily depend on detailed knowledge of the algorithm. A performative perspective on data integrates the way data connect social inequalities to algorithmic applications with many other forms in which algorithmic practices "cite" and thus iteratively continue existing social practices, such as surveillance. Thus, if an algorithm has a racist impact, the reason can also lie in the practices of screening or profiling that are extended with algorithmic means (Browne 2015) and not only the training data. Particularly non-white or lower-class persons often share a history of experiencing surveillance, which an algorithmic technology connects to a new social context, such as social media use.

In general, a political critique of data thus does not need insight into the oft-cited black box of machine learning (Pasquale 2015). A lot of issues can be addressed in asking how data enables algorithms to performatively connect different contexts. In all applications, there are at least three contexts that are differentially situated. One is the context of application with its respective practices, e.g. surveillance or medical diagnosis. The second is the context from which training data are gathered. In my surveillance example, this could be social media use, in the case of medical diagnosis, these are prior instances of similar diagnoses. The third context is the one in which training data is processed and the algorithms are programmed. Reframing my critique above with this triad, a representational critique only focuses on problems in the context of application and explains them by a wrong or biased representation of the context from which data are gathered in the context of programming. There are many more problems to observe. For example, the meaning in the context of application shifts (what is suspicious, what is a reliable diagnosis). Often, this shift is parasitical[5] on the context in

---

5 More on the use of this term in Matzner (2016).

which data are gathered (e.g. the presumed authenticity of social media data or the magnitude of medical images that went into training the algorithm).

Furthermore, also the practices in the context in which data are gathered can change. All of this concerns the relation of the context in which training data is gathered to the context of application. This does not mean that the context of data processing and programming does not matter. It may well be, for example, that the way surveillance data is processed cites the norm of "white prototypicality," thus leading to racist results (Browne 2010). White prototypicality is Lewis Gordon's term for the fact that whiteness and non-whiteness are asymmetrical performatives, as discussed in Chapter 3, p. 40. One is enacted by excluding the other, or in other terms: social norms install being white as normal and everything else as a deviation from that normalcy. As a consequence, only non-whites "have" a race, whiteness is invisible (Alcoff 2006). This explains the commonness of training data sets that exhibit white prototypicality. Such a dataset is more than just a biased representation of reality. Rather, it cites and thus continues a central practice in which the reality of race is re-created and sustained in our societies. As explained above, these practices are not just continued but also iteratively transformed. For example, they disappear within software applications that – despite years of writing to the contrary – still often come with a perception of neutrality. They move, via technology, to new areas – even to innocuous parts of our social lives as unlocking one's phone with fingerprints or face detection.

A critical engagement with these issues is political in the sense discussed in Chapter 3. When algorithms connect differently situated contexts, critical work needs to open up new relations between these forms of situatedness. Rather than following the algorithmic connections – and thus inevitably conforming to their epistemology, that is the new norms they establish – these new connections need to sidestep the algorithmic connections. They need to create encounters that make differences and continuities in situatedness visible, such as the extensions and re-contextualization of prevailing norms. At the same time, they need to proceed in a situated manner that takes seriously that these same norms are often asymmetrical and attain different meanings in different contexts. A situated manner also means not underestimating that these other situations "are not easily learned." This entails that the need to sidestep the algorithmic epistemology does not mean that the norms it cites can be sidestepped, too. It is all too probable to remain complicit in them.

7
ALGORITHMS AND SUBJECTS

Throughout this book, different subjects have already appeared: programmers, "click-workers" producing training data, users, people who are rated or assessed by algorithms, etc. Such subject positions correspond to differently situated perspectives. For example, a programmer might implement an algorithm for work, which needs attention to programming languages, details of software libraries, etc. For a user, running that algorithm might turn the computer into a music player. The notion of complementary abstractions explains that each of these perspectives brings some issues into view while foreclosing others. It also emphasizes that these subjects are not just given positions that take different points of view on algorithms or use them differently. Rather, subjects and algorithms are co-constituted as well.

Discussions of algorithmic subjectification, that is the constitution of subjects through algorithms are prominent in discussions about subjects that are rated, ranked, scrutinized, and surveilled by algorithms. Such debates are also thoroughly political and focus on discrimination, inequality, and power. I will begin this chapter by discussing these issues. Then I will move on to other subjects that are rather discussed regarding the way they constitute algorithms: in programming, data creation, and similar tasks. The politics in this case are often tied to a kind of investigative gesture of discovering the humans "behind" the algorithm. Often this takes the form of a claim: "Algorithms are not neutral because they are made by (these) humans."

Algorithmic subjectification

In Chapter 6, I have discussed how training data is considered a major inroad of social inequality into algorithms. Via training data, algorithms are

DOI: 10.4324/9781003299851-9

related to pre-existing practices that are "cited" by the algorithm, as I explained using a term inspired by Judith Butler. Citation in this sense means that the algorithm "accumulates the force of authority through the repetition or citation of a prior, authoritative set of practices" (Butler 1993, 228). This is an important difference to the diagnosis of a biased training set. For example, Ruha Benjamin states regarding a predictive policing algorithm that she has analyzed that if "a prediction matches the current crime rate, it is still unjust" (Benjamin 2019, 58). The reason is that the prevailing practice of policing is inherently discriminatory, in this case concerning race. In consequence, the problem is not that the algorithm is biased (regarding the current crime rate, it may be not) but that it cites this discriminatory practice. In this case, this citation is established via training data, but its meaning goes beyond it. That the algorithm "cites" also means to re-contextualize the established practice. The police officers will now follow orders from the algorithm rather than their chief or their intuition. The policing actions are veiled in an aura of objectivity that still prevails despite decades of critical work on algorithms and technology in general (Browne 2015; Eubanks 2017). These actions will also have a different source of legitimacy, grounded in performance metrics from computer science rather than for example the experience of police officers. Finally, it can provide police officers with an excuse not to reflect on what they are doing.

Part of this algorithmic "citation" in predictive policing is an illustrative example regarding the subjectifying force of algorithms. In Chapter 6, I have begun to use Butler's notion of citation mainly as an alternative to understanding the meaning of data as representation. Yet, Butler's main concern is subjectification. She picks up Althusser's notion of "interpellation." Althusser used this term to describe his take on Marxist ideology. He claimed that ideology works through specific acts that force people to change their daily practice. People are thus "hailed" or "interpellated" to conform to the power of the state, by such mundane but frequent acts as a police officer in the street calling "Hey you!" (Althusser 1977). Butler moves this idea of repeated, subject-forming calls to conform away from Marxist thought and joins it with a Foucauldian notion of power. According to Foucault, power creates subjects through what he calls subjectification. That is, there are no subjects, which are then forced by power in a second step. Being subjected to power and being a subject is the same thing. As Butler writes:

"Indeed, there is no 'one' who takes on a gender norm. On the contrary, this citation of the gender norm is necessary in order to qualify as a 'one,' to become viable as a 'one,' where subject-formation is dependent on the prior operation of legitimating gender norms".

(Butler 1993, 232)

However, this act is both constraining and enabling. The subject has to conform to norms – in this case, gender norms – but at the same time becomes a subject that has the agency to do all kinds of things. In this sense, algorithms in predictive policing perform a double interpellation: the police officers are hailed to control specific areas or specific people. These people or the inhabitants of this area, in turn, are interpellated as suspects. In both cases, this influences the respective subject positions. For those who become suspects, repeated searches and an increased police presence become a part of their lives. It could also be the case that predictive policing leads to a continuation of pre-existing practices, but with another legitimation. Thus, not only the changing but particularly the sustaining of norms is an important consequence of subjectification. These suspected subjects have little possibility to escape this interpellation because here the algorithm directs the legally sanctioned force of the police.

The police officers' subjectivity changes as well. As described above, the algorithm would have to cite pre-existing practices to a large enough extent that the suggested procedures still make sense as policing. However, police officers might carry out the same tasks with a different feeling of responsibility, shifting it to the algorithm – or with the constant feeling of indignation that such a machine is supposed to be superior to their own intuition honed by years of experience. In contrast to the suspects, they also have more possibilities to act against the suggestion of the algorithm. Importantly, however, it might just be easier to follow them. In consequence, to assess the subjectifying force of an algorithm, it is necessary to know the exact situation into which the algorithmic results are integrated. Is there an order or a suggestion to follow the algorithm? Can it be contested, by whom, which effort does this take, etc? As a general takeaway, the interpellative force of an algorithm must not always come with the citation of a strong source of authority such as the police. It can also just offer the path of least resistance.

Butler's reworking of interpellation as a citation of a norm entails that subjectification does not depend on the authority of a speaking subject. It also shifts the notion of power from the state to social norms such as sex and gender norms that have power without anyone "possessing" this power – not even a collective subject like "the state" or the "capitalist class." In her theory, there are strong and direct interpellating speech acts such as a doctor announcing: "It's a girl!" Yet, as I also discuss in Chapter 6, p. 127, she explains that a performative succeeds "not because an intention successfully governs the action of speech, but only because that action echoes prior actions, and accumulates the force of authority through the repetition or citation of a prior, authoritative set of practices" (Butler 1993, 228). Nowadays, the doctor announcing "It's a girl" may be replaced by a cloud of pink powder left behind by a popping balloon or pink cream in a cake, a performative most often supported by the gaze of a camera that will make it visible on social media. Yet, all these material artifacts, their usage, and their distribution in media repeat and cite an "authoritative set of practices," in this case of gender and birth. Quite generally, the (both astonishing and frustrating) stability of heteronormative sex and gender do not stem from the authority of subjects such as doctors but from the vast amount of different, distributed, and circumspect acts of power: how people look at each other in streets, how they dress, how they are required to dress, which toys they get as children, where the toilets are located, how many toilets are there, how it feels to enter a full subway cart, how it feels to enter an empty one late at night, what it means to behave, how people touch others, which jobs they are offered, which fields there are on forms, what the parents felt when the content of the balloon was pink, etc. Thus, following Foucault, the power to subjectify is not only in speech acts in the narrow sense but distributed through clothing, architecture, technology, bureaucracy, manners, morals, etc. The power of sex and gender is an effect of the sustained iteration of a norm throughout these examples and many more (see also Chapter 3, p. 35).

The subjectifying force of algorithms stems from their integration into this distributed and sustained power of a norm. They cite this norm, which means that they both continue and re-contextualize it. Algorithms today are involved in the entire variety of such performatives from the direct and state-sanctioned interpellations in predictive policing and automated border controls to the comparatively subtle suggestions of products to buy or pictures to like on social media. Online shopping is a good example to study the re-contextualization of subjectification through algorithms.[1] An online shop might for example use an algorithm that attempts to estimate the gender of the user. As discussed in Chapter 6, p. 129, one of the decisive features of algorithms is the ability to connect different situations via training data. Thus, the gender estimation might not only be based on the use of the online shop itself, but on more data such as the browsing history (accessible via cookies) or app usage (accessible via the operating system of the user's phone). Thus, the context of situations that are relevant to gender (as performed through the algorithm) is widened. At the same time, its subjectifying force is hidden. The online shop might present its selection of goods – and probably also the prices attached to them – based on gender estimation. Yet, it does not say "for women" or "for men" as a sign in a department store does. Neither does it say "for 54% male and 71% female." It says "personalized, for you!" Still, the selection might be just the same. In consequence, the impact that the available goods or clothing have on the performativity of gender remains, even if the user is no longer directly addressed by their gender. What is more, the fact that a decision based on gender does happen is hidden.

---

1 See Cheney-Lippold (2011) and Matzner (2016) for a detailed discussion.

In Chapter 5, p. 103 I discuss how a data object describing Facebook users is produced performatively for clients of Facebook that access the platform via an API. This object contains all kinds of information including gender, relationship status, interests, religion, and more (van der Vlist et al. 2021). All of this is exchanged only between Facebook and a client programming a website or an app for the smartphone but might again align that client's software with established norms encoded in Facebook's data – without that becoming apparent to the user.

A similar structure was also uncovered by a study that showed how big platforms distributed advertisements for employment skewed by gender (Imana, Korolova, and Heidemann 2021). In this case, each subject just sees advertisements. They have no way of knowing what they do not see. Thus, subjects are not addressed at all. They just see a different advertisement depending on all kinds of algorithmic measures that correlate with gender – not necessarily targeting gender explicitly. Yet, even without any direct address, just this distribution of advertisement contributes to perpetuating gender inequality, and thus also what it means to be situated as a gendered subject.

Further normalizing the norm is thus one of the potentials of algorithms to increase the power of subjectification. While someone might take offense or at least notice when they are treated based on a gender estimation, this becomes very difficult in this case.

Normalcy, exclusion, and liberal subjects

This re-contextualization of norms through algorithms needs to be considered in a situated manner. Safiya Umoja Noble has dedicated an entire book-length study to the power of search engines to enforce racism. She recounts how she was searching for things for her "stepdaughter and nieces" only to experience "the perfect storm of insult and injury" by the sexualized results that the search term "black girls" brought up (Noble 2018, 3). The power of such stereotypes is sustained by being part of normalcy for many others – persons for whom such results do not mean insult and injury but go rather unnoticed, or are even desired. Regrettably, insult and injury themselves are normal for many people. In consequence, I use the slightly more unwieldy term "normalcy" to denote the specific form of normality that results from an alignment with existing norms that allows them to go unnoticed – such as the ones described as "unmarked identities" (Alcoff 2006; see also the discussion in Chapter 3).

Normalcy and exclusion are thus just two facets of the same power structure that present themselves to differently situated subjects. This interdependence can also be found in data. Many models do not just collect data about the subjects that they want to identify or assess but also so-called "negative examples." These are data that do not contain the feature to be identified or that are to be assessed differently. For example, a predictive policing algorithm might not only work with data from high-crime areas but also from areas with a low prevalence of crime. In political terms, such models create normalcy from which deviance can be detected. Even seemingly innocuous models of the type "others who have bought this have also bought that" will learn to represent a commodified version of normal behavior, and suggest that behavior to others, solidifying for example a gender norm. In consequence, the subjectifying power of algorithms does not only depend on data about the subject but also on data about others. Thus, all the people who say "I have nothing to hide" or even give away their data voluntarily for well-working digital services potentially contribute to models that expose, discriminate against, or disadvantage others.

This relevance of data speaks to the fact that algorithms and subjects are co-constitutively related. Algorithms are not just an increasingly common element of subjectification. Even if the power might be distributed quite asymmetrically, many algorithms are in important regards constituted by user data. Thus, the question of whose data is used, who provides it voluntarily, etc. are questions that ask for the influence of subjects on algorithms. As argued in Chapter 6, the aim of such questions should not be a better representation of all subjects – this is the wrong perspective – but rather to scrutinize who can live with these algorithms, for whom they support the normality they live in, for whom are they a source of injustice and exclusion? As I have argued here, both normality and exclusion can only be understood as the interplay of prevailing norms and practices and the way they are shifted by algorithms.

The interdependence of normalcy and exclusion is also necessary to assess some prominent critiques of the relation of algorithms and subjects, particularly those using the idea of a "data double" (Lyon 2014) or "dividual" (Deleuze 1992). They refer to digital information about subjects that has an impact on subjects' lives via algorithms. Yet, they all oppose these data doubles to a "real" subject – often in showing how these data doubles become an imposition or more generally speaking a source of heteronomy for that subject (Matzner 2016). Such critiques do important work, because many discourses, particularly legal discourses are structured by this opposition. Yet, theoretically speaking, there are some issues with this way of posing the problem that also have political consequences. First of all, the opposition of a subject and its "data doubles" contains traces of a real world vs. virtual world Platonism that I discuss in Chapter 4. It also forms an instance of the representationalist critique which I show in need to be amended in Chapter 6.

Regarding the topic of this chapter, this opposition potentially continues a tendency of liberal theory to ignore the socio-technical dependence of subjects; in this case, the subjects who are opposed to the data doubles or dividuals (Matzner 2019b). Feminist (Pateman 1988) and critical race scholars (Mills 2011) have long taken issue with the traditional notion of an autonomous subject as the starting point of political thought. They argue that this idea generalizes particular – e.g. white, male – subject positions. These subjects are dependent in all kinds of ways on others – including many female and non-white others – yet are in a position that allows them to disavow that dependence.

The relational concept of subjectification that I use here, can be seen as a continuation of this line of thought. Yet, it adds many more elements to the dependence of subjects. In a sense, subjects "depend"[2] on everything that is involved in their relational co-constitution. Of course, technology is politically not in the same position as the exploited or appropriated non-white or non-male subjects as some argue (Atanasoski and Vora 2019). But the fact that some subject positions allow to disavow their constitutive relations – including those involving technology – while others cannot, mediates inequalities between these subjects. In this regard, the double character of power as both enabling and constraining is central – as well as the way in which both are unequally situated. Whether one easily conforms to the norms and actually endorses the subject position that results from it or one experiences them as insult and injury, all these subjectivities are a result of a similar power structure. Yet, for those whose lives align easily with the normalcy that this power structure entails, this feels much more enabled or even independent – autonomous – than for those who experience the constraining.

Haraway (1988; 1991) and Barad (Barad 2007) have emphasized particularly the technical and material entanglements of subjects. Such observations, however, should not lead to a general, anthropological reflection – or a new ontology, but again to a situated perspective. For example, scholars from disability studies have criticized Haraway's (Haraway 1991) notion of the cyborg as too celebratory of the possibility to tear down established dichotomies such as nature and culture that it forgets that dependence on technology or in this case prosthetics is not only a source of new possibilities but of disability (Siebers 2008, 63). It is thus important to consider the specific situation and ensuing power structures of the co-constitutive relations of technology or data and subjects.

For example, in *Discipline and Punish*, Foucault (1977) has described how record keeping in the medical and juridical systems contribute to subjectification. Of course, today such records still exist in much more complex forms. A medical record, with all the blood values, X-ray images, and various other measurements could also be described as a "data double." Yet,

2 In a relational, co-constitutive perspective, of course, that on which a subject depends does not pre-exist the subject but is co-constituted with it.

this double often helps sustain the life of the subject it "doubles" rather than force it into something it does not want – although that can happen in the medical sector, too. Yet, for many chronically ill persons, such a medical data double is constitutive of their subjectivity – in the very strong sense that they could not live without it.

Also, the bodies of "healthy" persons are increasingly constituted by data. Smartwatches, apps, and other "self-tracking" appliances measure the state of fitness, evaluate it algorithmically and use this evaluation to motivate persons to become more fit. This can happen through comparison to pre-set aims, to others on social platforms, or other elements of "gamification." Implicitly, such technologies take up a lesson from the critique of liberal subjects – but only halfway. That is, they illustrate that humans are not the rational, self-controlled beings they claimed or wanted to be since the Enlightenment. Humans are also effective, habitual beings. Yet, with these technologies, the promise is to become more self-controlled and rational. The ensemble of human and technology approaches a form of subjectivity that is much closer to the liberal ideal of subjectivity than human beings without it – at least for those who easily align with the norm of fitness and individualized self-management (Matzner 2019b). For others, such technologies are yet another way of forcing subjects to follow this norm to begin with.

The problem, thus, is neither the data nor the double *per se*. As long as they are aligned with the norms that govern the lives of subjects, they are not perceived as sources of heteronomy. They can even be considered as extending autonomy. Data are considered as external, heteronomous, as a "double," if they confront or oppose norms and power structures that have been constitutive of the subject so far (Matzner 2018).

The framing of data as something external to the subject runs the risk of forgetting these power relations that structure subjectivity in the first place. For many who do not live in a rather surveillance-free normalcy, algorithmic surveillance through "data doubles" is not a novel imposition but rather a continuation of the lives they are used to – *nolens volens*. Simone Browne cites the experience of a US-American person of color regarding the new security measures introduced after 9/11: "As for a permanent alert, a defensive attitude with which one lives anyway—it has not changed since" (Browne 2015, 122). In sum, a shift in perspective away from autonomous use vs. heteronomous imposition through technology is needed, toward a perspective on the detailed distribution of power along the many co-constitutive relations of subjectivity.

Many facets of subjectivity change through algorithms. I have already discussed algorithmic forms of suspicion in surveillance and predictive policing. Today, there are also algorithmic forms of fame (followers, likes, placing in feeds), dating (dating and matchmaking websites), academic quality (citation indexes and placement in special search engines such as Google Scholar), qualification (as in the models used to assess applicants), etc.

All these algorithms cite existing practices, that is they both continue and transform them. As in the case of surveillance, these transformations usually benefit some while being an obstacle, imposition, or even source of injury for others. Which of these is the case depends on how the transformations that are introduced by algorithms align with the previous situatedness of the subjects. Often, a transformation is experienced as beneficial if easily integrated into normalcy, that is a transformation that works in a way that the subjectifying, constitutive power regarding the own subject position is not experienced as heteronomy. Yet, such transformations need not always align with the stronger side of power relations. For example, many gender non-conforming and queer persons report that they prefer algorithmic dating on digital media to dating in clubs, bars, or other face-to-face situations, which for them always also means a risk of insult or harassment. Ute Kalender describes the experience of a man with disabilities who uses a car with an algorithmically assisted mode of driving. He reports that the "situation in the car is the only one in my life where I'm treated exactly the same. Just like everyone else" (Kalender 2023).

Algorithms and habitualization

There are critics who argue that the discussion on the level that I have presented so far, that is on the level of subjectifying power, does not suffice. They argue that the really problematic influence happens on a level that does not concern subjects anymore.

Many algorithmic processes happen indeed in the background and users are just presented with the results. I have already used the examples of an online shop and job advert distribution that uses a gender classification algorithm or is skewed regarding gender but presents the selection as personalized. Similarly, contents of social media feeds or search results just appear on the interface without any direct addressing or interpellation of a subject. The content, the results, and the ads are just there, no relation to the own subject position or situation is presented. Thus, the invocation of the subject position in question that defines classic examples of interpellation, is missing: "It's a girl." "*Boys* don't cry." "You are arrested under *suspicion* of … ." Many companies use A/B testing for new versions of their functions and interfaces. Facebook, in a notorious study even attempted to manipulate the mood of their users. The effect was measurable but small. The far bigger impact has been the fact that the terms and conditions of Facebook allowed such as study to be conducted without informing the users (Flick 2016). Such experiments and A/B tests follow the idea of quantifiable performance that I detail in Chapter 6, p. 124. Quite like the continuous speech recognition group at IBM that did not want to learn anything about language, but just build a recognizer that works, the subjects are no matter of interest in these experiments. Thus, they are not aimed at learning which kind of subjects the users are and in turn how to manipulate *such subjects*. Rather, after the A/B test, whatever works best (for whichever reason) is used. The stage of modeling a subject, of addressing it as a subject, is elided. No data double is involved.

Furthermore, many interfaces are structured in a way that is intended to make users react rather unreflectedly. "Accept" buttons are bright and noticeable, "deny" buttons small and grey. Repeated reminders not to miss out reach us with the affective humming and pinging of smartphones in order to bring users back to the platforms. Interface elements are laid out in a way that the "login," "play," or "try it now" buttons are seen before the terms and conditions, prices, or other caveats.

All of these phenomena give substance to the claim that algorithmic power today cannot be understood on the level of the subject. This argument is presented by Antoinette Rouvroy. She describes what she calls "algorithmic governmentality" as

> [e]ffected through the reconfiguration of informational and physical architectures and/or environments within which certain things become impossible or unthinkable, and throwing alerts or stimuli producing reflex responses rather than interpretation and reflection.
>
> (Rouvroy 2013, 155)

According to Rouvroy, this process "does not allow the process of subjectivation to happen, because it does not confront 'subjects' [...]."

> [T]he subjective singularities of individuals, their personal psychological motivations or intentions do not matter. What matters is the possibility of linking any trivial information or data left behind or voluntarily disclosed by individuals with other data gathered in heterogeneous contexts and to establish statistically meaningful correlations.
>
> (Rouvroy 2013, 157)

In many ways, this is a very good description of those algorithmic processes described above. Rouvroy's position is also quite pertinent to my analysis because she does not oppose this form of governance to the liberal subject that ignores the heteronomous conditions of the own position. Rather, she acknowledges that subjects are intersubjectively constituted by power. Yet, such subjects are still addressed and thus can confront this being addressed – among other things via law which is Rouvroy's main concern. In contrast, she calls the processes of algorithmic governmentality "data behaviorism" for it does not aim at the subject but at creating an environment that sends the right "alerts or stimuli producing [the] reflex responses" that are desired.

This analysis leaves the subject behind too quickly, however.[3] Subjects and algorithms are co-constituted also on a material level of environments. Subjectification happens through architecture, design, attire, record keeping, movement, and more. All of these subjectifying moments leave also embodied traces, which I call habitual following the works of Linda Martín Alcoff (2006) and Sarah Ahmed (2007). What seems to be the reflex response of a quasi-behaviorist creature is still the reaction of situated subjects – situated also in an embodied and material fashion.

Wendy Chun has already suggested that new media are centrally about habits. Yet, in her study the concept of habit is used in many different ways, explaining all kinds of things: correlation, information, memory, reason, and more (Chun 2016). She also discusses the norms that are captured and extracted from data and thus structure algorithmic processes as habits (Chun 2016, 59–62). In my analysis, I will stick to the notion of norm and normalcy, because as I have discussed above, they align with power in being opposed to exclusion or deviance. In contrast, habitualization is a product of power but does not align with it. One can be habitualized by experiences at either end of power relations. What I describe as habit is present between the lines in many parts of Chun's text, but only rarely explicit, as in this definition: "Habits are 'remnants' of the past – past goals/selves, past experiences – that live on in our reactions to the environment today" (Chun 2016, 95).

This view can be posited as a response to Rouvroy: the reaction to an environment – even an algorithmically predicted and attuned one – is the result of past experiences. However, it needs to be qualified as situated experience. Chun discusses the unreflected or "unconscious" quality of habits with regard to neuropsychological research, which works on humans and animals alike, paradoxically eradicating the situatedness that is postulated in the citation above from the scope of her theory (Chun 2016, 88).

Alcoff (2006) and Ahmed (2007) describe habitualization based on phenomenological research on embodiment. A typical example of embodiment is learning to drive a car or ride a bike. Once one has learned it, most of it happens unreflectedly, one could say as a "reflex." Yet, this is clearly a situated practice, as Alcoff reminds us by describing how these reflex-like reactions suddenly ceased to function and even became an irritation when she had to drive on the other side of the road in Australia (Alcoff 2006, 108). Iris Marion Young's famous study "Throwing like a girl" (1980) shows that this situatedness also entails subjectifying norms such as gender. The "girl" here is decidedly not a fact of nature but a girl that is demanded time and again to dress, move, position, comport, and express herself in particular ways, which again leads to embodied habitual reactions. Alcoff extends these

3 For the following, see Matzner (2019a) for a more detailed discussion.

analyses by fusing them with a Foucauldian notion of power. That way, even "natural" affective reactions can be traced to situated habits:

> Part of what the collective praxis creates are aspects of the self. Our preferences, our dispositions toward certain kinds of feelings in certain kinds of situations, what typically causes fear, anxiety, calmness, anger, and so on, are affected by our cultural and historical location. Sometimes people take such internal feelings as proof of a natural origin, as when a homosexual kiss elicits feelings of disgust. The feelings may well be quite real, but this is not proof that homosexuality is unnatural; physical reactions can be altered by knowledge and acquaintance.
>
> (Alcoff 2006, 115–16)

These observations can be extended to algorithms. If an algorithm creates a "reflex response" (Rouvroy) or a direct "physical reaction" (Alcoff) it connects with a situated, habitualized subject. The examples discussed here illustrate that such reactions will not be the same for all subjects. Again, it depends on how the relation between the subject and the algorithm cites – continues and transforms – preceding practices. For many, an algorithm might match their habits while for others whose habit is either structured by wariness and attention or whose habitual actions are disrupted, it will work differently.

This situatedness of course includes that people can relate to their habits. It is possible to train oneself not to buy one of the chocolate bars that are laid out suggestively for those waiting in line at the supermarket checkout; and one can learn to be attentive to the manipulative tricks and not always click on the bright red button. Yet, such processes are no simple matter of rationality winning over habit or affect. They are themselves socio-material, embodied processes – a de-habitualization one could say, which is in important regards also a re-habitualization. These again take time, resources, and a stable enough subject position to do so. This is one of the reasons why attempts and programs such as "digital detox" quickly turned into a rather elitist self-optimization (Helm and Matzner 2023), while for others the often called-for digital literacy programs would yet be another burden rather than a way to a more self-determined media use (Matzner et al. 2016).

Such forms of algorithmic subjectification that connects to habits can be even more difficult to notice than algorithmic norms that remain hidden such as the gender estimation in a store. They feel as if the algorithm could provoke a natural or physical reaction as Alcoff writes. This does not just make the politics of the algorithm hard to discern – it can lend the algorithm even more credibility because it seems to conform to what is natural.

"Algorithms are not neutral because they are made by humans"

Many studies that detail the negative impact of algorithms on human subjects link that impact to other human subjects: those who created the algorithm. The idea that "algorithms are not neutral because they are created by humans" can be found in the materials of NGOs (e.g. Algorithmwatch 2022), political institutions (e.g. European Union Agency for Fundamental Rights 2022), and of course many academic texts (e.g. Benjamin 2019, 50–51). Asking for the role of programmers, data scientists, management, exploited laborers, and more who partake in the co-constitution of an algorithm is of course very important. So is the question of who should be held responsible, or liable for the outcomes of algorithms. Yet, in the framing that "algorithms are created by humans," many forms of critical engagement with algorithms turn into the investigative gesture of finding the humans "behind" the algorithms. Put pointedly, algorithms just become a "channel" or "amplifier" that transports whatever is put in by one set of humans, the "creators," to another set of humans: those who suffer from bias, injustice, and discrimination.

Of course, it would neither make sense to just deal with the algorithms without taking these groups of humans into account. I am not arguing for a strong notion of non-human agency. Neither do I think that discussions on whether algorithms could be carriers of moral or legal attributes such as responsibility or liability are helpful. As I argue in detail in Chapter 3, p. 46 the practices that are concerned here are human practices – not ontologically but in their local, historical, and cultural specificity. This means also taking the specific subject positions involved seriously. Rather than importing notions such as "creation," "decision," etc. from a general idea of humanity, this means scrutinizing how not only the subject positions of those concerned by algorithmic results but also those involved in the creation of algorithms are constituted. While this of course entails many factors, in this section, I will discuss the co-constitution of algorithms and the subject positions of those involved in making algorithms.

Nick Seaver systematically theorizes (rather than just claims) the necessity of finding humans "behind" or "within" the algorithm. He argues against monolithic and too abstract notions of algorithms, which I also discuss in Chapter 1. Yet, he also questions the role of anthropology and similar empirical research in providing "the cultural to their technical; the thick description to their thin; the human to their computer" (Seaver 2018, 380). This position, Seaver argues, is so diametrically opposed to the concept of algorithms that it at the same time affirms it, because it "depends on it for coherence" (Seaver 2018, 380). Yet, the way he wants to dissolve this opposition is mainly by finding the many "people hidden within supposedly automatic systems" (Seaver 2018, 382).

With respect to an ethnographic study at a firm producing recommender systems for music, he writes:

[P]ress on any algorithmic decision and you will find many human ones: people like Brad or his manager deciding that a certain error threshold is acceptable, that one data source should be used over another or that a good recommendation means this, not that. These systems are, as a former head of recommendation at Spotify put it, 'human all the way down' (Heath 2015). There is no such thing as an algorithmic decision; there are only ways of seeing decisions as algorithmic.

(Seaver 2018, 378)

"Brad" is part of a team whose work Seaver has studied. He creates an algorithm that depends on gathering human input of all sorts: his own parameters, team members' feedback, and the data that users produce through their interactions using the product. This observation leads Seaver to frame "the essence of a contemporary algorithmic system: a steady accumulation of feedback loops, little circuits of interpretation and decision knit together into a vast textile. Every stitch is held together by a moment of human response [...]" (Seaver 2018, 377).

What Seaver proposes certainly is no continuation of what Chun (Chun 2008) calls the "fetishization" of code or similar instrumental views of the programmer as autonomous "creator," which I discuss in detail in Chapter 5, p. 82. He is quite attentive to the particular practices of programmers and the way they are organized. Yet, the influence is one-way: from humans to algorithms. Seaver cites "Conway's Law," which states "that organizations which design systems [...] are constrained to produce designs which are copies of the communication structures of these organizations" (Conway 1968, 31). Intended by its author as a formal analysis to improve software design, it became a part of "programmer lore" that Seaver picks up generalizing: "Social structures emboss themselves onto digital substrates" (Seaver 2018, 375).

The necessity to consider the mutual constitution of subjects purportedly "hidden within the algorithm" and algorithms themselves are most clearly discernible concerning those who prepare training data or do similar tasks on platforms such as Amazon's Mechanical Turk (AMT). As discussed in Chapter 6, p. 118, these tasks, so-called "HITs," are created by programmers or data scientists using a dedicated API or Amazon's interface. Both quite narrowly constrain how the directions look and how the requirements of who is accepted to work on them can be specified. Particularly, ascertaining these requirements is outsourced to the platform. Many of them are automatically gathered by algorithmic means, e.g. location, approval rates, or experience. Amazon also offers a metric that algorithmically qualifies so-called "master workers," who "have consistently demonstrated a high degree of success in performing a wide range of HITs across a large number of Requesters" (Amazon Mechanical Turk 2019). All the terms in this description remain vague (consistently, high degree, large number), to be specified in an internal, and probably changing algorithm. There are also self-reported qualifications that, however, have to conform to a strict survey-like structure with pre-given fields. AMT thus positions workers in a similar manner as it is known from social media platforms: forcing the user data into an algorithmically usable form and combining it with particular metrics that define access, visibility, success, etc. on the platform (Cover 2012).

Beyond these material conditions of platform labor, those working to provide training data also are epistemically situated by the algorithm. As I discuss in Chapter 6, machine learning uses any input data only regarding its utility for the performance of a specific algorithm. All data, even data used to critically investigate problems such as bias needs to conform to that performance-based epistemology. Varying a prominent figure of speech, the data workers need to learn to "see like an algorithm" – or to hear like it. As a student I was confronted with training data for speech recognition gathered from an automated telephone hotline system. This data exhibited a quite common phenomenon of human speech: when the system would not understand a term, the human dialogue partner would repeat it very slowly, clearly, and overpronounced. While this helps many human beings understand better, it was a problem for algorithms that are trained on large collections of ordinary speech, where this particular form of speaking rarely appears. Thus, for the algorithm, this common reaction made things worse, not better. In consequence, those preparing the data had to learn that the sections that were most clear for them to understand needed to be sorted out as a special problem for the algorithm.

Those who work in programming are not as tightly placed and controlled by algorithms – although workplace metrics are common also in this industry. They are also much better paid and work in much more comfortable circumstances. In Chapter 5, I show that even their work is very much pre-structured by algorithms. Programmers call libraries or services they have not themselves programmed and that they cannot scrutinize or access. This is either due to legal reasons or a consequence of the economy of distributed labor. Programmers need to have a lot of algorithms black-boxed in a way that renders them usable without understanding their functionality to do their work. After all, most programming is done as wage work in large teams and a specific working culture. This involves prestige and good payment, but often also constant pressure, long hours, and thus a sustained need to be effective. To be sure, programming and designing algorithms comprises a wide range of activities. There are some truly novel approaches that lead to academic prestige or market success (even if this is never the sole factor.)

Yet, there are also many programmers that have to use services or APIs that are very much geared toward a certain usage – if not explicitly governed by big platforms to enforce their aims also via code. Even in the wide space between these examples, bread and butter programming is very much combining pre-existing algorithms, oriented by yet another set of algorithms that facilitate design. In this regard, Seaver's image of "little circuits of interpretation and decision knit together into a vast textile" is quite apt – only that the pieces that are stitched together need to be considered as well as the humans doing the stitching, and not only humans do the stitching.

All of this is situated in practices where the interplay of code and algorithms structures the subject position of programmers. Algorithms need not just fulfill the functional requirements of the employer or the project. The code in which they are written also needs to do the necessary face work for the programmer and mediates the community of programming. I discuss – in Chapter 5, p. 92 – how this creates a particular boundary between an inside and an outside. Particularly, this community is structured by a specific view toward algorithms and information technology in general that informs which and how algorithms get designed and implemented. It includes a self-understanding of a privileged insight from the inside, that interacts in a complex fashion with the epistemic situation of programming just mentioned, where actually a lot needs to be black-boxed rather than transparent. This became part of the community and intersects with many other forms of social situatedness – including the many practices that anthropologists such as Seaver study. Programmers are not the homogenous group that their established self-understanding based on the experience of educated white men often implies. Yet, the "success stories" of having made it to the inside still influence the subject positions of programmers.

Finally, algorithms also need to establish the trustworthiness of their "author" for other programmers and commercial users – where the "author" can be individuals, organizations, or enterprises.

If Seaver claims that every "algorithmic decision" can be traced back to a "human decision," the situatedness of the subjects that I have quickly summarized here from Chapters 5 and 6 qualifies what it means to talk about their "decisions." First of all, already Friedman and Nissenbaum (1996) in their fundamental text on *Bias in Computer Systems* warned about so-called "emergent biases." They do not only occur in the context of machine learning but can be the result of the contingencies of the interoperation of two libraries or an established algorithm and a new data set, without having been anyone's decision. At most, they could be traced to human oversight. But that is not my concern here. Even the "decisions" that are "taken" are deeply structured by the particular situatedness of programmers or data workers, which is both a social situation and an epistemic situation regarding algorithms. While the social situation may very well include entitlement and the competence to decide for programmers, at the same time it has the potential to render many of the conditions and consequences of these decisions invisible with both the constant pressure to be effective in a highly distributed form of work with black-boxed technology and the way programming is at least implicitly working as a community.

Programmers: situated responsibility

Often, the aim of finding the human decisions within the algorithms is aimed at finding the responsible person. This comes with connotations of a conscious, informed, and autonomous decision. When Seaver opposes "algorithmic" and "human decision," he most probably does not have such a strong notion of autonomy in mind. Rather, he wants to dismantle too easy claims about algorithms as neutral, unbiased "deciders." He clearly considers humans at least socially situated to which I just added technological situatedness.

This does not mean that programmers are not responsible for what they do. It just shows the necessity of rethinking the concept of responsibility in light of the way in which programmers are subjectified and particularly the way in which algorithms and subjects co-constitute each other. As I discuss generally in Chapter 3, responsibility should not be understood as a full accounting of the factors that determine the own situation and decisions based on that account. Rather, responsibility derives from the insight into situatedness that is limited without knowing the extent of the limits. Responsibility thus turns from a moral into a political demand. It means a reflection on the way that the outside of the own position is just a view from the inside. Ideally, this turns responsibility literally into the ability to gather responses from those who live in that "outside," that is in differently situated positions. A responsible programmer, thus, should try to create some form of encounter with those who are concerned by the programs they write. Responsibility is the way in which one relates to others who are differently situated. This needs to be truly a relation, not just a transport of information or subjects to the inside. Because that transport invariably re-contextualizes everything to the epistemology of the own situation and precludes the ability to see from another's point of view. Given the considerations just mentioned, as an individual effort this will most likely have limited success, if not institutionalized as part of usual work routines. In the end, political responsibility needs to change the own situatedness, rather than just deciding differently within that situation.

Users: responsibilization

This rethinking of responsibility also concerns users. The increasing importance of the internet and digital technology is constantly accompanied by demands for more media literacy, privacy literacy, and data literacy. All of these literacies are aimed at enabling more responsible use of digital technologies. Most of the programs, methods, and curricula that are suggested can be summarized as attempts to turn users into programmers – or data scientists – at least on a basic level. Traces of this can even be found in the most politically informed versions, such as *Data Feminism* by D'Ignazio and Klein (2020). While the question of how much programming and data skills are necessary in digital societies certainly is relevant, it is no solution to the question of responsible users.

First, such proposals ignore that the same technology is something different for programmers and users, but neither has a better or more privileged view. *Both* have limits and in this particular case, both situations are a limit for the other. This leads to the development of sophisticated algorithms by programmers that try to guess and estimate the behavior of users which changes the outputs of the algorithm. At the same time, the users of social media platforms, for example, imagine a certain function of the algorithm, which in turn changes their behavior (Bucher 2017; Schulz 2022). In Chapter 6, p. 123, I describe how through social media platforms, both perspectives are algorithmically connected and influence each other. This complex interplay cannot be understood and responsibly treated without a thorough grasp of the difference in situatedness of users and programmers.

Second, such proposals ignore that responsibility cannot be grounded in a full accounting of the relations and factors that constitute the own situation. Even without the socio-material theory I develop in Chapter 3, for users the impossibility to do so is blatantly obvious: endless terms and conditions in complex legal language and for the majority of the world in a foreign language, constant updates and changes of features, an inextricable amount of intermediaries for even a single website accessed from a phone (mobile carrier, mobile operation system, website provider, data brokers listening in and providing additional data to advertising networks), etc. I have a graduate degree in computer science, I have banned anything not free or opensource from my phone, I block all the ads and scripts I can and still, there is *no way* of being sure what goes on on my phone. Still, many proposals for data- or privacy literacies suggest surmounting these difficulties at least a bit.

These suggestions derive from an understanding of the relationship between human beings and technology as instrumental: one needs a thorough understanding of the functions and their consequences which then can be rationally directed as appropriate means to the right ends. For programmers, this view is part of the self-understanding as a group with privileged insight. In this sense, a lot of data literacy proposals are at least implicitly inspired by this inner perspective of programmers. Taking situatedness into account for users means – as it does for programmers – to focus on relations to others beyond their own situation. Yet, for users, this focus on relations also needs to entail the refusal to take on the responsibility from these others. In social and political theory, the term responsibilization denotes the shift of responsibility from the entity that so far has been responsible (most often the state) to individuals (Harris and White 2018). This is what happens here: users that should study the terms and agreements, accept the cookies, understand the technology, etc. are then held responsible for what happens with the data and its algorithmic processing, e.g. infringements of their privacy (Matzner et al. 2016). In this case, true responsibility for users would mean to change the own situatedness, that is to say: I am not responsible, you are! "You" in this case could be the state, the platform, or other enterprises, administrators, programmers, and more. This does not mean that users do not have any responsibility. Yet, as for programmers, responsibility would be based on the acknowledgment that the possibilities to act for situated subjects depend on the way in which their own desires and aims align with the prevailing power structures and norms, that is on the particular subjectification taking place, as I have explained at the beginning of this chapter. Again, this is something that cannot be fully accounted for but still (or rather for that reason) can be the starting point of responsible political action. Referring to the discussion of Haraway in Chapter 3, this acknowledgment of the own situation is not an ontological task but a political one.

8
ALGORITHMS AND HUMANS

The rhetoric of autonomous systems, artificial intelligence, etc., abounds. The replacement – or displacement – of humans is a topic whenever there is some algorithmic progress. Yet, while it is true that algorithms fulfill tasks before being done by human beings, all algorithmic applications involve human subjects. Furthermore, they do not involve "humans" per se but differently situated subjects. In this chapter, I will show that even prominent cases of algorithmic autonomy such as self-driving cars mean a re-configuration of situated human–algorithmic ensembles rather than just a replacement of human subjects by algorithms.

It is certainly true that algorithms make many jobs obsolete. Yet, that never happens in the way that algorithms just replace the work that hitherto had been done by a human subject. For example, many stores now have self-service checkout. The workplace of the cashier is no longer needed. Yet, there is no algorithm doing the scanning of the merchandise. This task is delegated to the clients themselves. Algorithms just help to make fraud more difficult, e.g. by checking if the weight of the purchased article corresponds with the scanned one. Collecting the money is done by yet another set of algorithms for identifying coins and notes or reading cards and processing payments with the bank. In sum, the job of the cashier is replaced not by an algorithm but by a complex ensemble of human subjects, here the clients, and algorithms (Matzner 2019b).

The factual way in which the process takes place within such an ensemble has to be differentiated from the rhetorical attribution of agency to humans and algorithms. For example, Seaver takes the notion that algorithms are "humans all the way down" from engineers that do recommendation algorithms at Spotify, one of the largest music streaming services in the world. In

DOI: 10.4324/9781003299851-10

an interview, they state: "Discover Weekly is humans all the way down. Every single track that appears in Discover Weekly is because other humans being [sic] have said, 'Hey this is a good song, and here's why'" (Heath 2015). Linking the results of algorithms to human input, in this case, is intended to say something about the sophistication and quality of the recommendations – implying a certain difference between humans and algorithms that make human judgment preferable: human beings have taste, passion for music, etc., while algorithms calculate. This is less a statement about the actual function, which happens in a more relational manner, than marketing. Gillespie (2012) reports that Twitter, when faced with the accusation of censoring the "trending" topics on its website, reacted quite differently. They argued that "trends" are determined by an algorithm that uses the same, quite static – albeit secret – criteria in all situations. Here the fact that an algorithm selects the "trends" without human involvement was a key argument. Again, this rhetoric implies a difference between humans and algorithms: humans have politics and a weak character that could lead them to manipulate; algorithms work in a steady, knee-jerk, and thus neutral fashion; and again, the actual operation works in a much more relational fashion.

Still, it would be too simple to just consider such remarks as purely rhetorical. The relation between human subjects and algorithms also is structured by the way how either is enacted in discourse. Gillespie (2014) argues that regardless of how Twitter measures "trends," what makes them important, and thus what makes the measuring algorithm relevant, is that enough people treat them as important. The impact of the trends algorithm cannot be reduced to its metric but includes its perception which is structured by the accompanying view of the difference between humans and algorithms.

In the following, I will quickly discuss two recent examples that illustrate different facets of the way in which the difference between "the algorithm" and "the human" can become quite consequential in the co-constitutive relation of concrete algorithms and situated human subjects: self-driving cars and ChatGPT.

Algorithms and the human in self-driving cars: Legitimizing the rating of lives

Self-driving cars have become a kind of poster child for the ethics of algorithms. Their prominence is certainly understandable. They bring machine learning to an activity that many people know as first-hand experience. Furthermore, cars are already given much attention as an important status symbol. The medial appearances of successful actors and popstars, top managers, and leading politicians all share big, shiny, expensive cars. Most (male) movie heroes are seen behind the steering wheel of a car, be it in chase scenes – a staple of action movies –, while conquering the love interest in the passenger seat, or leaving the narrow confines of society in a road movie. The car industries and their commercials add even more content to this cultural constellation, where driving a car is not just a human activity, but a highly value-laden one, implying freedom, success, and even heroism.

Many current applications of machine learning are rather hidden, as part of search engines, social media platforms, hiring or credit decisions, etc. In contrast, everyone can imagine what a self-driving car would be like. At the same time, self-driving cars have also spurred a quite peculiar ethical discourse. Purportedly, there is an ethical problem that only algorithms have, not humans. The problem is based on the assumption of an unavoidable accident in the sense that both in the path of the car and in all possible change maneuvers, someone would be hurt – or in most statements of the problem killed. The ethical question is who should be killed in such a case. This is a variation of the so-called "trolley problems" known from moral philosophy (Foot 1967; Thomson 1976). In its original statement, a runaway tram goes down a track where it will hit five persons. There is however the possibility to steer it down another track where it would kill only one (Foot 1967, 8). Notably, this problem was not described by its inventor, Philippa Foot, as a moral problem in itself – the text she writes deals with the ethics of abortion – but rather as an illustration of certain moral points of view. The "trolley problem" for her is only one part of an argument, where it is opposed to another case: a judge is faced with an innocent person, yet there is an angry mob that demands that a culprit be found; otherwise, it will kill five hostages. The only way to avoid this is to frame the innocent person and have them executed (Foot 1967, 8). Foot's argument aims at the difference between these two cases, even if the outcome is the same in terms of number of lives and deaths. Despite that similarity, many still would think that the driver of the tram should change the track but that a judge should not frame an innocent person, even if that means the death of the hostages. Following Foot's paper, many versions of such problems have been proposed, where the difference is not always in the number of people dying, but also their age, wealth, character, and more. In all of these cases, the problems are an argumentative tool for discussing different theories in moral philosophy.

How come these arguably quite contrived hypothetical cases suddenly are considered real-world problems for an emerging technology? The argument for that appropriation is often not made explicit. It presupposes first that an accident is unavoidable and second that the car can predict that situation fast enough that it still can choose among different maneuvers. This is where the difference to humans comes in. Self-driving cars have much better sensors than human sight and hearing and they can process the input much faster. This informs the hope that self-driving cars will be safer in general because, through their faster reaction, they can evade accidents that humans cannot (Nyholm and Smids 2016, 1278).

Several authors have criticized the transfer of trolley problems to self-driving cars (JafariNaimi 2018; Nyholm and Smids 2016). Here, I want to show that it could only become plausible in the first place because of a particular conception of the difference between humans and algorithms. In this case, it is a very peculiar mix of two different conceptions.

All the premises that are necessary to discursively turn what would be a tragic accident for humans into a calculable and thus programmable event are based on a strong difference between humans and algorithms. The car has better sensors, faster processing time, and even additional information sources like networking with other cars. This way of conceiving the difference reduces the car to an algorithmic machine – implying a notion of algorithms that is based on determinist execution. In reality, the driving algorithms steer a physical car that, by the premises of the dilemma situation, drives so fast that it cannot brake anymore. While cars need to be able to change lanes at such speeds, omitting a potential obstacle, here the presumption is different. It is assumed that a car can *hit* an obstacle in a controlled manner at these speeds. While it is one thing to calculate who should die, it is another problem to make that happen in the physical world. No serious engineer would attempt to build a mechanism that intentionally crashes a car into a roadblock, killing the driver, in order to save a toddler that is only one meter away. This is one of the cases that the MIT Moral Machine experiment, an empirical survey that serves many different configurations of the trolley problem, presents (Awad et al. 2018). Those who discuss the trolley problem for self-driving cars only discuss the decision, quietly presupposing an idea of determinist execution by hardware that already fails to grasp the complexity of an algorithm running on a desktop computer (see Chapter 4) – let alone a computer driving at high speeds through traffic.

The plausibility of the situation thus derives from a particular, determinist view of algorithms that is strongly opposed to human beings. Yet, because of the features derived from this difference, the car suddenly seems lacking compared to human beings: it needs a component for ethical decisions.

This lack only appears because, in this single regard, a continuity – rather than a difference – to human drivers is drawn. We are used to the fact that the entities steering cars, human beings, happen to be capable of moral decisions – and as mentioned above, even very important, heroic ones. They are also beings with a wide range of possible activities, including speeding, talking on the phone while driving, and for some of them, sustaining their masculinity by letting the motor roar, that makes moral judgment necessary. Cars don't have either. What self-driving cars teach human beings is that driving a car is not a very special, let alone heroic skill. It can be done by processing sensor data in feedback loops that are complex but neither require intelligence in any human sense nor a moral being. Again, this does not mean that human beings no longer play a role. In a sense, the same thing happens as with the self-checkout: the task of driving is differently configured in a new human–algorithm ensemble, where the humans involved are not in the car, but, e.g., work for its manufacturer. Yet, the argument for the trolley problem still presupposes a morally capable – or at least programmable – entity in the car because there used to be one. However, in a self-driving car, there is none.

In sum, only that incoherent mixture of an essential difference between algorithms (ignoring their materiality) and humans on the one hand and an extension of what we have culturally been trained to consider a human driver to self-driving cars on the other hand can make it plausible to consider the trolley problem as a real-life problem. Of course that does not mean that self-driving cars do not have ethical problems. They have a lot. Yet, as JafariNaimi (2018) and Nyholm and Smids (2016) argue, they are a matter of estimating risks and decisions under uncertainty rather than determinist calculation and execution, of structural and systemic evaluations, as they have been informing decisions in the design and manufacture of cars for a long time (Evans 2008). The components that make a car self-driving are currently, and probably will be in the future, standardized, assessed, and tested, not unlike other components in a car. The actual path that a self-driving car takes is the outcome of the complex interplay of hundreds of components (Sprenger 2022) that again interact with the environment: road, weather, traffic, etc. In this interplay, accidents *happen*. They cannot and will not be solved algorithmically. Accidents would even happen to a presumed trolley-problem algorithm. The day on which the first such algorithm would kill a person in order to save the five children playing on the road that it had detected – but that did not exist – would be the end of this technology.

The plausibility of trolley problems as an ethical issue for self-driving cars is illustrative beyond that case. It speaks to the impact of the way in which specific relations of humans and algorithms situate how technology is discussed and accordingly also designed and used. This impact legitimizes views and practices that are highly problematic from a political point of view and go far beyond the common problem of apparent machinic neutrality. When the possibility of ethics only for algorithms in specific situations can be assumed, quite a lot becomes possible. Probably the most well-known publication on the issue of self-driving cars and trolley problems is a paper in the prestigious journal *Nature* reporting the results from the so-called "MIT Moral Machine Experiment" (Awad et al. 2018). This experiment was conducted on a website (https://www.moralmachine.net/) that presents everyone, who is interested, pairs of trolley-problem style situations. The basic setting is always the same: the car can stay in its lane or change it. In both cases, people will be killed: either by hitting a roadblock and killing all passengers and the driver or by killing everyone crossing at a traffic light or crosswalk ahead. The viewers are asked "What should the self-driving car do?" and have to decide among one of the two alternatives. The variation among the settings that are presented is in the subjects involved, which the experiment presents as members of different classes: babies in a stroller, pregnant persons, athletes, doctors, executives, large persons, homeless persons, old persons, criminals, dogs, and cats. Most of these have a binary gender, e.g. there are male and female doctors. Notably, babies, pregnant persons, criminals, and homeless persons, as well as dogs and cats, do not have a gender assigned (Awad et al. 2018, 61). This setup imports many (unmentioned) social norms and stereotypes into the experiment: binary gender and its relevance, high social status modeled by executives, low status by homeless, etc. (Awad et al. 2018, 61). Would that be an average social science survey, this would have probably been criticized. Yet, in this case, the categories carry the implication of being classifications of an algorithm and as such they are (unfortunately) plausible.[1]

The result of the study is essentially a list of worthy and less worthy lives – published in *Nature* in the year 2018. In the paper, it is innocuously titled "Preference in favour of sparing characters" (Awad et al. 2018, 61) and the sparing is related to the question in the experiment "What should the self-driving car do?" If the question would be reframed as what it essentially asks: "who should be systematically considered as less worthy of surviving an accident," the reactions would probably (hopefully) be different. The systematicity comes in through the fact that a postulated "trolley algorithm" would be shared by all cars of a manufacturer, or, as the authors of the study themselves suggest, legally mandated for all (Awad et al. 2018, 60). Yet, here the question is framed as a very confined action taken by a car in a defined situation, that is particular because it promises to algorithmically solve a hitherto tragic – even if very improbable – situation. This hinges on all the presuppositions discussed above: two clearly delineated and predictable alternatives; the reduction of the material situation to the execution of a determinist algorithm; and the purported need for an ethical decision for the car.

The framing here does more than rely on the presumed neutrality of algorithms – although that is part of its subtext. Trolley problems are not seen as the same decision that had been taken by humans now taken by a (neutral) algorithm. Rather, through the particular mixture of difference and continuity between human drivers and algorithms, the decision becomes something completely different: a specific algorithmic problem. Through this reframing, the problem becomes unlinked from established social, cultural,

---

1 Yet, the setup is also methodologically imprecise, because neither doctors nor criminals are included in the rating of social status and the unequal distribution of gendered subjects certainly skews the analysis of whether a specific gender should be spared, even if that is one of the main categories that are presented.

or ethical norms and concerns, such as the ones regarding publishing a list of more or less worthy lives.

The "Moral Machine Experiment" is not the first time that contemporary research on machine learning evokes odd similarities to eugenics, physiognomy, or similar "sciences" that were long believed to be surmounted as both scientifically wrong and politically discriminatory. In other prominent cases, researchers believed to detect homosexuality (Wang and Kosinski 2018) or criminality (Bowyer et al. 2020) in facial images. Wendy Chun has linked that resurgence to the historical roots of many statistical tools used today in machine learning. Many of them go back to the work of eugenicists or eugenically inspired thinkers, e.g. by Pearsons, Galton, or Fisher (Chun and Barnett 2021, chap. 4, 6). Yet, I do not think that this genealogy suffices to explain the sudden, matter-of-course acceptance of forms of thought largely held to be an aberration of the past – at least among the reviewers of good journals and quite some part of the academic and journalist communities taking up these results.

As I argue throughout the book, algorithms change the situatedness of practices. That change is both a continuation of practices and a recontextualization. In contrast, the particular framing of algorithms that I discuss here is structured by considering the algorithmic problem as something different from human practice and particular to algorithms. This includes disavowing or ignoring the relational situatedness of the algorithmic practice. Wang and Kosinski, the authors of the paper that claims to show the possibility to detect homosexuality from faces, seriously claimed that they were doing the "gay community" a favor by warning them about an imminent threat by possible misuse of face detection (Wang and Kosinski 2018, 35). This shows that the authors considered their algorithm as something completely removed from stereotypes and biases against homosexuals – fearing that both could eventually be connected. They did not comprehend at all how their algorithm was already in many ways a continuation (and recontextualization) of said biases and stereotypes.

In all these cases, the complexity of relational situatedness is disavowed by considering something a specific algorithmic solution to a particular, clearly delineated problem – implying a peculiar understanding of the difference between humans and algorithms. I guess that this recontextualization of the problem that does not consider it a *situated* recontextualization helps to understand the legitimizing force algorithms and particularly machine learning can have even for widely discredited modes of thought or belief.

Chatbots: Subjects situated by technology ≠ humans surmounted by technology

Emphasizing the need to consider the situatedness of subjects, including their co-constitution through technology and algorithms, as I do in this book, must be clearly differentiated from positions that argue for a continuum or a similarity of human beings and machines. As the examples from this chapter and also many others show: algorithms can mean a lesson in humility for human beings. Many things that until recently only humans were thought to be capable of are now done by algorithms. Yet, that does not mean that algorithms have become more similar to humans, let alone that they are on a trajectory to eventually surmount humans. As the discussions in Chapters 6 and 7 make clear, the results of algorithms and humans are only performatively the same or comparable. Yet, both achieve them in fundamentally different ways. Furthermore, algorithms never occupy the same position as humans did before. Introducing algorithms, as I have shown, means changing many relations in human–algorithmic ensembles. These changes also entail new subject positions – and sometimes a new understanding of what it means to be human.

During the time I was working on this book, quite a sensation in the field of machine learning happened when ChatGPT was released. This is maybe the best illustration for the issues just mentioned, even if the discussion necessarily will have a preliminary character.

ChatGPT is based on a large language model called GPT, a so-called "transformer" (Brown et al. 2020). Very generally speaking, such a model is trained on huge amounts of text to predict the most likely continuation of a sequence of words. Thus, based on an initial bit of text, it can continue generating text. In its chat version, these initial prompts are generated from input by users in a manner that they can chat with the algorithm. The sensation was that ChatGPT could write texts on all kinds of topics in all kinds of styles that were astonishingly good – for an algorithm. The software would have passed exams in law and business schools (Kelly 2023), wrote program code that actually worked, and several newspapers printed texts written by the software that went unnoticed. These successes were mainly due to two factors. The first was the innovation of transformer models. Artificial neural networks have been used to predict text for quite a while. In preceding approaches, however, language has been processed word by word. Transformers can process much bigger inputs in parallel and thus make use of positional information that is quite important for many languages. For example, adjectives or pronouns need to match verbs at a different location in a sentence. The second factor was sheer size: GPT-3, which initially was used in ChatGPT, considered a context of more than 2000 words and used more than 175 billion parameters to be adjusted using training data (Brown et al. 2020, 8).

Critics quickly pointed out that despite their success, such models did not even attempt to model any knowledge about the world or any form of reasoning. Rather, they are what Emily Bender called "stochastic parrots" (Weil 2023). They just repeat what they were given as data, yet not in a determinist fashion like a parrot but in a stochastic one. Given the data they have seen, they produce a likely next word. This illustrates the first point that I mention at the beginning of this section: the results of humans and algorithms may be comparable but are achieved in a completely different fashion. The emphasis on this fact was mainly directed at those who saw GPT as yet another step on the way to a truly intelligent AI or those who took it as yet another occasion to argue that humans are essentially algorithmic or data processors and that technology will enhance or surmount humanity (Weil 2023).

The opposition of humans on the one hand and a stochastic parrot on the other, however, does not settle another set of worries that were less concerned with fundamental issues of meaning or human understanding but with potential problems in specific applications. Here, a general humanism does not help much. Rather, a situated analysis of the concrete changes in human-algorithm ensembles is necessary. For example, schools and universities worry that students will be able to cheat in exams too easily, the creation and dissemination of manipulative content will become automatable and thus more widespread, and companies replacing humans with algorithms for economic reasons (e.g. in journalism) will be vulnerable to the errors and biases encoded in the models, and more. These issues concern the second aspect that I have mentioned above: the transformation of human–algorithmic ensembles and thus shifting subject positions for situated humans. This issue was, at the time I write this, not very present in discussions of ChatGPT and similar software. Rather, most of these worries were stated as the question "will we still be able to tell human and algorithmically created texts apart?" Yet, in this generality, this is not really the issue. In fact, in many cases, people do not care. For example, in Germany, where I live, but also in many other countries, many persons receive a quite important document each year that is algorithmically created: their tax assessment. Yet, this was introduced with very little public discussion. In this case, what the human "authors" of the documents did in the majority of cases was to put the right numbers into boilerplate text that is in large parts legally prescribed anyway and to perform a few checks against threshold values. There simply was little reason to doubt this could be automated, once both citizens and their employers were legally required to submit tax forms in an electronically readable format (again the distribution of tasks shifts).

Telling human and algorithmic texts apart, thus, is in most cases performing a certain function – and as the examples I mentioned show, a different function in each situation. For example, journalist texts – in contrast to tax statements – should be written by someone who follows certain standards that are less easily automated: checking sources, verifying claims, respecting privacy, etc. Knowing that a human being wrote the text thus makes it plausible – albeit does not guarantee – that these standards are respected. For schools and universities, the function is of course to make sure that the student who receives the grade also wrote the text. The rising demands to make sure that the distinction between human and algorithm always be guaranteed – through legal requirements, detection software, etc. – essentially demand that the current relation of humans and technology in each of these contexts and the function it performs stay the same. This may be an important demand in some cases. In others, however, algorithms like ChatGPT can be an occasion to reflect possible changes in subject positions and possible changes in human tasks. This reflection – decidedly – has nothing to do with the promethean or perfectionist ideas that many tie to AI (Weil 2023).[2] Rather, it is a situated rethinking of some of the relations that make up particular forms of subjectivity. For example, ChatGPT could lead us to question (again) why researching and reproducing or summarizing information still is the central task in so many exams in both schools and universities. Both have been important intellectual techniques that, however, have already fundamentally changed through the internet and digital media. Emphasizing the transfer of knowledge, its application, and creative use in exams and term papers would not only make cheating with Chatbots much more difficult but also adhere to demands that pedagogic theory has been making for decades – and the economy of schools and universities often counteracts.

In many other areas, ChatGPT serves as a reminder that a lot of texts that are produced by humans actually do not require much reflection or intelligence but are in fact repetitive creations by rote. Algorithmic or "robot journalism" for quite some time already produces such texts for sports results or financial news and increasingly other fields as well (Kotenidis and Veglis 2021). In other areas, such as cultural or political journalism, however, the author also functions as a possibility to identify positions and standpoints. Regular viewers, readers, and listeners learn to place different journalists and their points of view. Here naming and marking the author – as is done so far, remains important.

Such questions are never only questions of the quality of the text, but need to consider the larger changes in situatedness. As discussed in Chapter 3, p. 30, Lucas Introna argues that plagiarism detection software is mainly aimed at ascertaining the economic value of a degree (Introna 2016). Similar thoughts would hold for a chatbot detection software. In journalism but also administration, a related question would be what happens if in fact a

---

2 The very fact that ChatGPT inspires such thought illustrates again the limited view of humanity that informs these discourses. A truly human-like algorithm tasked to write a term paper would probably not duly spit out usable text but ask: if I help you pass the exam, what do I get?

significant part of text production can be automated. Will this be used to lay off persons? Or do they get new tasks, new liberties, and more time for what they do?

A further aspect of this situatedness is the emphasis that algorithms and particular AI currently get. Students can already hand in papers written by others – and do so. Regularly texts that are produced in journalism fail to meet standards and contain errors, misinformation, etc. Scientific papers need to be redacted or withdrawn due to mistakes. AI can now produce entirely made-up texts that however sound very credible. Human beings can do that also – and do it quite often. In consequence, curtailing dis-information, misinformation, and manipulative content, particularly on social media, is already an important challenge. Whichever means will be effective to do so, most probably will work regardless of whether the text was written by a manipulative human being or by an algorithm. This does not mean that there is no problem. In a sense, the problem is larger. In a world where an American president can just make arbitrary claims about the number of people present at his inauguration and is believed by a substantial amount of people, despite photographic evidence to the contrary, an AI-generated picture that supports the claim would most probably change the dynamics but not create a novel problem.

Finally, human authorship does not simply cease to matter for algorith-mically generated content - if it is considered in its situated function rather than as human creation. In 2018, Christie's auctioned an art piece called "Edward de Belamy" for 432,500 US dollars. It was presented as "created by an AI" (Vincent 2018). Yet, in the public discussion, most of the time it was described as produced by a French art group called "Obvious" (Alleyne 2018). This group quickly was accused of not giving credit to the author of the code they have been using, an artist and programmer called Robbie Barrat (Vincent 2018). On the other hand, it was Obvious who decided to print an image generated by Barrat's algorithm on canvas, sign it with the mathematical loss function they had used in the training algorithm for a more technical aura, and offer the result at Christie's. Similarly, in late 2022 and early 2023, thousands of people around the globe had fun with the newly available image generators, such as Dall-E, Stable Diffusion, or Midjourney. Images created by these algorithms were all over the web. Yet, the images that established photographers and artists such as Laurie Simmons or Charlie Engman produced using these algorithms made it into magazines and exhibitions. Of course, that is an old issue. Millions of people take photographs but only a few become celebrated photographers. Generally, the question of what it means to be an artist in the contemporary world is at least as old as Duchamps' famous fountain/urinal. This is not the place to discuss these questions. I just evoke them to show that the situat-edness of practices that are structured by norms and conventions of authorship does not change ad hoc by the introduction of algorithms. Of course, new technologies have the potential to fundamentally unsettle and displace these conventions, as photography and film did – although it remains to be seen if algorithmic content generation will have such far-reaching consequences. Yet, even if they do, these consequences will be quite different in differing situations, depending on existing norms and subject positions, their economic setting, and the different functions that are tied to notions such as author, creator, writer, etc. These will be iterations of known questions: how does automation change work? What qualifies a good student? How can public discourse be inclusive and just? This makes these questions not a bit less difficult. Yet, disregarding their situatedness and reducing them to general issues of technology vs. or with humankind will make a successful answer highly unlikely.

9
CONCLUSION

This book has presented a great number of various details: programming languages and paradigms, organizational principles in data centers, patterns on disks, data sets, and more. This follows the view that algorithms can only be insufficiently understood with too abstract and generalizing notions or first or fundamental principles such as computability or programmability. At the same time, all of this detail is not meant to just show how things are instead. All of the examples that I have discussed have been chosen because they relate to a more general, more abstract, and more sustained aspect of algorithms than just the individual case – but still, aspects understood in a situated manner. The general approach that I have applied throughout this book, considering the co-constitution of algorithms and their complements, of the abstract and the concrete, thus puts into practice the situated form of inquiry that I have developed in Chapter 3 with recourse to Barad, Haraway, and Foucault. Discussing all the details presented in this book as part of a co-constitutive relation aims at understanding different forms of situatedness – not in order to exhaust them but to sidestep or suspend existing concepts and distinctions that structure them. This includes historical situatedness: I discuss the current state of algorithms and relevant parts of its genealogy. It also includes admitting that such suspension and sidestepping can only ever be partial and cannot escape its own situatedness. Thus, the aims of this discussion are also partial and, in the sense that I describe in Chapter 3, political. It aims to acknowledge the plurality of those involved and to enable new connections to the political issues that concern them or should concern them: exclusion, discrimination, labor conditions, environmental impact, etc. Absent generalizing theories of algorithms as installments of

DOI: 10.4324/9781003299851-11

instrumental rationality, late modern capitalism, cybernetization, etc. this means to bridge the technical details and the political.

In this sense, discussions in this book have sidestepped common notions of bias by introducing the concept of citation to relate even an assumed bias-free machine learning algorithm to the concept of discrimination. It has suspended the usual discussions of efficiency and availability in tracing the algorithmically constituted administration of locality in data centers to relate it to the geo-politics and environmental politics of location. It has re-contextualized debates about the features of programming languages and paradigms to relate it to claims to communities and the politics of an inside and outside. It has situated common distinctions between human and algorithms to show their legit-imizing force for questionable politics. And so on.

This is, inherently, an open-ended endeavor – and one that can best be done in interaction. Thus, whoever wants to join, discuss, or contend: please be in touch. Ways to contact me are all over the internet, one is here: tobias.matzner@upb.de

REFERENCES

All URLs last accessed 24 March 2023.

Agre, Philip E. 1994. "Surveillance and Capture: Two Models of Privacy." *The Information Society* 10 (2): 101–127.

Ahmed, S. 2007. "A Phenomenology of Whiteness." *Feminist Theory* 8 (2): 149–168.

Ahmed, Sara. 2008. "Open Forum Imaginary Prohibitions: Some Preliminary Remarks on the Founding Gestures of the 'New Materialism'." *European Journal of Women's Studies* 15 (1): 23–39.

Albergotti, Reed, and Drew Harwell. 2020. "Apple and Google Are Building a Virus-Tracking System. Health Officials Say It Will Be Practically Useless." *Washington Post*, May 15, 2020. https://www.washingtonpost.com/technology/2020/05/15/app-apple-google-virus/

Alcoff, Linda Martín. 2006. *Visible Identities: Race, Gender, and the Self*. Studies in Feminist Philosophy. New York: Oxford University Press.

Alcoff, Linda Martín. 2015. *The Future of Whiteness*. Cambridge: Polity.

Algorithmwatch. 2022. "Busted Internet Myth: Algorithms Are Always Neutral." *AlgorithmWatch*. 2022. https://algorithmwatch.org/en/busted-internet-myth-algorithms-are-always-neutral/

Alleyne, Allyssia. 2018. "A Sign of Things to Come? AI-Produced Artwork Sells for \$433K, Smashing Expectations." *CNN*. October 25, 2018. https://www.cnn.com/style/article/obvious-ai-art-christies-auction-smart-creativity/index.html

Althusser, Louis. 1977. "Ideology and Ideological State Apparatuses." In *Lenin and Philosophy and Other Essays*, translated by Ben Brewster, 2nd ed. London: NLB.

Aly, Götz, and Karl Heinz Roth. 2004. *The Nazi Census: Identification and Control in the Third Reich*, translated by Edwin Black and Assenka Oksiloff. Philadelphia: Temple University Press.

Amazon Mechanical Turk. 2019. "Tutorial: Understanding Requirements and Qualifications." *Medium*. May 29, 2019. https://blog.mturk.com/tutorial-understanding-requirements-and-qualifications-99a26069fba2

Amoore, Louise. 2020. *Cloud Ethics: Algorithms and the Attributes of Ourselves and Others*. Durham: Duke University Press.

Angwin, Julia, and Jeff Larson. 2016. "Machine Bias." *Text/html. ProPublica*. May 23, 2016. https://www.propublica.org/article/machine-bias-risk-assessments-in-criminal-sentencing

Arendt, Hannah. 1998. *The Human Condition*. 2nd ed. Chicago: University of Chicago Press.

Arora, Payal. 2019. "General Data Protection Regulation—A Global Standard? Privacy Futures, Digital Activism, and Surveillance Cultures in the Global South." *Surveillance & Society* 17 (5): 717–725.

Atanasoski, Neda, and Kalindi Vora. 2019. *Surrogate Humanity: Race, Robots, and the Politics of Technological Futures*. Durham: Duke University Press.

Awad, Edmond, Sohan Dsouza, Richard Kim, Jonathan Schulz, Joseph Henrich, Azim Shariff, Jean-François Bonnefon, and Iyad Rahwan. 2018. "The Moral Machine Experiment." *Nature* 563 (7729): 59–64.

Backus, John. 1978. "Can Programming Be Liberated from the von Neumann Style?: A Functional Style and Its Algebra of Programs." *Communications of the ACM* 21 (8): 613–641.

Barad, Karen. 2007. *Meeting the Universe Halfway*. Durham: Duke University Press.

Barlow, John Perry. 2016. "A Declaration of the Independence of Cyberspace." *Electronic Frontier Foundation*. January 20, 2016. https://www.eff.org/de/cyberspace-independence

Baum, Leonard E, Ted Petrie, George Soules, and Norman Weiss. 1970. "A Maximization Technique Occurring in the Statistical Analysis of Probabilistic Functions of Markov Chains." *The Annals of Mathematical Statistics* 41 (1): 164–171.

Bender, Emily M., Timnit Gebru, Angelina McMillan-Major, and Shmargaret Shmitchell. 2021. "On the Dangers of Stochastic Parrots: Can Language Models Be Too Big?." In *Proceedings of the 2021 ACM Conference on Fairness, Accountability, and Transparency*, 610–623.

Benjamin, Ruha. 2019. *Race after Technology: Abolitionist Tools for the New Jim Code*. Medford: Polity.

Berry, David M. 2011. *The Philosophy of Software Code and Mediation in the Digital Age*. Basingstoke; New York: Palgrave Macmillan.

"BGP Hijacking." 2022. In *Wikipedia*. https://en.wikipedia.org/w/index.php?title=BGP_hijacking&oldid=1111742724

Binns, Reuben. 2017. "Fairness in Machine Learning: Lessons from Political Philosophy." *ArXiv Preprint ArXiv:1712.03586*.

Bishop, C. M. 2006. *Pattern Recognition and Machine Learning*. New York: Springer.

Blanchette, Jean-François. 2011. "A Material History of Bits." *Journal of the American Society for Information Science and Technology* 62 (6): 1042–1057.

Böhm, Corrado, and Giuseppe Jacopini. 1966. "Flow Diagrams, Turing Machines and Languages with Only Two Formation Rules." *Communications of the ACM* 9 (5): 366–371.

Bolter, J. David. 2001. *Writing Space: Computers, Hypertext, and the Remediation of Print*. 2nd ed. Mahwah: Lawrence Erlbaum Associates.

Bowker, Geoffrey C. 1993. "How to Be Universal: Some Cybernetic Strategies, 1943–70." *Social Studies of Science* 23 (1): 107–127.

Bowker, Geoffrey C., and Susan Leigh Star. 2000. *Sorting Things Out – Classification and Its Consequences*. Cambridge: MIT Press.

Bowyer, Kevin W., Michael C. King, Walter J. Scheirer, and Kushal Vangara. 2020. "The 'Criminality From Face' Illusion." *IEEE Transactions on Technology and Society* 1 (4): 175–183.

Braden, Robert T. 1989. "Requirements for Internet Hosts - Communication Layers." Request for Comments RFC 1122. Internet Engineering Task Force.

Braidotti, Rosi, and Timotheus Vermeulen. 2014. "Borrowed Energy." *Frieze* 165. http://www.frieze.com/issue/article/borrowed-energy/

Brey, Philip. 2005. "The Epistemology and Ontology of Human-Computer Interaction." *Minds and Machines* 15 (3–4): 383–398.

Brown, Tom B., Benjamin Mann, Nick Ryder, Melanie Subbiah, Jared Kaplan, Prafulla Dhariwal, Arvind Neelakantan, et al. 2020. "Language Models Are Few-Shot Learners." arXiv: 2005.14165.

Browne, Simone. 2010. "Digital Epidermalization: Race, Identity and Biometrics." *Critical Sociology* 36 (1): 131–150.

Browne, Simone. 2015. *Dark Matters: On the Surveillance of Blackness*. Durham: Duke University Press.

Bucher, Taina. 2017. "The Algorithmic Imaginary: Exploring the Ordinary Affects of Facebook Algorithms." *Information, Communication & Society* 20 (1): 30–44.

Bucher, Taina, and Anne Helmond. 2017. "The Affordances of Social Media Platforms." In *The SAGE Handbook of Social Media*, edited by Jean Burgess, Alice Marwick, and Thomas Poell, 223–253. London; New York: Sage Publications.

Buolamwini, Joy, and Timnit Gebru. 2018. "Gender Shades: Intersectional Accuracy Disparities in Commercial Gender Classification." In *Conference on Fairness, Accountability and Transparency*, 77–91. PMLR. http://proceedings.mlr.press/v81/buolamwini18a.html

Butler, Judith. 1993. *Bodies That Matter: On the Discursive Limits of "Sex."* New York: Routledge.

Butler, Judith. 2005. *Giving an Account of Oneself*. New York: Fordham University Press.

Campolo, Alex, Madelyn Sanfilippo, Meredith Whittaker, and Kate Crawford. 2017. "AI Now 2017 Report." New York: AI Now Institute.

Cantor, Georg. 1883. "Ueber unendliche, lineare Punktmannichfaltigkeiten." *Mathematische Annalen* 21 (4): 545–591.

Casilli, Antonio A. 2017. "Digital Labor Studies Go Global: Toward a Digital Decolonial Turn." *International Journal of Communication* 11: 3934–3954.

Casper, Monica J. 1994. "Reframing and Grounding Nonhuman Agency: What Makes a Fetus an Agent." *American Behavioral Scientist* 37 (6): 839–856.

Cheney-Lippold, John. 2011. "A New Algorithmic Identity: Soft Biopolitics and the Modulation of Control." *Theory, Culture & Society* 28 (6): 164–181.

Chun, Wendy Hui Kyong. 2004. "On Software, or the Persistence of Visual Knowledge." *Grey Room* 18: 26–51.

Chun, Wendy Hui Kyong. 2008. "On "Sourcery," or Code as Fetish." *Configurations* 16 (3): 299–324.

Chun, Wendy Hui Kyong. 2016. *Updating to Remain the Same: Habitual New Media*. Cambridge: MIT Press.

Chun, Wendy Hui Kyong. 2018. "Queerying Homophily." In *Pattern Discrimination*, edited by Clemens Apprich, Florian Cramer, Wendy Hui Kyong Chun, and Hito Steyerl, 59–98. Germany: meson press.

Chun, Wendy Hui Kyong, and Alex Barnett. 2021. *Discriminating Data: Correlation, Neighborhoods, and the New Politics of Recognition*. Cambridge: MIT Press.

Coleman, E Gabriella. 2012. *Coding Freedom: The Ethics and Aesthetics of Hacking*. Princeton University Press.

Church, Alonzo. 1936. An unsolvable problem of elementary number theory. *American Journal of Mathematics*, 58: 345. 10.2307/2371045

Confessore, Nicholas, and Danny Hakim. 2017. "Data Firm Says 'Secret Sauce' Aided Trump; Many Scoff - The New York Times." *New York Times*. March 6, 2017. https://www.nytimes.com/2017/03/06/us/politics/cambridge-analytica.html

Conway, Melvin E. 1968. "How Do Committees Invent?" http://www.melconway.com/research/committees.html.

Cover, Rob. 2012. "Performing and Undoing Identity Online: Social Networking, Identity Theories and the Incompatibility of Online Profiles and Friendship Regimes." *Convergence: The International Journal of Research into New Media Technologies* 18 (2): 177–193.

Cramer, Florian. 2018. "Crapularity Hermeneutics: Interpretation as the Blind Spot of Analytics, Artificial Intelligence, and Other Algorithmic Producers of the Postapocalyptic Present." In *Pattern Discrimination*, edited by Clemens Apprich, Wendy Hui Kyong Chun, Florian Cramer, and Hito Steyerl, 23–58. Lüneburg: meson press.

Crenshaw, Kimberlé Williams. 1995. "Mapping the Margins: Intersectionality, Identity Politics, and Violence Against Women of Color." In *Critical Race Theory – The Key Writings That Formed the Movement*, edited by Kimberlé Crenshaw, Neil Gotanda, Gary Peller, and Kendall Thomas, 357–383. The New Press.

Daston, Lorraine. 2019. "The Coup d'Oeil: On a Mode of Understanding." *Critical Inquiry* 45 (2): 307–331.

Dean, Jeffrey, and Sanjay Ghemawat. 2004. "MapReduce: Simplified Data Processing on Large Clusters." In *OSDI'04: Sixth Symposium on Operating System Design and Implementation*, 137–150. San Francisco.

Decker, Gero, Oliver Kopp, and Alistair Barros. 2008. "An Introduction to Service Choreographies (Servicechoreographien – Eine Einführung)." *It - Information Technology* 50 (2): 122–127.

Deleuze, Gilles. 1992. "Postscript on the Societies of Control." *October* 59: 3–7.

Deng, Jia, Wei Dong, Richard Socher, Li-Jia Li, Kai Li, and Li Fei-Fei. 2009. "ImageNet: A Large-Scale Hierarchical Image Database." In *2009 IEEE Conference on Computer Vision and Pattern Recognition*, 248–255.

Denham, Elisabeth. 2020. "Letter RE: ICO Investigation into Use of Personal Information and Political Influence." 2020. https://ico.org.uk/media/action-weve-taken/2618383/20201002_ico-o-ed-l-rtl-0181_to-julian-knight-mp.pdf

Diakopoulos, Nicholas. 2015. "Algorithmic Accountability." *Digital Journalism* 3 (3): 398–415.

D'Ignazio, Catherine, and Lauren F. Klein. 2020. *Data Feminism*. Cambridge: MIT Press.

Dijkstra, Edsger W. 1968. "A Case against the GO TO Statement." http://www.cs.utexas.edu/users/EWD/ewd02xx/EWD215.PDF

Dijkstra, Edsger W. 1970. "Notes on Structured Programming." http://www.cs. utexas.edu/users/EWD/ewd02xx/EWD249.PDF

Dourish, Paul. 2015. "Protocols, Packets, and Proximity - The Materiality of Internet Routing." In *Signal Traffic: Critical Studies of Media Infrastructures*, edited by Lisa Parks and Nicole Starosielski, 184–204. The Geopolitics of Information. Urbana: University of Illinois Press.

Dourish, Paul. 2016. "Algorithms and Their Others: Algorithmic Culture in Context." *Big Data & Society* 3 (2): 1–11.

Drucker, Johanna. 2011. "Humanities Approaches to Graphical Display." *Digital Humanities Quarterly* 005 (1).

Dyer, Richard. 1997. *White*. London; New York: Routledge.

Ensmenger, Nathan. 2018. "The Environmental History of Computing." *Technology and Culture* 59 (4): 7–33.

Eubanks, Virginia. 2017. *Automating Inequality: How High-Tech Tools Profile, Police, and Punish the Poor*. New York: St. Martin's Press.

European Union Agency for Fundamental Rights. 2022. *Bias in Algorithms: Artificial Intelligence and Discrimination*. Luxembourg: Publications Office of the European Union. https://data.europa.eu/doi/10.2811/536044.

Evans, Leonard. 2008. "Death in Traffic: Why Are the Ethical Issues Ignored?" *Studies in Ethics, Law, and Technology* 2 (1): 1–11.

Flick, Catherine. 2016. "Informed Consent and the Facebook Emotional Manipulation Study." *Research Ethics* 12 (1): 14–28.

Foot, Philippa. 1967. "The Problem of Abortion and the Doctrine of the Double Effect." *Oxford Review* 5: 5–15.

Foucault, Michel. 1977. *Discipline and Punish: The Birth of the Prison*. New York: Vintage.

Foucault, Michel. 2011. *The Government of Self and Others: Lectures at the Collège de France, 1982–1983*, edited by Frédéric Gros. Basingstoke: Palgrave Macmillan.

Fredman, Sandra. 2016. "Substantive Equality Revisited." *International Journal of Constitutional Law* 14 (3): 712–738.

Friedman, Batya, and Helen Nissenbaum. 1996. "Bias in Computer Systems." *ACM Transactions on Information Systems* 14 (3): 330–347.

Fuchs, Christian. 2022. *Digital Capitalism*. Media, Communication and Society, volume 3. Abingdon; New York: Routledge.

Fuller, Matthew, ed. 2008. *Software Studies: A Lexicon*. Leonardo Books. Cambridge: MIT Press.

Galison, Peter. 1994. "The Ontology of the Enemy: Norbert Wiener and the Cybernetic Vision." *Critical Inquiry* 21 (1): 228–266.

Galloway, Alexander R. 2006a. *Protocol: How Control Exists after Decentralization*. MIT Press. Cambridge: MIT Press.

Galloway, Alexander R. 2006b. "Language Wants To Be Overlooked: On Software and Ideology." *Journal of Visual Culture* 5 (3): 315–331.

Galloway, Alexander R. 2012. *The Interface Effect*. Cambridge, UK; Malden: Polity.

Gillespie, Tarleton. 2012. "Can an Algorithm Be Wrong?" Limn. February 2, 2012. https://limn.it/articles/can-an-algorithm-be-wrong/

Gillespie, Tarleton. 2014. "The Relevance of Algorithms." In *Media Technologies*, edited by Tarleton Gillespie, Pablo Boczkowski, and Kirsten Foot, 167–194. Cambridge: MIT Press.

Gillespie, Tarleton. 2018. *Custodians of the Internet: Platforms, Content Moderation, and the Hidden Decisions That Shape Social Media.* New Haven: Yale University Press.

Gödel, Kurt. 1931. "Über formal unentscheidbare Sätze der Principia Mathematica und verwandter Systeme I." *Monatshefte für Mathematik und Physik* 38 (1): 173–198.

Google. 2023. "Firebase." 2023. https://firebase.google.com/

Greenlee, Loren. 2023. "How Parts Pairing Kills Independent Repair." *iFixit.* February 19, 2023. https://de.ifixit.com/News/69320/how-parts-pairing-kills-independent-repair

Greenwald, Glenn. 2014. *No Place to Hide: Edward Snowden, the NSA, and the U.S. Surveillance State.* New York: Metropolitan Books.

Haraway, Donna. 1988. "Situated Knowledges: The Science Question in Feminism and the Privilege of Partial Perspective." *Feminist Studies* 14 (3): 575–599.

Haraway, Donna. 1991. "A Cyborg Manifesto – Science, Technology, and Socialist-Feminism in the Late Twentieth Century." In *Simians, Cyborgs and Women: The Reinvention of Nature.* New York: Routledge.

Harris, John, and Vicky White. 2018. "Responsibilization." In *A Dictionary of Social Work and Social Care*, edited by Vicky White and John Harris. Oxford: Oxford University Press.

Hayles, N. Katherine. 1999. *How We Became Posthuman.* Chicago: University of Chicago Press.

Hazas, Mike, and Lisa P. Nathan, eds. 2019. *Digital Technology and Sustainability: Engaging the Paradox.* Abingdon: Routledge.

Heath, Alex. 2015. "Spotify Is Getting Unbelievably Good at Picking Music — Here's an inside Look at How." *Business Insider.* September 3, 2015. https://www.businessinsider.com/inside-spotify-and-the-future-of-music-streaming

Helmond, Anne, David B. Nieborg, and Fernando N. van der Vlist. 2019. "Facebook's Evolution: Development of a Platform-as-Infrastructure." *Internet Histories* 3 (2): 123–146.

Helm, Paula, and Matzner, Tobias. 2023. "Co-addictive Human–machine Configurations: Relating Critical Design and Algorithm Studies to Medical-psychiatric Research on 'problematic Internet use'". *New Media & Society.* 10. 1177/14614448231165916

Hilbert, David, and Wilhelm Ackermann. 1928. *Grundzüge Der Theoretischen Logik.* Berlin: Verlag von Julius Springer.

Hirschman, Dan. 2017. "Artificial Intelligence Discovers Gayface. Sigh." *Scatterplot* (blog). September 11, 2017. https://scatter.wordpress.com/2017/09/10/guest-post-artificial-intelligence-discovers-gayface-sigh/

Hollerith, Herman. 2020. "An Electric Tabulation System." 2020. http://www.columbia.edu/cu/computinghistory/hh/

Holt, Jennifer, and Patrick Vonderau. 2015. "Where the Internet Lives - Data Centers as Cloud Infrastructure." In *Signal Traffic: Critical Studies of Media Infrastructures*, edited by Lisa Parks and Nicole Starosielski, 71–93. Urbana: University of Illinois Press.

Hopper, Grace Murray. 1952. "The Education of a Computer." In *Proceedings of the 1952 ACM National Meeting (Pittsburgh) on - ACM '52*, 243–249. Pittsburgh: ACM Press.

Hopper, Grace Murray. 1978. "Keynote Address." In *History of Programming Languages*, 7–20. New York: Association for Computing Machinery.

Hunter, Tatum, and Gerrit De Vynck. 2021. "The 'Most Serious' Security Breach Ever Is Unfolding Right Now. Here's What You Need to Know." *Washington Post*. December 20, 2021. https://www.washingtonpost.com/technology/2021/12/20/log4j-hack-vulnerability-java/

Husberg, Nisse, and Jouko Seppänen. 1974. "ANALITIK: Principal Features of the Language and Its Implementation." *ACM SIGSAM Bulletin* 8 (3): 24–25.

Imana, Basileal, Aleksandra Korolova, and John Heidemann. 2021. "Auditing for Discrimination in Algorithms Delivering Job Ads." In *Proceedings of the Web Conference 2021*, 3767–3778. WWW '21. New York: Association for Computing Machinery.

Introna, Lucas D. 2016. "Algorithms, Governance, and Governmentality: On Governing Academic Writing." *Science, Technology & Human Values* 41 (1): 17–49.

Ipeirotis, Panagiotis G., Foster Provost, and Jing Wang. 2010. "Quality Management on Amazon Mechanical Turk." In *Proceedings of the ACM SIGKDD Workshop on Human Computation*, 64–67.

Irani, Lilly. 2015. "The Cultural Work of Microwork." *New Media & Society* 17 (5): 720–739.

ISO. 2000. "ISO/IEC 7498-1:1994." https://www.iso.org/standard/20269.html

JafariNaimi, Nassim. 2018. "Our Bodies in the Trolley's Path, or Why Self-Driving Cars Must *Not* Be Programmed to Kill." *Science, Technology, & Human Values* 43 (2): 302–323.

Jelinek, Frederick. 2005. "Some of My Best Friends Are Linguists." *Language Resources and Evaluation* 39 (1): 25–34.

Jelinek, Frederick. 2009. "The Dawn of Statistical ASR and MT." *Computational Linguistics* 35 (4): 483–494.

Jelinek, Frederick, Lalith Bahl, and Robert Mercer. 1975. "Design of a Linguistic Statistical Decoder for the Recognition of Continuous Speech." *IEEE Transactions on Information Theory* 21 (3): 250–256.

Jiahao, Chen. 2016. "'This Guy's Arrogance Takes Your Breath Away.'" *Medium* (blog). May 30, 2016. https://medium.com/@acidflask/this-guys-arrogance-takes-your-breath-away-5b903624ca5f

Kalender, Ute. 2023. "Queer-Crip Perspectives on the Cyborg Figure in the Context of Artificial Intelligence." In *Queer Reflections of AI: Uncertain Intelligences*, edited by Michael Klipphahn-Karge, Ann-Kathrin Koster, and Sara Morais dos Santos Bruss. London: Routledge.

Kelly, Samantha Murphy. 2023. "ChatGPT Passes Exams from Law and Business Schools | CNN Business." *CNN*. January 26, 2023. https://www.cnn.com/2023/01/26/tech/chatgpt-passes-exams/index.html

Kirschenbaum, Matthew G. 2008. *Mechanisms: New Media and the Forensic Imagination*. Cambridge: MIT Press.

Kitchin, Rob. 2014. "Big Data, New Epistemologies and Paradigm Shifts." *Big Data & Society* 1 (1): 1–12.

Kitchin, Rob. 2017. "Thinking Critically about and Researching Algorithms." *Information, Communication & Society* 20 (1): 14–29.

Kittler, Friedrich. 1992. "There Is No Software." *Stanford Literature Review* 9 (1): 81–90.

Kleinberg, Jon, Sendhil Mullainathan, and Manish Raghavan. 2016. "Inherent Trade-Offs in the Fair Determination of Risk Scores." *ArXiv:1609.05807.* http://arxiv.org/abs/1609.05807

Knuth, Donald Ervin. 1997. *The Art of Computer Programming.* 3rd ed. Reading: Addison-Wesley.

Kocher, Paul, Jann Horn, Anders Fogh, Daniel Genkin, Daniel Gruss, Werner Haas, Mike Hamburg, et al. 2019. "Spectre Attacks: Exploiting Speculative Execution." In *40th IEEE Symposium on Security and Privacy (S&P'19).*

Kotenidis, Efthimis, and Andreas Veglis. 2021. "Algorithmic Journalism—Current Applications and Future Perspectives." *Journalism and Media* 2 (2): 244–257.

Kwan, Campbell. 2021. "Apple Settles Lawsuit to Allow Developers to Use Payment Systems Outside of App Store." *ZDNet.* August 26, 2021. https://www.zdnet.com/article/apple-settles-lawsuit-to-allow-developers-to-use-payment-systems-outside-of-app-store/

Laat, Paul B. de. 2019. "The Disciplinary Power of Predictive Algorithms: A Foucauldian Perspective." *Ethics and Information Technology* 21(4): 319–329.

Lash, Scott. 2007. "Power after Hegemony: Cultural Studies in Mutation?" *Theory, Culture & Society* 24 (3): 55–78.

Leith, Douglas J. 2021. "Mobile Handset Privacy: Measuring the Data Ios and Android Send to Apple and Google." In *Security and Privacy in Communication Networks: 17th EAI International Conference, SecureComm 2021, Virtual Event, September 6–9, 2021, Proceedings, Part II 17*, 231–251. Springer.

Lemke, Thomas. 2021. *The Government of Things: Foucault and the New Materialism's.* New York: NYU Press.

Lessig, Lawrence. 2006. *Code Version 2.0.* New York: Basic Books.

Li, Xiaochang. 2017. "Divination Engines: A Media History of Text Prediction." PhD Thesis, New York University.

"LibreSignal Issue #37." 2016. *GitHub.* 2016. https://github.com/LibreSignal/LibreSignal/issues/37.

Lipp, Moritz, Michael Schwarz, Daniel Gruss, Thomas Prescher, Werner Haas, Anders Fogh, Jann Horn, et al. 2018. "Meltdown: Reading Kernel Memory from User Space." In *27th USENIX Security Symposium (USENIX Security 18).*

Little, Gregg, Lydia B. Chilton, Max Goldman, and Robert C. Miller. 2010. "TurKit: Human Computation Algorithms On Mechanical Turk." In Proceedings of the 23nd annual ACM symposium on User interface software and technology (UIST '10), 57–66. New York: ACM.

Lyon, David. 2003. *Surveillance As Social Sorting: Privacy, Risk, and Digital Discrimination.* London: Routledge.

Lyon, David. 2014. "Surveillance, Snowden, and Big Data: Capacities, Consequences, Critique." *Big Data & Society* 1 (2): 1–13.

MacKenzie, Donald. 2018. "'Making', 'Taking' and the Material Political Economy of Algorithmic Trading." *Economy and Society* 47 (4): 501–523.

MacKenzie, Donald A. 2021. *Trading at the Speed of Light: How Ultrafast Algorithms Are Transforming Financial Markets.* Princeton: Princeton University Press.

Mann, Monique, and Tobias Matzner. 2019. "Challenging Algorithmic Profiling: The Limits of Data Protection and Anti-Discrimination in Responding to Emergent Discrimination." *Big Data & Society* 6 (2): 1–11.

Manovich, Lev. 2001. *The Language of New Media*. Leonardo. Cambridge: MIT Press.

Marlinspike, Moxie. 2014. "The New TextSecure: Privacy Beyond SMS." *Signal Blog*. February 24, 2014. https://signal.org/blog/the-new-textsecure/

Mateescu, Alexandra, Douglas Brunton, Alex Rosenblat, Desmond Patton, Zachary Gold, and Danah Boyd. 2015. "Social Media Surveillance and Law Enforcement." *Data Civil Rights* 27: 2015–2027.

Matzner, Tobias. 2016. "Beyond Data as Representation: The Performativity of Big Data in Surveillance." *Surveillance & Society* 14 (2): 197–210.

Matzner, Tobias. 2017. "Opening Black Boxes Is Not Enough – Data-Based Surveillance In Discipline and Punish And Today." *Foucault Studies* 23: 27–45.

Matzner, Tobias. 2018. "Surveillance as a Critical Paradigm for Big Data?" In *The Politics and Policies of Big Data: Big Data, Big Brother?*, edited by Ann Rudinow Saetnan, Ingrid Schneider, and Nicola Green, 68–86. Abingdon; New York: Routledge.

Matzner, Tobias. 2019a. "Plural, situated subjects in the critique of artificial intelligence." In *The Democratization of Artificial Intelligence*, edited by Andreas Sudmann, 109–121. Bielefeld: transcript.

Matzner, Tobias. 2019b. "The Human Is Dead – Long Live the Algorithm! Human-Algorithmic Ensembles and Liberal Subjectivity." *Theory, Culture & Society* 36 (2): 123–144.

Matzner, Tobias. 2022. "Algorithms as Complementary Abstractions." *New Media & Society*, February, online first. 10.1177/14614448221078604

Matzner, Tobias. 2023. "Understanding the Affective Impact of Algorithmic Publics." In *Affective Formation of Publics: Places, Networks, and Media*, edited by Margreth Lünenborg and Birgitt Röttger-Rössler. London: Routledge.

Matzner, Tobias, Philipp K Masur, Carsten Ochs, and Thilo von Pape. 2016. "Do-It-Yourself Data Protection—Empowerment or Burden?" In *Data Protection on the Move*, edited by Gutwirth Serge, Ronald Leenes and Paul De Hert, 277–305. Dordrecht: Springer.

Matzner, Tobias, and Carsten Ochs. 2019. "Privacy." *Internet Policy Review* 8 (4).

McCulloch, Warren S., and Walter Pitts. 1943. "A Logical Calculus of the Ideas Immanent in Nervous Activity." *The Bulletin of Mathematical Biophysics* 5 (4): 115–133.

McPherson, Tara. 2012. "Why Are the Digital Humanities So White? Or Thinking the Histories of Race and Computation." *Debates in the Digital Humanities*. 2012. https://dhdebates.gc.cuny.edu/read/untitled-88c11800-9446-469b-a3be-3fdb36bfbd1e/section/20df8acd-9ab9-4f35-8a5d-e91aa5f4a0ea#ch09

Mills, Charles W. 2011. *The Racial Contract*. Ithaca: Cornell Univ. Press.

Mitchell, Tom M. 1997. *Machine Learning*. New York: McGraw-Hill.

Mitra, Tanushree, C.J. Hutto, and Eric Gilbert. 2015. "Comparing Person- and Process-Centric Strategies for Obtaining Quality Data on Amazon Mechanical Turk." In *Proceedings of the 33rd Annual ACM Conference on Human Factors in Computing Systems*, 1345–1354. Seoul: ACM.

Moore, Gordon E. 1965. "The Experts Look Ahead. Cramming More Components onto Integrated Circuits." *Electronics* 38 (8): 114–119.

Mühlhoff, Rainer. 2020. "Human-Aided Artificial Intelligence: Or, How to Run Large Computations in Human Brains? Toward a Media Sociology of Machine Learning." *New Media & Society* 22 (10): 1868–1884.

Munn, Luke. 2018. *Ferocious Logics: Unmaking the Algorithm*. Lüneburg: meson press.

Naderi, Babak. 2018. "Who Are the Crowdworkers?" In *Motivation of Workers on Microtask Crowdsourcing Platforms*, edited by Babak Naderi, 17–27. Cham: Springer International Publishing.

Nakamoto, Satoshi. 2008. "Bitcoin Whitepaper." https://bitcoin.org/bitcoin.pdf

Nakamura, Lisa. 2010. "Race and Identity in Digital Media." In *Mass Media and Society*, edited by James Curran und Michael Gurevitch, 336–347. ed. London: Hodder Arnold.

Naur, Peter, and Brian Randell. 1969. "Software Engineering: Report of a Conference Sponsored by the Nato Science Committee, Garmisch, Germany, 7th-11th October 1968."

Negroponte, Nicholas. 1995. *Being Digital*. New York: Knopf.

Neubert, Christoph. 2015. "'The Tail on the Hard- Ware Dog': Historical Articulations of Computing Machinery, Software, and Services." In *There Is No Software, There Are Just Services*, edited by Irina Kaldrack and Martina Leeker. Lüneburg: meson press.

Newell, Allen, and Herbert A. Simon. 1976. "Computer Science as Empirical Inquiry: Symbols and Search." *Communications of the ACM* 19 (3): 113–126.

Noble, Safiya Umoja. 2018. *Algorithms of Oppression: How Search Engines Reinforce Racism*. New York: NYU Press.

Nyckel, Thomas. 2022. *Der agentielle Realismus Karen Barads: eine medienwissenschaftliche Relektüre und ihre Anwendung auf das Digitale*. Bielefeld: transcript.

Nyholm, Sven, and Jilles Smids. 2016. "The Ethics of Accident-Algorithms for Self-Driving Cars: An Applied Trolley Problem?" *Ethical Theory and Moral Practice* 19 (5): 1275–1289.

O'Neil, Cathy. 2017. *Weapons of Math Destruction: How Big Data Increases Inequality and Threatens Democracy*. First paperback edition. New York: B/D/W/Y Broadway Books.

Pariser, Eli. 2011. *The Filter Bubble: What the Internet Is Hiding from You*. London: Viking.

Parisi, Luciana. 2019. "Media Ontology and Transcendental Instrumentality." *Theory, Culture & Society* 36 (6): 95–124.

Parks, Lisa. 2015. "Water, Energy, Access - Materializing the Internet in Rural Zambia." In *Signal Traffic: Critical Studies of Media Infrastructures*, edited by Lisa Parks and Nicole Starosielski, 115–136. The Geopolitics of Information. Urbana: University of Illinois Press.

Parks, Lisa, and Nicole Starosielski, eds. 2015. *Signal Traffic: Critical Studies of Media Infrastructures*. The Geopolitics of Information. Urbana: University of Illinois Press.

Pasquale, Frank. 2015. *The Black Box Society: The Secret Algorithms That Control Money and Information*. Cambridge: Harvard Univ. Press.

Pateman, Carole. 1988. *The Sexual Contract*. Stanford: Stanford University Press.

Pentenrieder, Annelie. 2020. *Algorithmen im Alltag: Eine praxistheoretische Studie zum informierten Umgang mit Routenplanern*. Frankfurt am Main: Campus Verlag.

Pentland, Alex. 2014. *Social Physics: How Good Ideas Spread-the Lessons from a New Science*. New York: Penguin.

Pinch, Trevor. 2011. "Review Essay: Karen Barad, Quantum Mechanics, and the Paradox of Mutual Exclusivity." *Social Studies of Science* 41 (3): 431–441.

Poster, Mark. 1990. *The Mode of Information: Poststructuralism and Social Context*. Chicago: University of Chicago Press.

Raymond, Eric S. 2004a. "ID10T Error." *The Jargon File*. April 1, 2004. http://www.catb.org/jargon/html/I/idiot.html

Raymond, Eric S. 2004b. "The Jargon File, Version 4.4.8." April 1, 2004. http://www.catb.org/jargon/

Rieder, Bernhard. 2020. *Engines of Order*. Amsterdam: Amsterdam University Press.

Rohlfing, K. J., P. Cimiano, I. Scharlau, T. Matzner, H. M. Buhl, H. Buschmeier, E. Esposito, et al. 2020. "Explanation as a Social Practice: Toward a Conceptual Framework for the Social Design of AI Systems." *IEEE Transactions on Cognitive and Developmental Systems*, 1–18.

Rosenberg, Daniel. 2013. "Data before the Fact." In *Raw Data Is an Oxymoron*, edited by L. Gitelman, 15–40. Cambridge: MIT Press.

Rosenblueth, Arturo, Norbert Wiener, and Julian Bigelow. 1943. "Behavior, Purpose and Teleology." *Philosophy of Science* 10 (1): 18–24.

Ross, Joel, Lilly Irani, M. Six Silberman, Andrew Zaldivar, and Bill Tomlinson. 2010. "Who Are the Crowdworkers?: Shifting Demographics in Mechanical Turk." In *CHI '10 Extended Abstracts on Human Factors in Computing Systems*, 2863–2872. CHI EA '10. Atlanta: ACM.

Rössler, Beate. 2021. *Autonomy: An Essay on the Life Well Lived*, translated by James C. Wagner. English edition. Cambridge: Polity.

Rouse, Joseph. 2004. "Barad's Feminist Naturalism." *Hypatia* 19 (1): 142–161.

Rouvroy, Antoinette. 2013. "The End (s) of Critique: Data-Behaviourism vs. Due-Process." In *Privacy, Due Process and the Computational Turn – The Philosophy of Law Meets the Philosophy of Technology*, edited by Katja de Vries Mireille Hildebrandt, 143–167. London: Routledge.

Russell, Stuart J., and Peter Norvig. 2016. *Artificial Intelligence: A Modern Approach*. Third edition, Global edition. Boston: Pearson.

Šajn, Nikolina. 2022. "Briefing Right to Repair." PE 698.869. Brussels: European Parliamentary Research Service. https://www.europarl.europa.eu/thinktank/de/document/EPRS_BRI(2022)698869

Sandvig, Christian. 2014. "Seeing the Sort: The Aesthetic and Industrial Defense of 'The Algorithm.'" *Media-N, Journal of the New Media Caucus* (blog). November 22, 2014. http://median.newmediacaucus.org/art-infrastructures-information/seeing-the-sort-the-aesthetic-and-industrial-defense-of-the-algorithm/

Sandvig, Christian. 2015. "The Internet as the Anti-Television - Distribution Infrastructure as Culture and Power." In *Signal Traffic: Critical Studies of Media Infrastructures*, edited by Lisa Parks and Nicole Starosielski, 225–245. Urbana: University of Illinois Press.

Schmieg, Sebastian. 2017. *I Will Say Whatever You Want In Front Of A Pizza*. Video loop, website, url, lecture performance, Prezi. http://i-will-say-whatever-you-want-in-front-of-a.pizza

Schulz, Christian. 2022. "A New Algorithmic Imaginary." *Media, Culture & Society*, November, online first. 10.1177/01634437221136014

Schwartz, Roy, Jesse Dodge, Noah A. Smith, and Oren Etzioni. 2020. "Green AI." *Communications of the ACM* 63 (12): 54–63.

Seaver, Nick. 2017. "Algorithms as Culture: Some Tactics for the Ethnography of Algorithmic Systems." *Big Data & Society* 4 (2): 1–17.

Seaver, Nick. 2018. "What Should an Anthropology of Algorithms Do?" *Cultural Anthropology* 33 (3): 375–385.

Seier, Andrea. 2018. "New Materialism Meets Practice Turn. A Reading of Transgender Knowledge." In *Connect and Divide. The Practice Turn in Media Studies*, edited byUlrike Bergermann, Monika Dommann, Erhard Schüttpelz, and Jeremy Stolow. Berlin: Diaphanes Verlag.

Sharwood, Simon. 2015. "Buggy? Angry? LET IT ALL OUT Says Linus Torvalds." January 19, 2015. https://www.theregister.com/2015/01/19/got_bugs_got_anger_just_get_them_out_says_linus_torvalds/

Siebers, Tobin. 2008. *Disability Theory*. Ann Arbor: University of Michigan Press.

Siegert, Bernhard. 2015. *Cultural Techniques: Grids, Filters, Doors, and Other Articulations of the Real*. New York: Fordham Univ. Press.

Simondon, Gilbert. 2016. *On the Mode of Existence of Technical Objects*, translated by Cécile Malaspina and John Rogove. Minneapolis: Univocal Pub.

Spivak, Gayatri Chakravorty. 1985. "The Rani of Sirmur: An Essay in Reading the Archives." *History and Theory* 24 (3): 247–272.

Sprenger, Florian. 2015. *The Politics of Micro-Decisions: Edward Snowden, Net Neutrality, and the Architectures of the Internet*. meson press.

Sprenger, Florian. 2022. "Microdecisions and Autonomy in Self-Driving Cars: Virtual Probabilities." *AI & Society* 37 (2): 619–634.

Srnicek, Nick, and Alex Williams. 2015. *Inventing the Future: Postcapitalism and a World without Work*. Brooklyn: Verso Books.

Stallman, Richard. 2015. *Free Software Free Society: Selected Essays of Richard M. Stallman*. Third edition. Boston: Free Software Foundation.

Starosielski, Nicole. 2015. *The Undersea Network*. SST, Sign, Storage, Transmission. Durham and London: Duke University Press.

Striphas, Ted. 2015. "Algorithmic Culture." *European Journal of Cultural Studies* 18 (4–5): 395–412.

Sweeney, Latanya. 2013. "Discrimination in Online Ad Delivery." *Communications of the ACM* 56 (5): 44–54.

Tejo, Matthew. 2022. "Why Twitter Didn't Go Down: From a Real Twitter SRE." Substack newsletter. *Matthew's Writing* (blog). November 22, 2022. https://matthewtejo.substack.com/p/why-twitter-didnt-go-down-from-a

Thomson, Judith Jarvis. 1976. "Killing, Letting Die, and the Trolley Problem." *The Monist* 59 (2): 204–217.

Totaro, Paolo, and Domenico Ninno. 2014. "The Concept of Algorithm as an Interpretative Key of Modern Rationality." *Theory, Culture & Society* 31 (4): 29–49.

Turing, A. M. 1937. "On Computable Numbers, with an Application to the Entscheidungsproblem." *Proceedings of the London Mathematical Society* s2-42 (1): 230–265.

Vincent, James. 2018. "How Three French Students Used Borrowed Code to Put the First AI Portrait in Christie's." *The Verge*. October 23, 2018. https://www.theverge.com/2018/10/23/18013190/ai-art-portrait-auction-christies-belamy-obvious-robbie-barrat-gans

Vlist, Fernando N van der, Anne Helmond, Marcus Burkhardt, and Tatjana Seitz. 2021. "The Technicity of Platform Governance: Structure and Evolution of

Facebook's APIs." 20. WORKING PAPER SERIES. Siegen: University of Siegen: Collaborative Research Center 1187 Media of Cooperation.

Vogelmann, Frieder. 2017. "Critique as a Practice of Prefigurative Emancipation." *Distinktion: Journal of Social Theory* 18 (2): 196–214.

Wang, Yilun, and Michal Kosinski. 2018. "Deep Neural Networks Are More Accurate than Humans at Detecting Sexual Orientation from Facial Images." *Journal of Personality and Social Psychology* 114 (2): 246.

Washick, Bonnie, and Elizabeth Wingrove. 2015. "Politics That Matter: Thinking about Power and Justice with the New Materialists." *Contemporary Political Theory* 14 (1): 63–89.

Weil, Elizabeth. 2023. "You Are Not a Parrot." *Intelligencer*. March 1, 2023. https://nymag.com/intelligencer/article/ai-artificial-intelligence-chatbots-emily-m-bender.html

Welch, Lloyd R. 2003. "Hidden Markov Models and the Baum-Welch Algorithm." *IEEE Information Theory Society Newsletter* 53 (4): 10–13.

Whitehead, Alfred North, and Bertrand Russell. 1927. *Principia Mathematica.* 2nd ed. 3 vols. Cambridge: Cambridge University Press.

Wiener, Norbert. 2019. *Cybernetics: Or, Control and Communication in the Animal and the Machine.* Second edition, 2019 reissue. Cambridge: The MIT Press.

Wilkes, M. V., David J. Wheeler, and Stanley Gill. 1982. *The Preparation of Programs for an Electronic Digital Computer: With Special Reference to the EDSAC and the Use of a Library of Subroutines.* Charles Babbage Institute Reprint Series for the History of Computing, v. 1. Los Angeles: Tomash Publishers.

Wirth, Niklaus. 1976. *Algorithms + Data Structures=programs.* Englewood Cliffs: Prentice-Hall.

Wittgenstein, Ludwig. 1969. *On Certainty*, edited by G. E. M. Anscombe and G. H. von Wright. Oxford: Basil Blackwell.

Wittgenstein, Ludwig. 2009. *Philosophische Untersuchungen =: Philosophical investigations*, translated by G. E. M. Anscombe, P. M. S. Hacker, and Joachim Schulte. Rev. 4th ed. Chichester: Wiley-Blackwell.

Wu, Xiaolin, and Xi Zhang. 2016. "Automated Inference on Criminality Using Face Images." *ArXiv Preprint ArXiv:1611.04135*, 4038–4052.

Young, Iris Marion. 1980. "Throwing like a Girl: A Phenomenology of Feminine Body Comportment Motility and Spatiality." *Human Studies* 3 (2): 137–156.

Yusoff, Kathryn. 2018. *A Billion Black Anthropocenes or None.* Minneapolis: University of Minnesota Press.

Zerilli, Linda M. G. 1998. "Doing without Knowing: Feminism's Politics of the Ordinary." *Political Theory* 26 (4): 435–458.

Ziewitz, Malte. 2016. "Governing Algorithms: Myth, Mess, and Methods." *Science, Technology, & Human Values* 41 (1): 3–16.

Zuiderveen Borgesius, Frederik, Damian Trilling, Judith Moeller, Balázs Bodó, Claes H De Vreese, and Natali Helberger. 2016. "Should We Worry about Filter Bubbles?" *Internet Policy Review. Journal on Internet Regulation* 5 (1). https://policyreview.info/articles/analysis/should-we-worry-about-filter-bubbles

INDEX

For Product Safety Concerns and Information please contact our EU
representative GPSR@taylorandfrancis.com Taylor & Francis Verlag GmbH,
Kaufingerstraße 24, 80331 München, Germany

Printed and bound by CPI Group (UK) Ltd, Croydon, CR0 4YY

08/06/2025

01897008-0007